PRAISE FOR *THE PRICING PLAYBOOK*

For large, matrixed organizations, pricing decisions require structure, clarity, and alignment. *The Pricing Playbook* offers exactly that, making it a strong resource for RGM and commercial leaders in global businesses.

—**Michael Kantor,** CEO,
Promotion Optimization Institute,
Adjunct Professor, Saint Joseph's University

In a highly elastic environment, short-term price moves can quickly destroy value for FMCG companies. This book shows how advanced analytics can support RGM strategies that grow consumption, not just margins.

—**Alberto de Marchis,** CFO France,
The Kraft Heinz Company

Grounded in pricing theory but written for practitioners, *The Pricing Playbook* provides a clear and practical framework for building effective revenue management strategies in complex organizations, thoughtfully integrating the realities of AI-enabled decision-making. It is especially relevant for leaders responsible for turning pricing insight into real commercial impact.

—**Harry Ergan,** Vice President,
Head of Revenue Growth Management,
The Ajinomoto Group

Profitable revenue growth management (RGM) is at the heart of every FMCG/CPG top performer today. Holistic RGM, aligning brand strategic objectives with shelf pricing, price pack design, and customized trade and promotion plans, becomes the backbone of the commercial planning process.

As the "pricing lever" is the most strategic value driver in RGM, solid pricing playbooks are crucial to navigate increasingly complex pricing decisions. In this book, Ingo Reinhardt not only explains foundational theory but also offers practical examples of how to incorporate customer- and data-driven pricing decisions into your playbooks as RGM enters the era of AI.

—**Pol Vanaerde,** Chair,
EPP Pricing Platform

THE
PRICING
PLAYBOOK

INGO REINHARDT

THE PRICING PLAYBOOK

A PRACTICAL GUIDE TO REVENUE GROWTH MANAGEMENT IN THE AGE OF AI

WILEY

This edition first published 2026
© 2026 by John Wiley & Sons, Ltd.

All rights reserved, including rights for text and data mining and training of artificial intelligence technologies or similar technologies. No part of this publication may be reproduced, stored in a retrieval system, or transmitted, in any form or by any means, electronic, mechanical, photocopying, recording or otherwise, except as permitted by law. Advice on how to obtain permission to reuse material from this title is available at http://www.wiley.com/go/permissions.

The right of Ingo Reinhardt to be identified as the author of the editorial material in this work has been asserted in accordance with law.

Registered Offices
John Wiley & Sons, Inc., 111 River Street, Hoboken, NJ 07030, USA
John Wiley & Sons Ltd, New Era House, 8 Oldlands Way, Bognor Regis, West Sussex, PO22 9NQ, UK

For details of our global editorial offices, customer services, and more information about Wiley products visit us at www.wiley.com.

The manufacturer's authorized representative according to the EU General Product Safety Regulation is Wiley-VCH GmbH, Boschstr. 12, 69469 Weinheim, Germany, e-mail: Product_Safety@wiley.com.

Wiley also publishes its books in a variety of electronic formats and by print-on-demand. Some content that appears in standard print versions of this book may not be available in other formats.

Trademarks: Wiley and the Wiley logo are trademarks or registered trademarks of John Wiley & Sons, Inc. and/or its affiliates in the United States and other countries and may not be used without written permission. All other trademarks are the property of their respective owners. John Wiley & Sons, Inc. is not associated with any product or vendor mentioned in this book.

Limit of Liability/Disclaimer of Warranty
While the publisher and the authors have used their best efforts in preparing this work, including a review of the content of the work, neither the publisher nor the authors make any representations or warranties with respect to the accuracy or completeness of the contents of this work and specifically disclaim all warranties, including without limitation any implied warranties of merchantability or fitness for a particular purpose. No warranty may be created or extended by sales representatives, written sales materials or promotional statements for this work. The fact that an organization, website, or product is referred to in this work as a citation and/or potential source of further information does not mean that the publisher and authors endorse the information or services the organization, website, or product may provide or recommendations it may make. This work is sold with the understanding that the publisher is not engaged in rendering professional services. The advice and strategies contained herein may not be suitable for your situation. You should consult with a specialist where appropriate. Further, readers should be aware that websites listed in this work may have changed or disappeared between when this work was written and when it is read. Neither the publisher nor authors shall be liable for any loss of profit or any other commercial damages, including but not limited to special, incidental, consequential, or other damages.

Library of Congress Cataloging-in-Publication Data is Available:

ISBN 9781394396900 (Cloth)
ISBN 9781394396917 (ePub)
ISBN 9781394396924 (ePDF)

Cover Design: Wiley
Cover Images: © Phantip/stock.adobe.com

Set in 11/16pts and Minion Pro by Straive, Chennai, India.
Printed and bound by CPI Group (UK) Ltd, Croydon, CR0 4YY

This book is dedicated to everyone I've had the privilege of working with.

CONTENTS

LIST OF FIGURES — xiii
LIST OF TABLES — xix
PREFACE — xxi

CHAPTER 1
INTRODUCTION — 1

CHAPTER 2
FOUNDATIONS — 7
2.1 Terminology — 7
    2.1.1 Pricing — 8
    2.1.2 Revenue Growth Management — 8
    2.1.3 Playbook — 11
2.2 The Role of Pricing in the Firm — 12
    2.2.1 Relevance of Pricing — 12
    2.2.2 Value Creation and Value Capture — 15
    2.2.3 Evolution of Pricing and RGM Roles in Companies — 18
2.3 Theoretical Foundations — 19
    2.3.1 Microeconomics — 20
        2.3.1.1 Demand Functions — 21
        2.3.1.2 Price Elasticity of Demand — 29
        2.3.1.3 Challenges with Multiple Products — 34
        2.3.1.4 A Note on Value — 38

	2.3.2	Behavioral Economics	40
	2.3.3	Macroeconomic Effects on Pricing and RGM	44
2.4	Pricing and RGM in Practice		47
	2.4.1	Pricing Research	47
		2.4.1.1 Market Data Assessment	48
		2.4.1.2 Surveys	58
		2.4.1.3 Expert Judgment	71
		2.4.1.4 Further Considerations	79
	2.4.2	Traditional RGM Methods	82
		2.4.2.1 Pricing	83
		2.4.2.2 Price-Pack Architecture	100
		2.4.2.3 Promotions	104
		2.4.2.4 Trade Terms	108
		2.4.2.5 Channel Mix	113
		2.4.2.6 Bringing It All Together	115
	2.4.3	Beyond Pay-Per-Unit: Pricing Models	115
	2.4.4	Current Technology Solutions	117
	2.4.5	Pricing Myths	120
		2.4.5.1 Myth: Costs Do Not Matter in Pricing	120
		2.4.5.2 Myth: Pricing Is All About Value to "the Customer"	122
		2.4.5.3 A Corollary Myth: It Is Always Better to Differentiate Prices Between Customers	124
		2.4.5.4 Myth: Price Elasticity Is a Single Number	126
		2.4.5.5 Myth: Identified Behavioral Effects Can Be Applied Directly	127
2.5	Further Reading		128
	2.5.1	Books	129
	2.5.2	Professional Societies and Conferences	131
		2.5.2.1 Societies and Professional Organizers	131
		2.5.2.2 Conferences for Pricing and RGM	132

CHAPTER 3
BUILDING THE RGM PLAYBOOK — 135

- 3.1 Pricing and RGM Strategy — 136
  - 3.1.1 Pricing Strategy Framework — 137
  - 3.1.2 Simple Examples — 138
    - 3.1.2.1 David and Goliath — 139
    - 3.1.2.2 AOL — 140
    - 3.1.2.3 Oil Lamps — 141
- 3.2 Integrating into a Pricing Framework — 142
  - 3.2.1 Step 1 – RGM Process — 144
    - 3.2.1.1 Step 1.1 – Strategy — 144
    - 3.2.1.2 Step 1.2 – Execution — 158
    - 3.2.1.3 Step 1.3 – Improvement — 166
  - 3.2.2 Step 2 – People and Organization — 174
  - 3.2.3 Step 3 – Technology — 176
    - 3.2.3.1 Tools — 177
    - 3.2.3.2 Data — 177
- 3.3 International RGM Considerations — 178
- 3.4 How to Build Your RGM Playbook — 186

CHAPTER 4
DIGITALIZATION OF PRICING AND RGM — 187

- 4.1 Digitalization — 188
  - 4.1.1 Terminology — 188
  - 4.1.2 Origins and Developments — 190
- 4.2 Evolution of RGM in the Digital Age — 192
  - 4.2.1 Recap Core RGM Challenges — 193
  - 4.2.2 First Wave: From Siloed to Integrated Teams — 195
  - 4.2.3 Second Wave: Toward Integrated Solutions — 197
  - 4.2.4 Toward the Revenue Manager of Tomorrow — 201
    - 4.2.4.1 Tomorrow – The Revenue Manager as a Change Agent — 201
    - 4.2.4.2 The Day After – Hypotheses on the Changing Role — 202

CONTENTS

- 4.3 Generative AI for RGM — 203
  - 4.3.1 Introduction to AI, GenAI, and Other Variants — 204
    - 4.3.1.1 GenAI — 206
    - 4.3.1.2 Agentic AI — 209
    - 4.3.1.3 Agent-Based Modeling — 210
  - 4.3.2 The RGM Core Challenge for AI — 212
    - 4.3.2.1 Virtual Shoppers — 217
    - 4.3.2.2 Virtual Shopping Situation — 220
    - 4.3.2.3 Further Considerations — 221
  - 4.3.3 AI in RGM — 222
    - 4.3.3.1 Data Integration — 224
    - 4.3.3.2 Sales Forecasting — 226
    - 4.3.3.3 Offer Optimization — 228
    - 4.3.3.4 Recommendation and Management of Offer Changes — 231
    - 4.3.3.5 Integrating the RGM GenAI Layers — 233
  - 4.3.4 Are AI Agents the Future of RGM? — 234
- 4.4 Use Cases in RGM for CPG Companies — 237
  - 4.4.1 Trade offs Between RGM Levers — 238
  - 4.4.2 Promotion Fine-Tuning — 239
  - 4.4.3 Strategic Pricing Shift from High-Low to EDLP — 240
- 4.5 Use Cases in Other Industries — 243
  - 4.5.1 Telecommunications (Telco) — 244
  - 4.5.2 Automotive — 245
  - 4.5.3 Retail — 246
  - 4.5.4 B2B (Business-to-Business) — 247
  - 4.5.5 Hospitality — 248

CHAPTER 5
WAY AHEAD: THE MARKET-LED ORGANIZATION — 249

BIBLIOGRAPHY — 253
ABOUT THE AUTHOR — 263
INDEX — 265

LIST OF FIGURES

Figure 2.1: Pricing and RGM — 9
Figure 2.2: History of RGM development — 10
Figure 2.3: Comparison of profit levers — 13
Figure 2.4: Value creation vs. value capture — 15
Figure 2.5: Principal pricing objectives (stylized) — 16
Figure 2.6: Tradeoff between profit and revenue — 18
Figure 2.7: Linear demand — 22
Figure 2.8: Isoelastic demand — 23
Figure 2.9: Normal demand — 24
Figure 2.10: Profit optimization — 25
Figure 2.11: Revenue optimization — 26
Figure 2.12: Visualization of price elasticity — 30
Figure 2.13: Point price elasticity for linear demand — 32
Figure 2.14: Arc price elasticity — 33
Figure 2.15: Price elasticity and profit optimum — 35
Figure 2.16: Price elasticity dependent on competitor's price change — 36
Figure 2.17: Price elasticity depends on market dynamics — 37
Figure 2.18: Being rational is not easy — 40
Figure 2.19: Homo oeconomicus vs. Homo sapiens — 41
Figure 2.20: Example of decoy pricing — 43

LIST OF FIGURES

Figure 2.21: Key macro trends relevant for RGM — 44
Figure 2.22: Macro trends have a direct RGM impact — 46
Figure 2.23: Overview of pricing research methods — 48
Figure 2.24: Linear regression example — 51
Figure 2.25: Actual and estimated sales with promotions in weeks 7 and 10 — 54
Figure 2.26: Simple AB test — 55
Figure 2.27: Example of effects for AB testing — 57
Figure 2.28: Van Westendorp questionnaire — 59
Figure 2.29: Van Westendorp Price Sensitivity Meter — 60
Figure 2.30: From the too-expensive plot to the demand function — 61
Figure 2.31: Gabor–Granger questionnaire (excerpt) — 62
Figure 2.32: Gabor–Granger results (example) — 63
Figure 2.33: MaxDiff survey example — 64
Figure 2.34: Output MaxDiff survey – importance ranking — 65
Figure 2.35: Example of conjoint analysis (for TVs) — 67
Figure 2.36: Conjoint output – relative importance of value drivers — 68
Figure 2.37: Conjoint output – relative importance of attribute levels — 69
Figure 2.38: Input price elasticity assessment — 72
Figure 2.39: Output price elasticity assessment — 73
Figure 2.40: Profit and revenue curves based on expert judgment — 74
Figure 2.41: Importance and performance rating — 75
Figure 2.42: Value driver assessment from expert judgment — 76
Figure 2.43: Attribute level output based on expert judgment — 76
Figure 2.44: Attribute level output based on expert judgment (example: Product 1) — 78
Figure 2.45: Value map — 78
Figure 2.46: RGM levers — 83
Figure 2.47: Cost-plus pricing — 84
Figure 2.48: Competitive pricing — 86
Figure 2.49: Example of competitive pricing getting out of control — 87
Figure 2.50: Example price elasticity table — 88
Figure 2.51: Value-based pricing — 90
Figure 2.52: Overview of behavioral pricing effects — 93

List of Figures

Figure 2.53: Survey results vs. actual sales — 96
Figure 2.54: Price recommendations from different pricing methods — 98
Figure 2.55: Step-by-step price build up — 99
Figure 2.56: Alignment of consumption occasion and product size — 100
Figure 2.57: Brand ladder — 101
Figure 2.58: Price-pack architecture — 103
Figure 2.59: Brand- and pack-size-architecture — 104
Figure 2.60: Promotion dynamics — 105
Figure 2.61: Promotion effectiveness — 106
Figure 2.62: Promotion levers — 108
Figure 2.63: Price waterfall (example) — 109
Figure 2.64: Example Excel pricing tool — 117
Figure 2.65: Costs matter for profit optimization! — 121
Figure 2.66: Pricing is all about value to the customer! — 123
Figure 2.67: Customer segmentation and personas — 124
Figure 2.68: Price differentiation — 125
Figure 3.1: Strategy framework – the kernel of good strategy — 137
Figure 3.2: Pricing strategy framework — 139
Figure 3.3: Pricing framework — 143
Figure 3.4: Strategic trade off between profit and revenue — 146
Figure 3.5: Examples of statements of corporate objectives — 147
Figure 3.6: Key trends relevant for RGM in the second half of 2025 — 148
Figure 3.7: General strategy — 149
Figure 3.8: RGM guidelines — 150
Figure 3.9: BCG growth-market share matrix — 153
Figure 3.10: Net revenue targets per category and channel (2026) — 154
Figure 3.11: Overview of pricing instruments — 156
Figure 3.12: Overview of trigger events for pricing actions — 157
Figure 3.13: Integration of different data inputs — 158
Figure 3.14: Key analyses per RGM lever (selection) — 159
Figure 3.15: Overview of the key RGM processes (example) — 161
Figure 3.16: Example portfolio/PPA optimization process — 162
Figure 3.17: SRP and list price process — 163

LIST OF FIGURES

Figure 3.18: Promotion process — 164
Figure 3.19: Five elements of a successful sell-in story — 166
Figure 3.20: Example set of KPIs — 167
Figure 3.21: KPI overview for assessing RGM success — 169
Figure 3.22: Strategic KPI monitoring (Balanced Scorecard) — 172
Figure 3.23: The RGM organizational structure — 174
Figure 3.24: Responsibilities for key activities — 176
Figure 3.25: Tools to use — 177
Figure 3.26: Required data inputs — 178
Figure 3.27: Global governance — 180
Figure 3.28: Global, regional, local price coordination — 183
Figure 3.29: Impact of gray market share — 183
Figure 3.30: Gray market assessment (case study) — 185
Figure 4.1: The digitalization journey — 189
Figure 4.2: The history of digitalization — 192
Figure 4.3: RGM levers — 194
Figure 4.4: Evolution of RGM in CPGs — 196
Figure 4.5: From siloed departments to integrated RGM teams — 196
Figure 4.6: Example of PPA vs. pricing analysis — 198
Figure 4.7: Increasing integration — 199
Figure 4.8: Data sources — 200
Figure 4.9: Google searches for GenAI and Agentic AI over the past five years — 204
Figure 4.10: Example workflow of an LLM predicting the next word — 208
Figure 4.11: Overview of different AI applications — 208
Figure 4.12: Summary of AI types — 211
Figure 4.13: Price elasticity measurement via regression analysis — 213
Figure 4.14: Model parameters vs. model performance — 215
Figure 4.15: Demand and Virtual Shoppers — 216
Figure 4.16: The Virtual Shoppers technology — 218
Figure 4.17: From Virtual Shoppers to demand prediction — 219
Figure 4.18: Virtual Shoppers predict demand for different offers — 220
Figure 4.19: The GenAI halo effect in RGM — 223
Figure 4.20: Four core layers for using (Gen)AI in RGM — 224

List of Figures

Figure 4.21: Integration of key data sources into a single model — 225
Figure 4.22: Offer optimization using AI — 230
Figure 4.23: Example of prompt-based RGM optimization — 232
Figure 4.24: Strategic importance of AI layers — 234
Figure 4.25: Integration of GenAI, Agentic AI, and agent-based models — 235
Figure 4.26: Price increase vs. de-gramming — 239
Figure 4.27: Promotion optimization — 241
Figure 4.28: High-Low pricing vs. EDLP — 242

LIST OF TABLES

Table 2.1: Computation of impact of value drivers — 14
Table 2.2: Example data linear regression — 49
Table 2.3: Overview of typical discount and bonus elements — 111
Table 2.4: Overview of pricing and RGM tool categories — 119

PREFACE

I wrote this book over the past 12 months – essentially in two stages. First, in the first half of 2025, I wrote Chapter 2 on the fundamentals of pricing and revenue growth management (RGM) and Chapter 3 on how to define a pricing and RGM playbook. Then in late summer and fall, I worked on Chapter 4 – the role of GenAI, Agentic AI, and agent-based modeling in RGM. This turned out to be much more of a moving target than anticipated. The idea of Agentic AI was just emerging, and with it the potential of exciting applications in RGM. However, it is still very open what role Agentic AI will play and how the different parts of the AI story best fit together. In this book, I will present my view.

From speaking with our customers and prospects, we know that some in the field expect AI to soon provide them with a button they can press and then some AI Agent does all the RGM optimization work for them – and they can just lean back, watch, and do not need to understand the dynamics driving sales in their market. There are two important caveats to this. First, I argue in this book that this future is still a few years out based on developments in other areas. Human abilities will be augmented by AI technology and not replaced any time soon.

Second, in essentially all professions – especially highly technical and automated ones such as pilots, ship captains, surgeons, astronauts, or nuclear plant controllers – professionals need to know the fundamentals of their field by hand. While RGM is not a formal profession with a defined curriculum, there is a relevant body of knowledge everyone should know. For example, every RGM professional should know how to compute a product's profit-optimal price after determining its price elasticity by hand. This book is not a comprehensive compendium of all details of RGM work. Rather, we provide an overview of many of the basic concepts and list sources for further study.

This book grew out of the webinars we have hosted over the past few years. Therefore, I want to thank everyone who has participated in those webinars, which have motivated and pushed us every time to come up with new content and further develop our ideas. Also, I want to thank Medeina Musteikytė for helping design the figures in this book, Charlotte Harris for helping with the formatting of the bibliography, footnotes, captions, etc. throughout the book, and Skirmante Bikaite and the rest of the Buynomics marketing team for supporting the book development process. Your support is invaluable. Any mistakes in this book are my responsibility.

—Ingo Reinhardt

Cologne, November 2025

CHAPTER ONE

INTRODUCTION

When They Say It's Not About Money, It's About Money.
—Abe Martin, 1916

This book is about pricing and revenue growth management (RGM). It is aimed at everyone with a professional or personal interest in the topic. What makes the field fascinating is that it has – at the same time – grown from ancient roots in moral philosophy, is based on elegant theoretical underpinnings in economics, and, first and foremost, has grown out of a practical necessity. In modern free-market societies, value creation happens almost exclusively within companies that have at least some freedoms in selecting the products they produce and how they market, price, and sell them. In the long run, only persistent profitability can ensure the survival of a company. Therefore, it is crucial for their survival and success that professionals master the art and science of pricing. This is particularly true as more advanced artificial intelligence (AI) and machine learning (ML) technologies are being introduced into the field and increasingly support teams in their analysis and decision-making. To get started, let's justify these claims.

The ancient roots of pricing: Pricing is as old as money, and the question of how to set prices and offer products has long played a central part in people's lives. Therefore, it comes as no surprise that ancient writings such as the Code of Hammurabi (eighteenth century BC) or the Bible had some advice to give to their readers. For example, the Bible in Leviticus 25:14 states that "when you make a sale or buy from your neighbor, you shall not wrong one another." In this and other examples, the emphasis is typically on fairness to ensure peace within the community. This idea lives on in pricing methods such as cost-plus pricing with an accepted markup on costs.

The elegant theoretical underpinnings in economics: Mathematical optimization of revenue or profit was made possible by neoclassical economists such as Alfred Marshall, who developed quantitative models around the end of the nineteenth century to understand how supply and demand are matched.[1] Using the mathematics of calculus, economic models allowed studying the dynamics of markets. For example, how does a product's sales volume depend on its price? The answer to this question is typically expressed by one of the central actors in pricing: the price elasticity. Here is an outline of arguably the most relevant insight for price optimization.[2] The price elasticity of a product measures how strongly sales volumes change because of the price changes. For example, if the price is increased by 10% and as a result the sales volume declines by 20%, the price elasticity (ε) is $-20\% / 10\% = -2$. Then, there is a beautiful relationship between the price elasticity of a product and its percentage margin $\left(m = \dfrac{p-c}{p}\right)$ at the price (p) that optimizes profit for unit costs (c). That is:[3]

$$\varepsilon \cdot m = -1.$$

---

[1] Marshall (2009 [1890]).
[2] For more details see Chapter 2, Section 2.3.
[3] In Section 2.3, we will show why this relationship is true.

For example, if the price elasticity of a product is −2 for all prices, then the profit-optimal margin is 50%. With unit costs of €100, the optimal price is €200. With this, it is easy to compute the price optimum if the price elasticity is known. Also, this relationship shows that in the revenue optimum, the price elasticity is −1. This is because for a (hypothetical) product without variable costs, the margin is 100% in the above equation, and the profit optimum is equal to the revenue optimum. It is important to note that this relationship is only valid in the one-product case – that is, there is no interdependence with competitor products or the own portfolio to consider. In Section 2.3, we will explain this in more detail.

The practical necessity: When a company wants to sell a product, there are several decisions it needs to make. These include the selection of sales channels, the number of product variations in the portfolio, and the product prices. Good decision-making considers a range of aspects, including customers' preferences and willingness to pay, competition, costs, strengths, weaknesses, opportunities, and threats.

Different industries offer different degrees of freedom. For example, companies that sell a commodity with little opportunity for differentiation must stay close to the "market price" – that is, the price of competitors. Further, in many industries with a long tradition, price metrics and price levels have been established, and simple heuristics are available. For example, many restaurants compute their prices by multiplying the cost of making a meal by four. This results in a gross margin of 75%.

On the other side of the spectrum, there is the pricing in newly developed industries. For example, in the ride-sharing industry, which emerged in the 2010s, competitors Uber and Lyft followed very different pricing strategies with Uber using a dynamic pricing model to match supply (drivers) and demand (customers) and Lyft relying on a more traditional pricing structure consisting of a base fee plus a per-mile and per-minute rate.[4]

---

[4] See Bradford (2021); Danu (2021); Hawkins (2015).

New product pricing is very difficult, and it can be off for even the most iconic products. When Apple first introduced the iPhone in 2007, the initial price tag for the 8 GB version in the US market was $599. This turned out to be too expensive, and Steve Jobs, then chief executive officer (CEO) of Apple, reduced the price to $399, which earned him the wrath of customers who had already paid $599 for the phone. In the end, Apple offered these customers a $100 voucher.[5]

Pricing and – more broadly – revenue growth management are fascinating fields that are constantly gaining in importance. This is particularly true since the return of inflation in 2022. For example, the occurrence of the term "price elasticity" in earnings calls has quadrupled in 2022 over previous years, highlighting the importance of pricing for C-level executives.[6]

Furthermore, in 2025, US tariffs brought the concept of price elasticity further into the public spotlight. Also, the widely reported surge in egg prices was an excellent example of the importance of price elasticity. Despite a 228% price increase, demand dropped by just 4%, implying a price elasticity near zero.[7]

Now, consumer goods companies face a perfect storm of challenges: surging input costs, shifting consumer preferences, intensifying retailer pressure, and global uncertainties. The cost of raw materials continues to fluctuate unpredictably, driven by geopolitical conflicts, inflation, and supply chain disruptions. For example, the war in Ukraine significantly impacted the global supply of critical commodities, creating ripple effects across industries.

Another example is cocoa, a key ingredient in chocolate, in which data revealed a price surge to almost $9,500 per metric ton in 2024, marking a

---

[5] BBC News (2007).
[6] Buynomics (2023).
[7] Foley (2025).

nearly 50% increase within three months and more than doubling compared to the previous year.[8]

Despite these challenges, we find that, based on our experience in the field over two decades and the hundreds of professionals we interact with on a regular basis, a comprehensive, practical guide to pricing and RGM is missing. Today, as pricing professionals have access to an increasing body of advanced AI and ML technologies, such as the one that we are building at Buynomics, we strongly believe that for the best use of such technologies, professionals need to have a solid understanding of the underlying methods and principles. And they need to understand how to apply the technologies to build effective commercial organizations and implement the best pricing and RGM strategy for their companies. This is the motivation for writing this playbook – particularly considering the recent advancements in AI and how pricing and RGM can benefit from them. In this playbook, we want to achieve the following three objectives:

- Provide an **overview of the basic concepts** of pricing, such as value pricing, price elasticities, and behavioral pricing (Chapter 2).
- Provide a **framework for developing a pricing and RGM playbook** that helps define and implement the pricing strategy within the organization (Chapter 3).
- Discuss **recent developments in the different forms of AI** such as GenAI, Agentic AI, and agent-based modeling – and how they affect pricing and RGM. Particularly, we discuss their application and demonstrate these in a few practical use cases (Chapter 4).

---
[8] International Cocoa Organization (2025).

CHAPTER TWO
FOUNDATIONS

In this chapter, we introduce the basic concepts, methods, and practical tool of pricing and revenue growth management (RGM). If you are new to the field, we recommend to thoroughly go through this section. If you are already a veteran, flipping through is sufficient. Also, this chapter can be used as a reference and a refresher for key concepts and ideas. Specifically, Section 2.1 covers the basic terminology. In Section 2.2 we discuss the role of pricing and RGM in the firm. Section 2.3 covers the theoretical foundations of key pricing terms and Section 2.4 their practical application. Section 2.5 closes with some suggestions for further information on pricing and RGM.

2.1 TERMINOLOGY

We define the three central terms of pricing, RGM, and playbook that will be used throughout the book.

2.1.1 Pricing

In this book, we define the term *pricing* more narrowly as the process of setting a monetary value on a product or service. Price setting involves determining the appropriate price level considering customers' willingness to pay for the product, competition, costs, other market conditions, and the objective such as profit or revenue maximization. The price set for a product generally has a significant impact on its sales volume and profitability. The different aspects to consider when setting a price will be explored on the following pages.[9] Of the different RGM levers, pricing has received the most attention, both in theory and practice, because it is the most accessible and often most easy to implement.

2.1.2 Revenue Growth Management

In comparison to pricing, we use the term revenue growth management (RGM) more broadly as the process of increasing a company's revenue or profit – not only through price setting, but also through the optimization of promotions, product features, the whole product portfolio, net and gross price levels – and managing other functions of the firm including distribution, marketing, finance, etc. (see Figure 2.1). It involves analyzing and understanding the market, customers, and competitors in order to identify opportunities for growth and implementing strategies to capitalize on those opportunities.

The goal of RGM is to drive sustainable revenue growth through a combination of tactics such as:

- **Identifying untapped customer segments or markets:** Conducting in-depth market segmentation and demand analysis uncovers new

---

[9] See Kotler and Keller (2005), Nagle et al. (2017), and Simon (2015) for more details.

Figure 2.1 Pricing and RGM

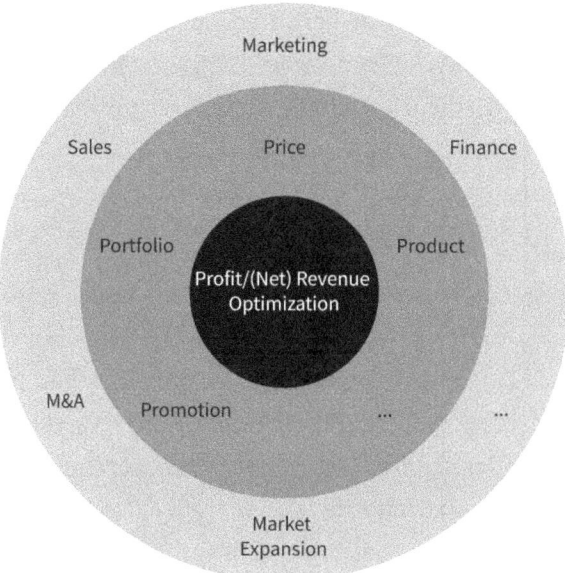

growth opportunities, with success measured by customer acquisition rates and incremental revenue contribution.

- **Launching new products or services:** Developing differentiated offerings aligned to emerging consumer needs strengthens competitive positioning, with return on investment (ROI) tracked through new product revenue share and speed-to-market metrics.
- **Upselling or cross-selling to existing customers:** Leveraging customer insights and purchase history to increase wallet share drives higher customer lifetime value (CLV), measured by average order value and retention uplift.
- **Optimizing pricing through data analysis and market research:** Applying elasticity modeling, competitive benchmarking, and scenario planning enables margin expansion, with impact measured through gross margin improvement and revenue per unit.

- **Implementing effective promotion and marketing campaigns:** Executing targeted, data-driven campaigns enhances conversion and brand equity, with performance assessed by ROI, cost per acquisition (CPA), and customer engagement scores.
- **Improving distribution channels and partnerships:** Strengthening logistics efficiency and forming strategic alliances increase market penetration, with effectiveness measured through channel profitability, on-shelf availability, and partnership-driven revenue.

This is a general overview of key tasks and goals. Later, we will become more specific on some of these ideas. RGM involves a holistic and data-driven approach to improving revenue growth, rather than relying on isolated tactics such as cutting prices or increasing marketing spend. It requires a deep understanding of products, customers, and competition, as well as the ability to continuously analyze and adapt to changing market conditions.

RGM has developed in many stages throughout the twentieth century (Figure 2.2), with the development of increasingly elaborate marketing and sales promotions from the 1920s, the professionalization of market research from the 1950s, through the increasing use of technology starting in the 1980s, to the advent of AI-based holistic optimization of all RGM levers starting in the past decade.

In this book, we refer to RGM as a tool for (net) revenue and profit optimization. The term RGM emerged from fixed capacity price optimization, particularly in industries such as aviation, where the prices of a fixed

Figure 2.2 History of RGM development

Marketing & sales promotions	Market research	Technology for automation	AI-based holistic optimization

1920   1930   1940   1950   1960   1970   1980   1990   2000   2010   2020

number of seats on a plane must be set to optimize revenue.[10] In such businesses with limited capacity, total costs are typically fixed, so that revenue and profit maximization are almost indistinguishable. This is because the cost difference between operating an empty plane and a full plane is minimal. Therefore, in such cases revenue and profit maximization are essentially identical. In those capacity-constrained industries, the term revenue management is more common. In industries with relevant variable costs such as fast-moving consumer goods (FMCG), the term revenue growth management (RGM) is more common – both to highlight the fact that revenue and profit optimization are different (as we will show on the following pages) and to emphasize the specific attention to growth in these industries.

2.1.3 Playbook

A playbook is a comprehensive guide or set of instructions that outline a specific process or system to achieve a particular goal or outcome. Playbooks are commonly used in sports, business, and military contexts, and can range from simple to highly complex, depending on the situation. In sports, a playbook is a collection of plays and strategies that a team uses to coordinate and execute their game plan. It can include offensive and defensive plays, as well as specific instructions for individual players or units. In a business context, a playbook can provide detailed steps for sales and marketing processes, customer service procedures, or crisis management protocols. It can also include information on best practices, potential challenges, and solutions for different scenarios.

With this playbook we want to provide the theoretical background for key concepts and show a wide range of practical applications to help pricing and RGM professionals across industries improve the quality of their

---

[10] For RGM in aviation, see Belobaba et al. (2015) and Clarke and Smith (2004).

work and by doing so support their organizations in achieving persistent success.

2.2 THE ROLE OF PRICING IN THE FIRM

Why do pricing and RGM matter to firms? Let's start with the standard answer and then add some nuance.

2.2.1 Relevance of Pricing

The importance of pricing is often justified by some version of the following argument. If you consider the general profit function of the firm:

$$\text{profit} = (\text{price} - \text{variable costs}) \cdot \text{volume} - \text{fixed costs},$$

then there are four levers that drive the firm's profit: price, variable costs, volume, and fixed costs. The question is, which is most impactful? Using the average economics of 2,463 companies from the Compustat database, Marn and Rosiello compared the impact of a separate 1% improvement in each of the four levers.[11] Figure 2.3 shows that the 1% improvement in price results in an 11.1% increase in operating profits, whereas a 1% increase in the other three levers only results in an operating profit improvement between 2.3% and 7.8%. Therefore, they concluded that pricing is the most effective profit lever.

Qualitatively, the narrative to support the primacy of pricing goes like this: Costs are difficult to reduce further, because companies have already put massive efforts into cost cutting and because diminishing returns only

---
[11] Marn and Rosiello (1992).

Figure 2.3 Comparison of profit levers

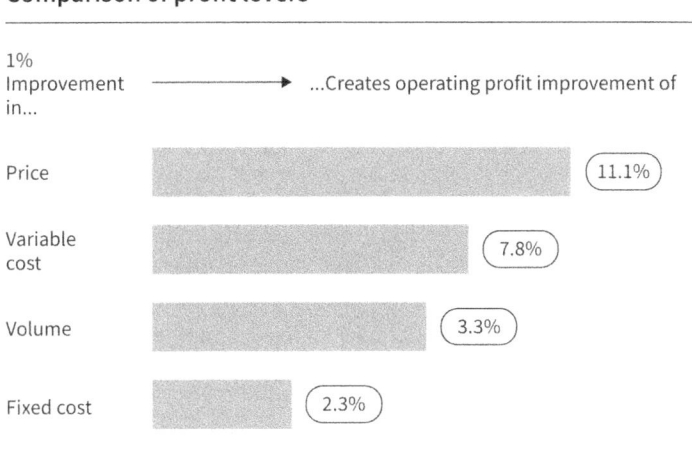

*Based on average economics of 2,463 companies in Compustat database

allow for minor improvements of fixed and variable costs. Sales volumes are also difficult to grow further because growth would have to come at the expense of competitors who will certainly fight back. Pricing on the other hand has received only limited attention in the past and now offers the best improvement opportunities.

Quantitatively, this computation is based on the (often implicit) assumption that prices can be increased by 1% without a loss in sales volume. That means that the price elasticity is 0. Table 2.1 shows the computation behind the values shown in Figure 2.3. For simplicity, the values are normalized to a price of €100 and sales of 100 units in the status quo. Variable costs of 72% of price and the fixed costs of 20% of revenue are implied from the values shown in Figure 2.3.[12] Then, the impacts are computed by improving each driver in isolation by 1% (e.g., price increase by

---

[12] Marn and Rosiello (1992) do not explicitly provide these in their paper.

Table 2.1 Computation of impact of value drivers

	Status quo		1% improvement		
Driver	value	Profit	Value	Profit	Profit improvement (%)
Price	€100	€902	€101	€1,002	11.1
Variable cost	€71	€902	€70	€973	7.8
Volume	100	€902	101	€932	3.3
Fixed cost	€2,046	€902	€2,026	€923	2.3

1%, fixed cost reduction by 1%) with everything else staying the same (ceteris paribus condition).

However, a price elasticity of 0 is rare. Certainly, it does not apply to the average of 2,463 companies. If we apply a price elasticity of −1, then the increase in operating profit is 7.9%, at a price elasticity of −2, it is 4.7%. Therefore, in this example, if the combined price elasticity is −1, then variable cost improvements are as profitable as price improvements, and between −2 and −3, volume and fixed cost improvements become more beneficial than price improvements.

Hence, the success of an improvement in pricing crucially depends on how well the effects of a price increase on sales volumes are understood and can be mitigated. There are certainly several options that we will also discuss in some detail in this playbook such as differentiated price changes within a portfolio of products or product size changes instead of a price change. With this, some of the volume effects can be, for example, compensated by movements of customers within the own portfolio to more high-value products.

Therefore, to really understand the importance of pricing and RGM, we need to take a much deeper look next, at their role in the two central tasks of every company.

2.2.2 Value Creation and Value Capture

A company has two principal tasks: value creation and value capture (see Figure 2.4). The former is performed across different departments from procurement to production, logistics, and others. The latter is guided by the company's strategy and largely implemented via its pricing and RGM functions – and it is the key to achieving the company's long-term profitable existence. Therefore, a well-executed pricing strategy supports the overall strategy of the company. For example, if a company follows a growth strategy, this would benefit from a pricing strategy that emphasizes increasing sales volumes over profit. In contrast, a company that is already close to its natural market share and can only grow further at great cost would benefit from a pricing that balances sales increase with profit growth.

Figure 2.4 Value creation vs. value capture

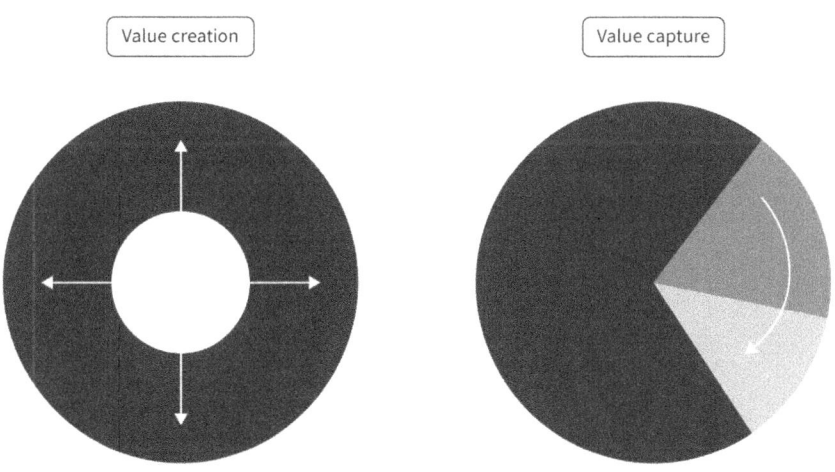

To understand the relationship between long-term value creation and capture, it is useful to differentiate between three principal objectives that companies can pursue (see Figure 2.5):

- **Sales or market share optimization:** This implies prices at the lower end of the industry to attract customers new to the market and from competitors. Sales maximization is not a sustainable strategy, as competitors often join in lowering prices igniting a price war – and this typically results in a money-losing endeavor for all.
- **Revenue maximization:** This generally implies higher prices than sales maximization. However, a pure (net) revenue maximization strategy is not necessarily profitable.

Figure 2.5 Principal pricing objectives (stylized)

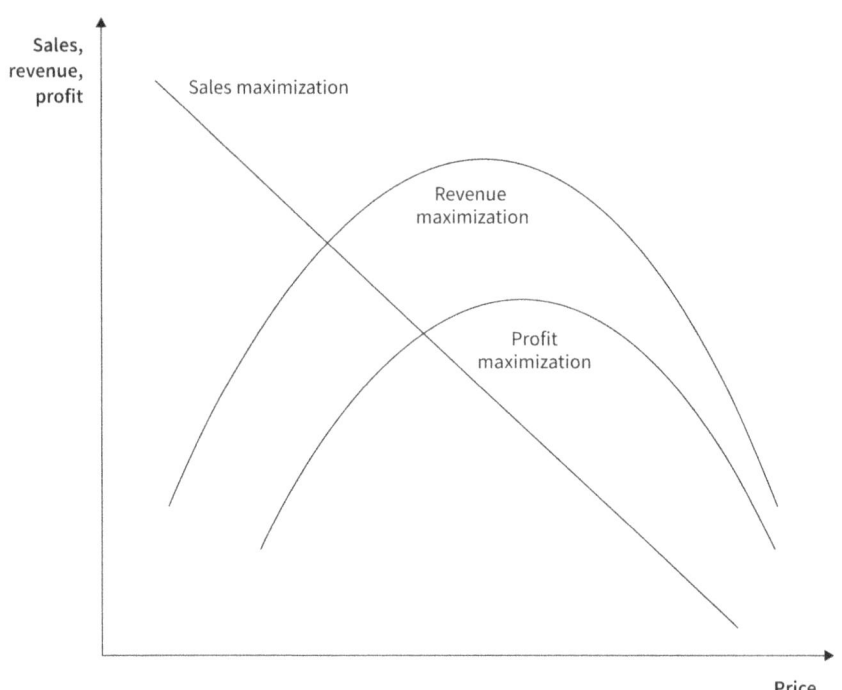

- **Profit maximization:** This objective generally leads to the highest price levels that can be justified. Few companies follow a pure profit maximization objective, as this often implies prices above the market level. Also, identifying the profit-maximizing portfolio in a complex market environment is difficult.

In our experience, most companies aim for an objective between revenue and profit maximization, which is commonly termed a **profitable growth objective**. Depending on the overall strategy, this may be closer to the revenue or profit optimum. Here it is important to note that if a company only sells a single product, then there is direct tradeoff between profit and revenue. Between the profit and the revenue optimum, a higher price increases profit and reduces revenue and a lower price reduces profit and increases revenue.

If a company sells many products, differentiates the offer between different routes to market or is confronted with other complexities, then there are typically many profit and revenue combinations that it can end up in. Most of these are inefficient in that profit or revenue can be increased without reducing the other. These inefficiencies can result from poor pricing decisions or changes in the environment such as competitors' offer changes or macroeconomic variations (e.g., rise of inflation or regulation). Figure 2.6 shows that there is an efficient boundary between profit and revenue that can be reached with a combination of measures. The task of pricing and RGM is to identify the measures (e.g., prices, offer structure, differentiation between channels, trade terms) to steer the company closer to the efficient boundary and manage the tradeoff between profit and revenue according to the company's strategy.

To summarize, pricing and RGM are important because they manage a company's relationship between value creation and value capture, and they identify measures to move closer to the efficient boundary between profit and revenue maximization. Based on our experience, many companies operate 2–4% of revenue below their efficient frontier. If you are a

Figure 2.6   Tradeoff between profit and revenue

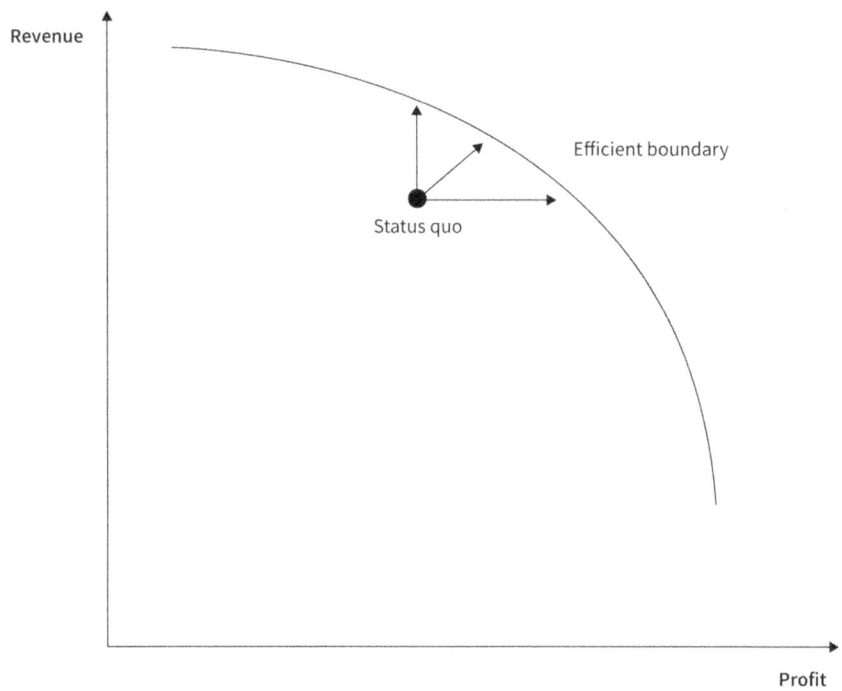

€20 billion company and decide to move only in the profit direction, this is a €400 million to €800 million opportunity to be captured via pricing and RGM.

2.2.3   Evolution of Pricing and RGM Roles in Companies

The role of pricing and RGM has evolved significantly in the past decades. Initially, pricing and RGM were primarily focused on setting prices for products and services based on simple methods such as cost-plus pricing. However, with the advent of new technologies and increased competition, pricing and revenue growth management have become much more complex. Today, pricing and revenue growth managers are responsible for optimizing pricing strategies, increasing revenue and profitability, and enhancing value to the customer. This involves using data-driven analyses to understand shopper behavior and market trends, developing pricing models that consider customer segmentation and willingness to pay, and constantly monitoring and adjusting prices in response to market conditions. Another important aspect of the role of pricing and revenue growth managers is to work cross-functionally with other departments, such as sales, marketing, and product development, to ensure that pricing strategies align with overall business objectives and customer needs. This requires strong communication and collaboration skills, as well as the ability to analyze and interpret data from a variety of sources.

Overall, the role of pricing and revenue growth managers has evolved from a primarily cost-based approach to a more strategic and customer-focused approach that requires a deep understanding of data analysis, market trends, and customer behavior. In Chapter 4, we will discuss the evolution of RGM in the age of AI in more detail.

2.3 THEORETICAL FOUNDATIONS

This is one of the most important sections in this book. Here, we will introduce the tools that are central to the work of pricing professionals and that we will use throughout the rest of this book. These include the microeconomic and behavioral foundations of pricing. It is important to note that although more and more of the actual computations using these methods – such as calculating how the sales in a product portfolio depend on price changes – will be performed by computers, it is vitally important for professionals to understand the underlying ideas and dynamics, and to be able to perform sense checks.

2.3.1   Microeconomics

How does a price change affect sales, and what prices optimize revenue or profit? These are key questions, which pricing and RGM professionals face frequently. Neoclassical economists such as Alfred Marshall developed quantitative models around the end of the nineteenth century to provide the tools to answer these questions.[13] Using the mathematics of calculus, they developed models to study the dynamics of supply and demand in specific cases such as:

- **Monopoly (one supplier):** Sales only depend on one's own actions (price or product changes).
- **Oligopolistic competition (few suppliers):** Sales depend on own and competitors' actions. This is the most relevant and most difficult to study, because the actions of others need to be considered. The field of game theory studies the interactions between competitors.[14]
- **Polypolistic competition (many suppliers):** Here, no single supplier affects the market price. Therefore, everyone will sell at the market price, because no one will be able to sell anything above the market price, and selling below the market price only loses money.

Economists typically draw the line between few and many by applying the dog arithmetic. Dogs can count to 4 or 5 (few), everything above that is considered many. In practical pricing work, professionals mostly assume (implicitly) the monopoly case, as only here you can compute a price elasticity that only depends on one's own price. We will do the same, but then

---

[13] Marshall (2009).
[14] For a good introduction and overview see Osborne (2003).

also discuss the challenges of considering competitor's actions for RGM optimization. Next, we look at demand dynamics in more detail.

2.3.1.1 Demand Functions

First, we start with demand. Figure 2.7 shows a linear demand function – the standard demand function used in most models. Mathematically, it is written as

$$V(p) = a + b \cdot p.$$

Here, $V(p)$ is the demand as a function of price p. The variable a denotes the maximum demand if p is 0, and b is the slope of the demand function. Typically, b is negative and denotes the volume that is lost if p is increased by 1 unit. For example, if the maximum sales potential for a product is 1,000 units, and you lose 200 units with every €1 of price increase, the demand function is:

$$V(p) = 1{,}000 - 200p.$$

Then, at a price of €5 or more no one will buy the product anymore.

This formalization is very useful, as we will see on the following pages. However, it is also important to understand the underlying dynamics that produce a linear demand function. Specifically, what it implies about customers' willingness to pay. In the above example, 400 customers are willing to pay a price of €3 and 200 customers will buy at a price of €4.[15] That means 200 customers have a willingness to pay between €3 and €4, and because demand is linear, one customer is lost every € $\frac{1}{200}$ = €0.005 – or every 0.5 cents. Therefore, a linear demand function implies that willingness to pay

---

[15] This is produced by the demand function by inputting the price of €3: 1,000 − 200 · €3 = 400; and for €4: 1,000 − 200 · €4 = 200.

is evenly distributed among customers such that if you sort them by their willingness to pay, they stand equidistant between the maximum price anyone is willing to pay and €0. In this example, there is one shopper every 0.5 cents, from €0 to €5. This is indicated in Figure 2.7 along the price axis.

Thinking of demand in terms of the implied distribution of willingness to pay among customers is a useful framework that we will use throughout this book to better understand a wide range of topics, such as the effects of competition and choices between products within a portfolio.

In addition to the linear demand function, two further demand function are relevant for pricing. First, the isoelastic demand function with

$$V(p) = a \cdot p^b.$$

Figure 2.7 Linear demand

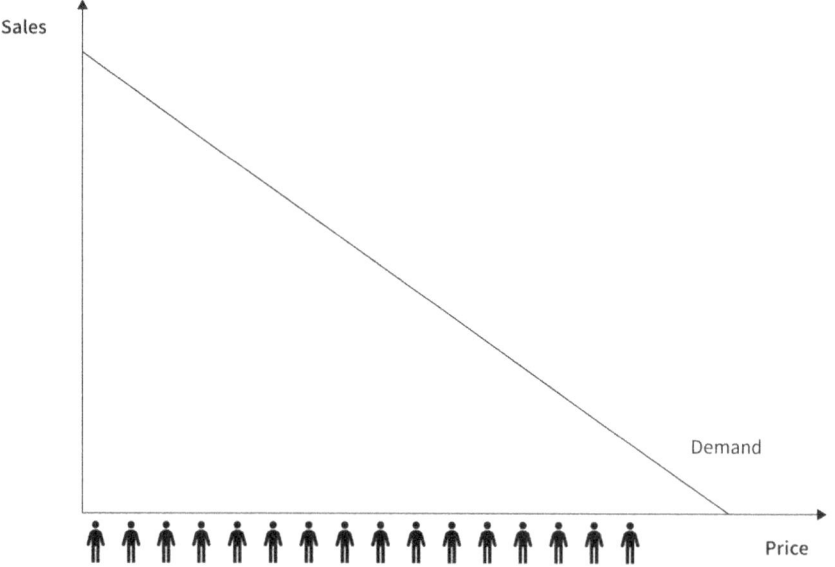

It is important because it has a constant price elasticity ε, as we will see in a few pages. So, when pricing managers use the same price elasticity at different price points, they assume an isoelastic demand function, as shown in Figure 2.8.

Isoelastic demand implies that if shoppers are standing along the price axis and are sorted by their willingness to pay, the distance between two adjacent shoppers decreases as the price decreases. Specifically, the distance decreases in proportion to the price. For example, if you gain 20% more shoppers from a price reduction from €4.00 to €3.00 (a 25% price reduction) you will also gain 20% more shoppers from a price reduction from €2.00 to €1.50 (a 25% price reduction).

Figure 2.8   Isoelastic demand

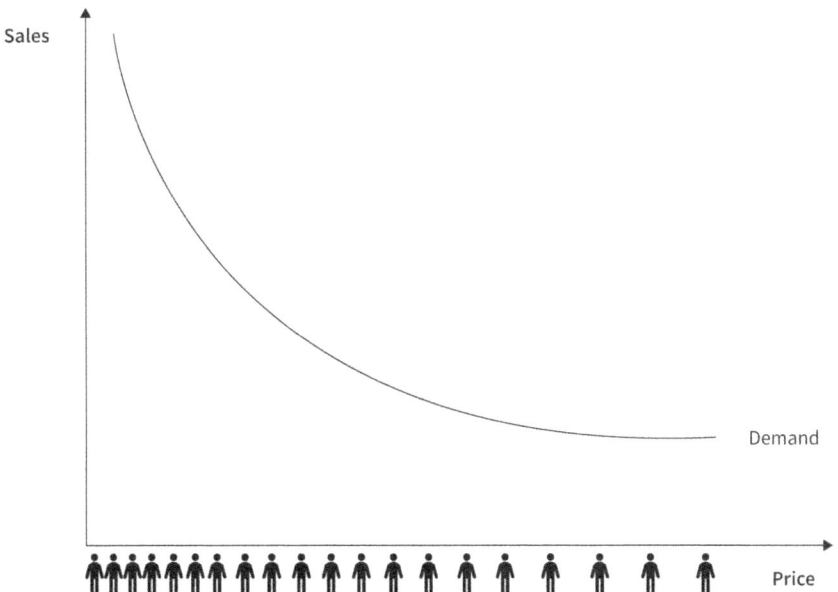

Second, empirical demand functions determined from surveys or sales data suggest that willingness to pay for products frequently follows a normal distributed, as shown in Figure 2.9. Here, most of the shoppers are willing to pay a price close to the mean, and only a few are willing to pay an extremely low or high price. This demand function is less widely used in pricing, but it is useful because it is close to actual demand and because the normal distribution has thin tails (few outliers), so demand changes do not overreact in the case of large price changes.

With these demand functions, we can do several useful things. For example, we can identify profit or revenue optimizing prices (Figures 2.10 and 2.11). The math required for this is straightforward and every pricing and RGM professional should go through the procedure occasionally to refresh the memory of the key mechanics.

Figure 2.9 Normal demand

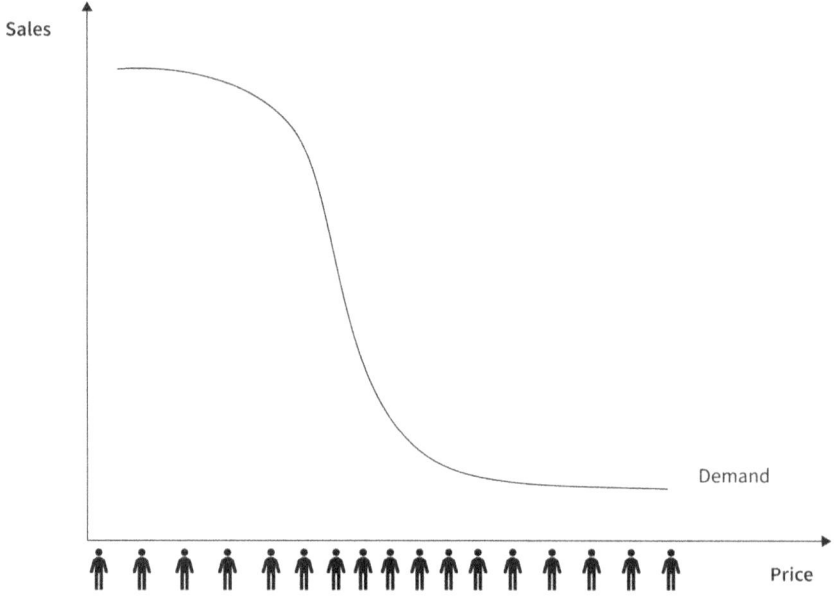

Figure 2.10 Profit optimization

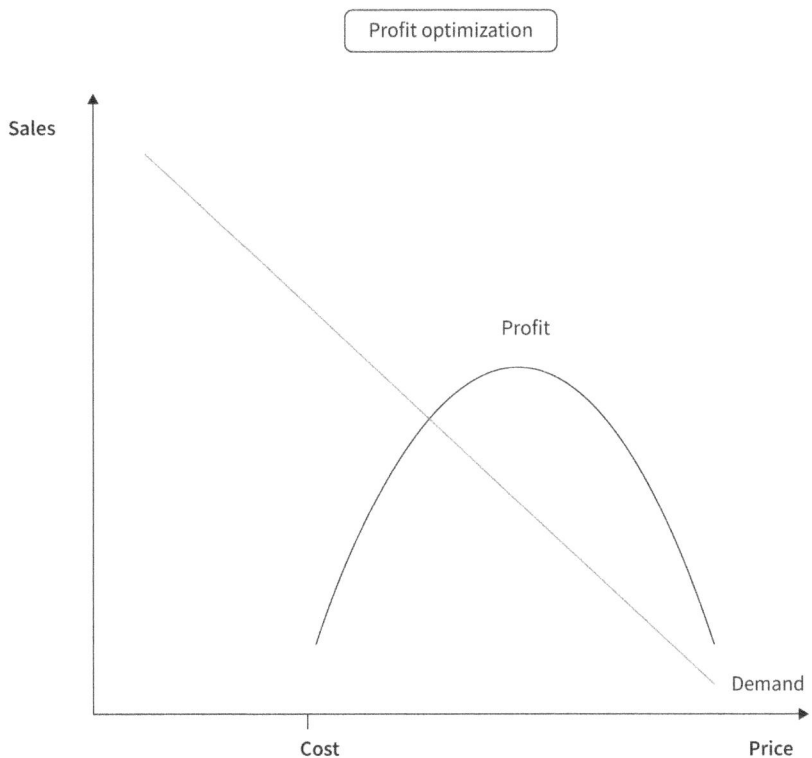

Let's look at a company's gross profit $\pi(p)$ as a function of price p, where c are the unit costs, and $V(p)$ is the sales volume depending on price. As a reminder, in pricing we only need to consider variable costs, and we can always ignore fixed costs in the profit optimization calculation. Therefore:

$$\pi(p) = (p-c) \cdot V(p)$$

$$= p \cdot V(p) - c \cdot V(p)$$

Figure 2.11 Revenue optimization

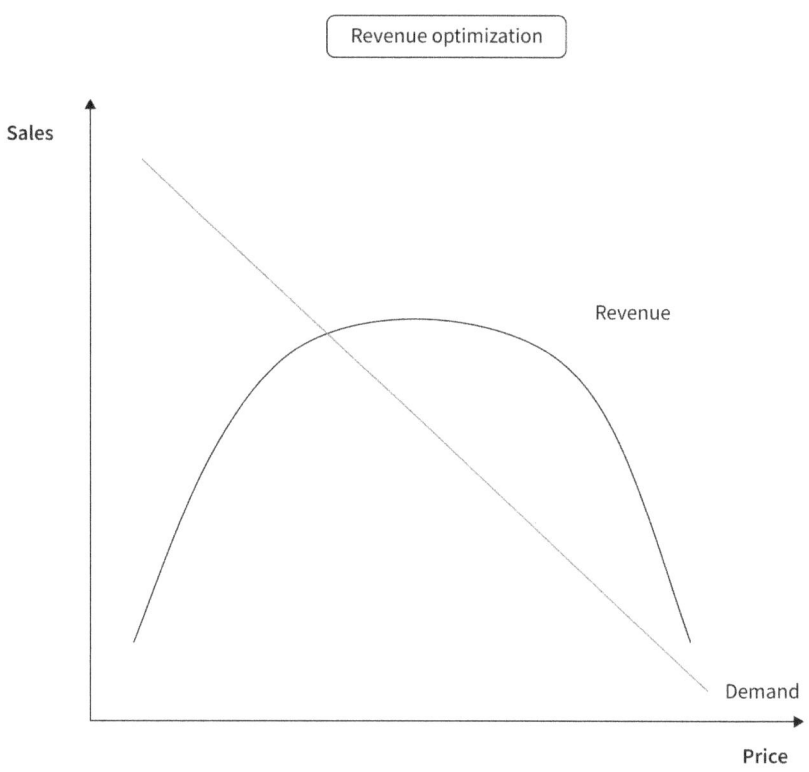

Then, to optimize profit, we consider the derivative and set it to 0 to determine the optimum.

$$\Rightarrow \frac{\partial \pi(p)}{\partial p} = p \cdot \frac{\partial V(p)}{\partial p} + V(p) - c \cdot \frac{\partial V(p)}{\partial p} \stackrel{!}{=} 0$$

$$\Rightarrow p = -\frac{V(p)}{V'(p)} + c \qquad (2.1)$$

To better understand this profit optimum, let's look at two specific cases. First, in the case of **linear demand** with $V(p) = a + bp$ and $V'(p) = b$, we get:

$$p = -\frac{a+bp}{b} + c$$

$$\Leftrightarrow p = -\frac{a}{2b} + \frac{c}{2}$$

Then the profit optimum is half of the maximum price anyone is willing to pay ($\frac{a}{-b}$), where the demand function crosses the x-axis, plus half of the variable costs ($\frac{c}{2}$). With the specific numbers from the previous example – that is, $a = 1{,}000$, $b = -200\frac{1}{€}$, and $c = €2$ – we get:

$$p = -\frac{1{,}000}{2 \cdot -200\frac{1}{€}} + \frac{€2}{2} = €2.50 + €1.00 = €3.50$$

Second, in the case of **isoelastic demand** with $V(p) = a \cdot p^b$ and $V'(p) = a \cdot b \cdot p^{b-1}$, we get:

$$p = -\frac{a \cdot p^b}{a \cdot b \cdot p^{b-1}} + c$$

$$\Leftrightarrow p = \frac{b}{b+1} \cdot c$$

Here, the profit optimum only depends on the exponent b, which determines the markup $\dfrac{b}{b+1}$ on the unit costs c. For example, if $b = -2$ and $c = €2$, then:

$$\Leftrightarrow p = \dfrac{-2}{-2+1} \cdot €2 = 2 \cdot €2 = €4.$$

We note that if $b > -1$, then there is no profit optimum.

Next, we can directly apply these results to determine the revenue optimum. If there are no variable costs, then profit (p_{prof}) and revenue (p_{rev}) optima are identical. Therefore:

$$p_{rev} = p_{prof}(c=0) = -\dfrac{V(p)}{V'(p)}$$

In the case of linear demand, we get:

$$p = -\dfrac{a}{2b}$$

With the numerical example from above:

$$p = -\dfrac{1{,}000}{2 \cdot -200\frac{1}{€}} = €2.50$$

For isoelastic demand, we have the peculiar situation that no unique revenue optimum exists, because if b is -1, then the revenue at every price is the same and optimal. If b is not -1, then no revenue-optimal price exists.

It is an important application of these optimization criteria to identify the best price change after a cost increase. There are different lines of thought in pricing on how to answer this question, and a value pricing fundamentalist might argue that costs should not be considered in setting prices – only value to the customer matters.[16] Here, we will simply apply the optimization criteria for linear and isoelastic demand.

For **linear demand** we have the profit-optimizing price:

$$p = -\frac{a}{2b} + \frac{c}{2}$$

If the price is profit optimal before the cost increase by Δc, then the price needs to be increased by half of the absolute cost increase Δc.

For **isoelastic demand** we have the profit-optimizing price:

$$p = \frac{b}{b+1} \cdot c$$

If the price is profit optimal before the cost increase, then the price needs to be increased by the same percentage change as the cost change.

Consider this example: We sell a product with $c =$ €100 at the profit-optimal price of €200. Now costs are increased by €10. With linear demand, we need to increase the price by €5 to €205, and with isoelastic demand the price needs to be increased by the same percentage that costs increase. Here, this is $\frac{€10}{€100} = 10\%$. Therefore, the profit-optimal price after the cost increase is €220. The large difference between the implied price changes shows how important it is to not only know the price elasticity (-2 in both examples), but also what the underlying demand function looks like.

2.3.1.2 Price Elasticity of Demand

Here, it is now the right place to introduce the concept of the **price elasticity of demand**, or for short, price elasticity. The idea of this concept is to have a measure of how strongly the sales of a product change as a result of

---

[16] We will discuss the different pricing methods in Section 2.4.2.

Figure 2.12 Visualization of price elasticity

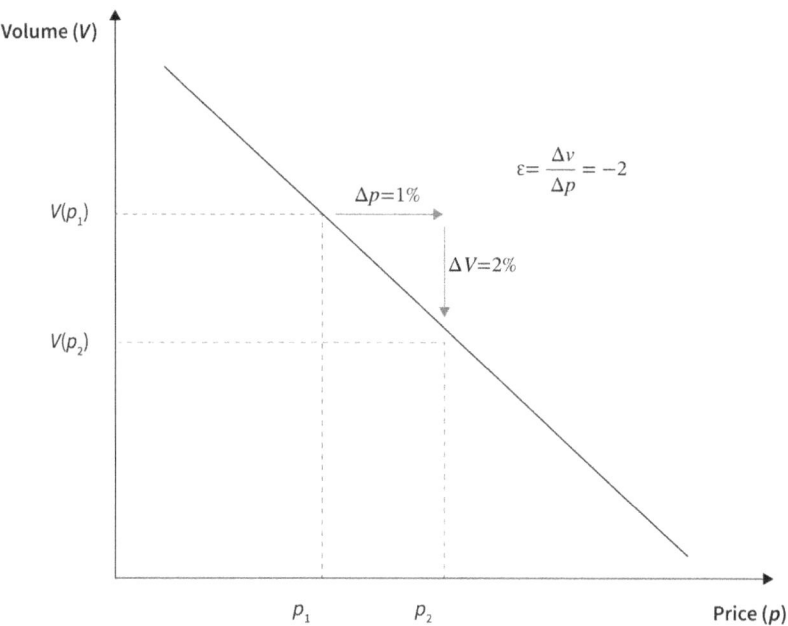

a price change. In Figure 2.12, a 1% increase in price leads to a 2% reduction in sales, because after the price increase the product is now too expensive for some buyers. The price elasticity (ε) is then defined as

$$\varepsilon = \frac{\text{percentage sales change}}{\text{percentage price change}}$$

In the example of Figure 2.12, the price elasticity at price p_1 is $\varepsilon(p_1) = \frac{-2\%}{1\%} = -2$. That's simple enough, and for the typical back-of-the-envelope calculations of how sales react to price changes, most pricing professionals will use this understanding. However, for a more precise understanding, the price elasticity needs to be defined with more care, because in general, the price elasticity varies with price and the magnitude of a price change.

Therefore, we need to distinguish between two types of price elasticity: point elasticity (price elasticity in a price point) and arc elasticity (price elasticity between two price points). First, to define a unique price elasticity at a specific price point, we use the following idea. If the demand function is not linear, then the price elasticity as defined above changes if we change the magnitude of the price change. Therefore, this equation does not yield a unique price elasticity value for price changes of 1%, 5%, or 10%. To determine a unique price elasticity value $\varepsilon_{point}(p)$ for a price point p, we reduce the price increase Δp further and further, and the limit of this process as Δp goes to 0, is called the **point elasticity**:

$$\varepsilon_{point}(p) = \frac{\frac{\Delta V}{V}}{\frac{\Delta p}{p}} = \frac{\frac{dV}{V}}{\frac{dp}{p}} = \frac{dV}{dp}\frac{p}{V} \qquad (2.2)$$

Figure 2.13 shows the point elasticities along a linear demand curve. For all linear demand curves the point elasticity at the midpoint, the price that corresponds to half of the maximum sales, is -1. For prices below the midpoint, the elasticity is above -1 and goes to 0 as the price goes to 0. Here, demand is called **inelastic**, because the percentage volume change is less than the percentage price change. For prices above the midpoint, the elasticity is below -1 and goes to minus infinity as the price goes to the maximum price with positive sales. Here, demand is called **elastic**, because the percentage volume change is larger than the percentage price change.

Formally, the point price elasticity ε at price p for linear demand is

$$\varepsilon(p) = \frac{bp}{a+bp},$$

Figure 2.13 Point price elasticity for linear demand

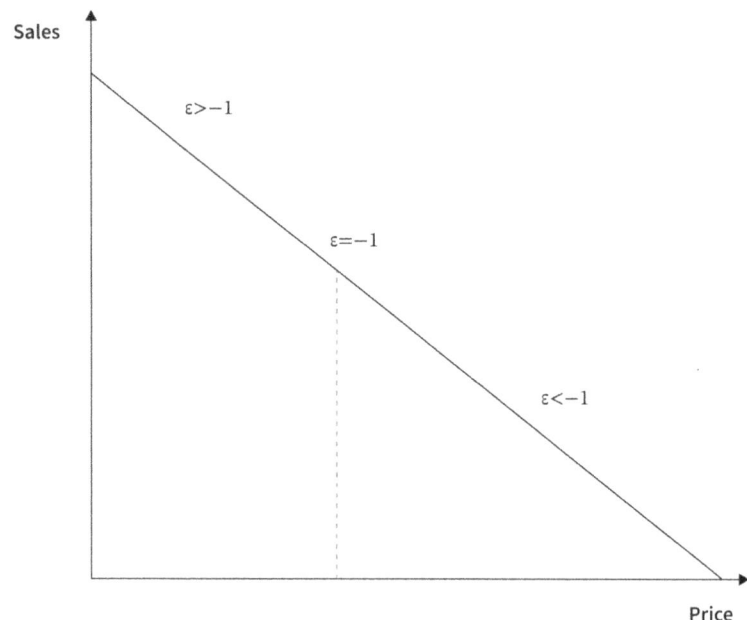

where a is the maximum sales volume and b is the slope (typically negative). For a linear demand function, the price elasticity can change strongly if the price is changed. For example, with $a = 1{,}000$ and $b = -100\frac{1}{€}$, the price elasticity at a price of €6 is $\varepsilon(€6) = \dfrac{-100\frac{1}{€} \cdot €6}{1{,}000 - 100\frac{1}{€} \cdot €6} = -1.5$. At a price of €7, it is −2.3. Price elasticities can change strongly with a price change. Therefore, pricing and RGM professionals need to be careful with using static price elasticities in the case of linear demand. For isoelastic demand $V(p) = a \cdot p^b$, this is much different, and the price elasticity is simply $\varepsilon = b$.

In practice, many professionals use what is called the **arc elasticity**. This is the price elasticity between two price points p_1 and p_2 (see Figure 2.14):

$$\varepsilon_{arc} = \frac{\dfrac{V_2 - V_1}{V_2 + V_1}}{\dfrac{p_2 - p_1}{p_2 + p_1}}$$

If the two price points move closer and closer toward each other, the arc elasticity and the point elasticity become identical.

Figure 2.14   Arc price elasticity

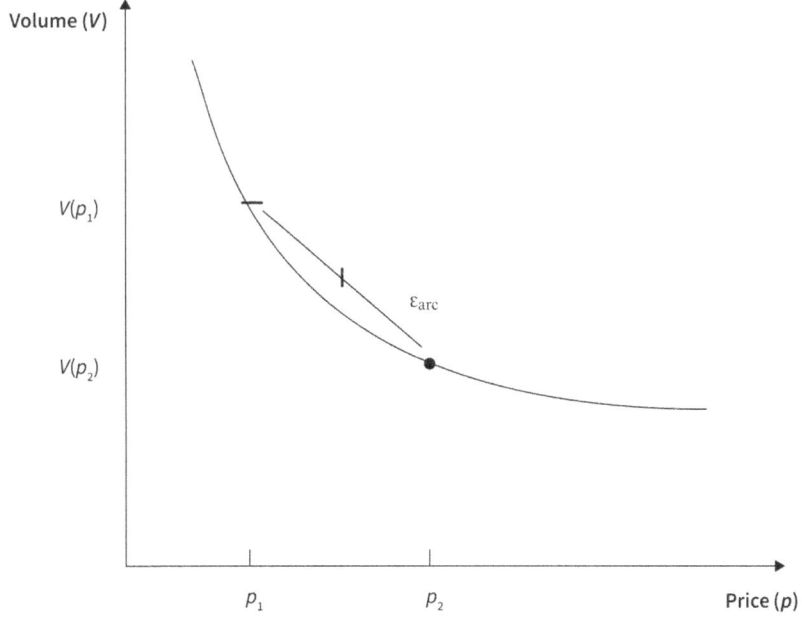

Using Equations (2.1) and (2.2), we can now derive a very useful insight that links price elasticity (ε), margin (m), and the profit optimum. That is, in the profit optimum, the following condition holds true:

$$p = -\frac{V(p)}{V'(p)} + c = -\frac{V(p)}{\frac{\varepsilon \cdot V(p)}{p}} + c$$

And hence:

$$\frac{p-c}{p} \cdot \varepsilon = m \cdot \varepsilon = -1$$

That means, in the simple one-product case, we find that margin times price elasticity is −1 for the profit-optimal price point. In the example in Figure 2.15, if the price elasticity is −2, then the profit-optimal margin is 50%, so with unit costs of €100, the profit-optimal price is €200. Further, for a price elasticity of −3, the profit-optimal margin is 33.33%, etc. If price elasticities are known, this is a very useful tool to determine if a price is optimal, or if not, whether it needs to be increased or decreased. Specifically, if $m \cdot \varepsilon > -1$, then the margin is too low, and the price needs to be increased. If $m \cdot \varepsilon < -1$, then the margin is too high, and the price needs to be reduced.

Further, because without variable cost ($c = 0$) profit and revenue optimization are identical, we immediately see that in the revenue optimum, the price elasticity is −1. If $\varepsilon < -1$ (elastic demand), a price increase decreases revenue. If $\varepsilon > -1$ (inelastic demand), a price increase increases revenue.

2.3.1.3 Challenges with Multiple Products

The previous rule ($m \cdot \varepsilon = -1$) is obviously very useful for profit and revenue optimization. However, there is a catch. This rule only applies in the one-product case. That is, when there are (1) no competitors that react to

Figure 2.15 Price elasticity and profit optimum

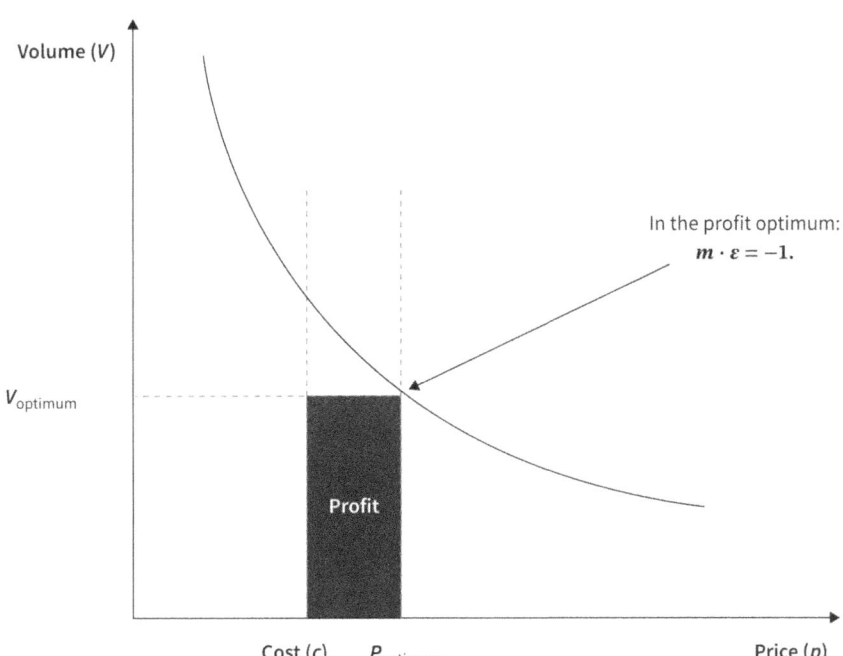

your price changes or make their own changes independently and you are (2) not optimizing the prices of a complete portfolio, where some of the lost sales after a price increase go to another product in the portfolio. This simplification is often forgotten by pricing and RGM professionals when they apply concepts like a price elasticity, because the simple relationship between a product's price and demand does, of course, also depend on other factors.

To understand the effects of competitor price changes, consider a market with two substitute products. One is your product and the other is your competitor's. To keep it simple, let's assume that the total demand in this market is constant. For example, the product may be an important spare part to an expensive machine, and the machine's owners will always buy from one of the two providers within a reasonable price range around the current prices. Then, if we increase the price by 10%, and the competitor does not change the price, our price elasticity is −2. If the competitor also increases the price by 10%, then our price elasticity is 0, as total demand is constant, and the relative price position has not changed. Figure 2.16 shows how our price elasticity (if we increase our price by 10%) depends on the competitor's price change and may even become positive if the competitor increases the price by more than 10%. This highlights that the price elasticity for a product depends on many other factors in a market.

Figure 2.17 shows an overview of how a product's price elasticity depends on other offer changes in a product category. These range from a single product price change to a price change together with a promotion and to a price increase of the whole portfolio combined with a price-pack

Figure 2.16 Price elasticity dependent on competitor's price change

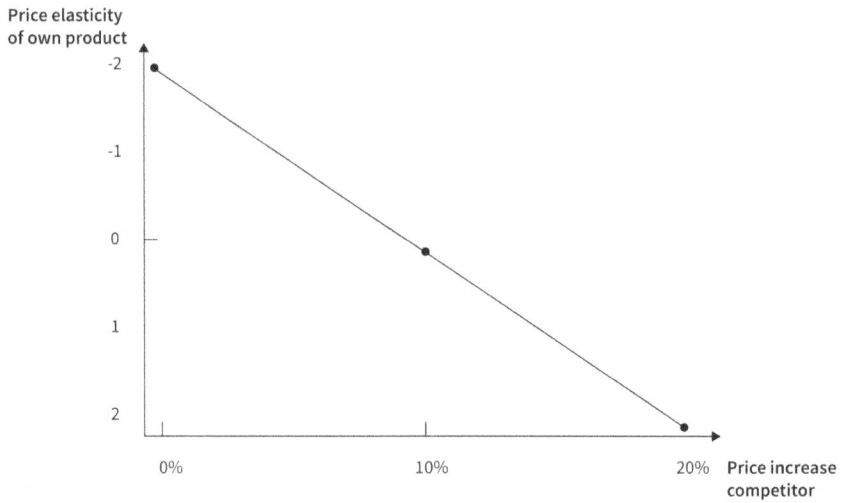

Figure 2.17   Price elasticity depends on market dynamics

Example values.

architecture (PPA) change. Price elasticities can vary greatly, and the different dynamics are difficult to assess other than with advanced simulation technologies (see Chapter 4).

Price optimization with competition is difficult as can already be inferred from the fact that textbooks in microeconomics typically focus on the two-product case (one own and one competitor product).[17] In practice, most professionals face a situation with significantly more complexity and often dozens of own and many more competitor products that are close substitutes. In such situations, price optimization is very difficult and needs to be addressed with an appropriate pricing or RGM strategy. Different alternatives are discussed in Chapter 3. As a general heuristic, a variation of the condition $m \cdot \varepsilon = -1$, discussed before in this playbook, is useful. If the objective is profit maximization, then in cases with more than one product in a category (own or competition), $m \cdot \varepsilon = -1$ should constitute a lower bound for all prices, as some of the lost sales from a price increase stay within the own portfolio. Further, lower prices may lead to a price war with competitors who lose sales because of our price reduction.

---

[17] See, for example, Mas-Colell et al. (1995).

2.3.1.4 A Note on Value

Value is a key concept in pricing and RGM to determine a product's price. However, it is often not clear what it means. This is probably best captured in Oscar Wilde's statement in *The Picture of Dorian Gray*[18]: "Nowadays people know the price of everything and the value of nothing." This would make its use in pricing to determine a product's price circular. Therefore, we need to spend some space in this book introducing the concept of value properly.

Classical authors such as David Ricardo or Karl Marx defined a product's value in terms of the resources required to make it.[19] These authors had mostly undifferentiated commodity products in mind such as bread and wine, that did not easily allow for price differentiation. So, the only way for producers to earn a surplus profit (a Ricardian rent) was from superior resources such as more fertile land. The shift in perspective to understand value from the customer's perspective came much later in the nineteenth century with the rise of product differentiation – specifically with different product brands that were perceived differently by customers.

For practical pricing and RGM, the key question is how to determine and work with the value of a product or its features. This can be easy as in some business-to-business (B2B) cases. For example, if your product saves a business one hour of labor a day for a specific necessary task, and one hour of labor costs the business $100, the value of your product to that business is $100 per day, and that is the maximum the business will be willing to pay for it. For business-to-consumer (B2C) cases, determining customers' willingness to pay can be more difficult. Section 2.4.1 provides an overview of the most common techniques to measure value to the customer. Here, it is important that value to the customer is not a single number – that would mean that the product has the same value to all

---

[18] Wilde (1891, p. 49).
[19] Ricardo (1817); Marx (1867).

customers – but a distribution of different values to different customers. Specifically, if to each customer the value of a product is the maximum they are willing to pay for it, then the distribution over the different values in a customer segment can be converted into a demand function (as described in Section 2.3.1) and used – for example via price elasticities – for profit or revenue optimization or for price differentiation across a product portfolio (see Section 2.4.2). Throughout this playbook, we will work with the following understanding of value.

For a single buyer (e.g., end user or company), the value of a product is the maximum willingness to pay (WTP) for that product if it is the only alternative. If alternatives are offered within a portfolio or from a competitor, the observed WTP can be different in a specific situation. For example, a buyer's (maximum) WTP for an orange juice is €7, and it is €5 for an apple juice. Then, €7 and €5 are the values this buyer attributes to the two products. If the orange juice is offered at a price of €4 and the buyer chooses the product that maximizes their utility computed by subtracting the product price from its value, then the utility of the orange juice is €7 − €4 = €3. In this case, the buyer will only buy apple juice if it is priced below €5 − €3 = €2 and produces a utility of at least €3. This differentiation can cause some confusion. Therefore, it is important to differentiate between the WTP of a product to a specific buyer, which does not change, and a context-specific buying decision, that depends on all offers in a market. If there are attractive alternatives in a market, then a buyer might not be willing to pay their (maximum) WTP for a product. Buyers are only willing to pay the WTP if there are no alternatives.

Further, we often hear terms like "value to the customer" when describing groups of customers or customer segments. However, it should be clear that typically not everyone in the group has the same WTP for a product and assuming it serves primarily as a simplification. In reality, the (maximum) WTP differs within groups of buyers. It follows some distribution and that distribution determines the demand function for that product.

For example, if the value attributed to a product is uniformly distributed among a group of buyers between zero and some maximum, then this results in a linear demand function for that product. This closes the circle and links value to the demand functions and concepts like price elasticity with our understanding of product value.

2.3.2 Behavioral Economics

Behavioral economics as a field of study challenges the key assumption of classical microeconomics that market participants (buyers and sellers) act rationally – which we used in this chapter up to now. Rather, it focuses on observed irrationalities in actual human decision-making and the factors that influence it. As we are all human, such irrationalities are self-evident for us, as the example in Figure 2.18 highlights. Even though we know that the two lines are of equal length, it is very hard to see it.

One of the key contributors to the development of behavioral economics is Daniel Kahneman, who won the Nobel Prize in Economics in 2002.

Figure 2.18 Being rational is not easy

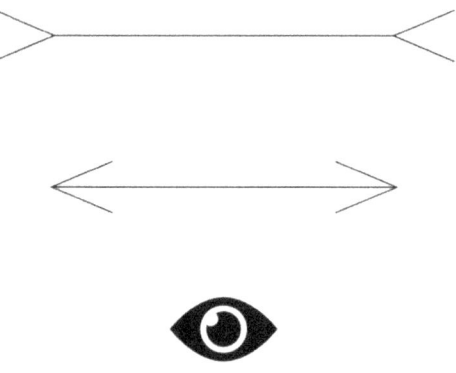

"I know that the two lines (without the arrows) have the same length, but I just can't see it!"

Figure 2.19 Homo oeconomicus vs. Homo sapiens

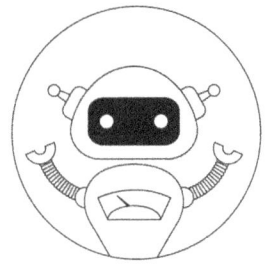

Homo sapiens (System 1)

- Irrational
- Uses simple decision heuristics
- Takes shortcuts that result in inconsistent behavior

Homo oeconomicus (System 2)

- Rational
- Maximizes utility
- Considers all alternatives
- Consistent decisions

In his book, *Thinking, Fast and Slow*, Kahneman introduced the concept of two modes of thinking (see Figure 2.19): System 1, which is intuitive, automatic, and often driven by emotions, and System 2, which is analytical, deliberate, and slow. Kahneman argues that System 1 thinking can lead to errors and biases, and that these biases can be used to better understand human behavior and decision-making.[20] To illustrate the differences between the two systems, we call the rational system that is envisioned by the microeconomic reasoning shown here to introduce demand functions and price elasticity "Homo oeconomicus" and the more irrational System 1 "Homo sapiens" – which is how real people make decisions.

Another important contributor to the field is Richard Thaler, who won the Nobel Prize in Economics in 2017. Thaler introduced the concept of "mental accounting," which suggests that individuals categorize their money into separate mental accounts, leading to irrational behavior. For

---

[20] Kahneman (2011).

example, individuals may be willing to pay more for a product if it is labeled as a "luxury item" than if it is labeled as a "basic item." The works of Kahneman, Thaler, and others have led to a number of important developments in economics, including the development of new models of decision-making under uncertainty, the study of social preferences and group behavior, and the application of insights from psychology to policy design.

One of the most important applications of behavioral economics has been the development of the concept of "nudges," which are small changes in the choice environment that encourage certain behaviors without limiting freedom of choice. The idea of nudging was popularized by Richard Thaler and Cass Sunstein in their book, *Nudge: Improving Decisions About Health, Wealth, and Happiness*. Nudges have been used in a variety of policy areas, including health care, retirement planning, and environmental policy.[21] Behavioral economics has been used to study a wide range of phenomena, from financial market bubbles and crashes, to social norms, and shopper decision-making.

Overall, behavioral economics has provided a valuable addition to classical microeconomics, offering a more nuanced understanding of human behavior and decision-making. Its insights have been used to inform policy and to shed light on a wide range of economic phenomena, making it a key area of study for economists and policymakers alike.[22]

Many of the heuristics that humans use in decision-making that have been studied in behavioral economics can also be applied to pricing and RGM. Examples of such heuristics include[23]:

- **Substitution:** A complex decision is replaced with a simpler one. For example, complex products that consist of hundreds of attributes are reduced to a simple decision between brands and a few

---

[21] Thaler and Sunstein (2008).
[22] Camerer (2011); Mullainathan and Shafir (2013).
[23] For a general overview on behavioural economics, see Kahneman (2017). For an overview on behavioural pricing, see Chen et al. (2021).

key features. For pricing, this can be used by optimizing a product with a focus on these key features.
- **Anchoring:** For people, it is much easier to evaluate something in relation to something known. For example, if customers must come up with their willingness to pay for some product that they do not know, their assessment can be anchored with a reference price (e.g., "Was €99, now . . .").

The starting point of behavioral pricing is the recognition rooted in behavioral economics that customers are often not rational but rather use a range of simplifying heuristics to make purchasing decisions. For example, a pricing manager might decide to add a third product to a product range to serve as a decoy to make the other products appear cheaper. Figure 2.20 shows a well-known example case. First, a wine vendor only offered the two bottles priced at €10 and €30. In this case, most customers go for the €10 bottle, because they are risk-averse and do not want to spend more than needed. If then the €50 bottle is added, the €30 bottle looks much more reasonable to most people, and they switch from the €10 to the €30 bottle. This behavior is considered irrational, because

Figure 2.20   Example of decoy pricing

the preference between the €10 and €30 bottle should not be affected by the addition of the €50 bottle. However, this is what happens consistently in human decision-making, and it can be very profitable to consider such common and empirically stable behavioral patterns in setting up an offer.

The specific application of behavioral pricing will be discussed in Section 2.4.2.

2.3.3 Macroeconomic Effects on Pricing and RGM

Pricing and RGM do not happen in isolation, but always in the context of a number of key macro trends that can affect the outcomes, objectives, or options available to pricing managers. Figure 2.21 shows an overview of such trends relevant at the time of writing this book. The selection and importance of these trends will surely change over time, but it is important to analyze how such trends affect pricing and RGM decision-making.

Figure 2.21   Key macro trends relevant for RGM

   Persistent inflation makes pricing more difficult – and more important.

   Change in shopper behavior: increasing share of private labels and discounter channels.

   Regulatory changes in ESG legislation (e.g., HFSS, carbon taxes) will increase.

   A global pandemic might return.

   Technological change accelerates and impacts product development and business models.

   Capital market requirements are acting as catalyst for business model and ESG changes.

For example, **inflation** reached levels of 9% in the United States and in the European Union (EU) during 2022, levels that have not been seen for decades.[24] Inflation and pricing are – obviously – intimately intertwined. Pricing is strongly affected by commodity price increases, directly via their own and indirectly via their competitors' COGS,[25] who also need to increase prices to protect their margins. Further, price increases in other categories can negatively impact shoppers' budgets. For example, if electricity prices increase, people might have to reduce the number of visits to the movies they can afford. Coming from a more stable world of low inflation, this put significant pressure on RGM teams and increased the need to use advanced analytics and improve processes to analyze market dynamics and make better decisions. In Section 3.2.1 we will take a closer look at how to use this playbook to optimize the response to a rapid increase and decrease in inflation.

Another key influence comes from **regulatory changes**. For example, regulations in the United Kingdom aim to reduce the consumption of products with high fat, sugar, or salt (HFSS)[26] contents by limiting the use of promotions and placement in stores. This limits the set of options for RGM.

Further, **capital markets** have a direct effect on pricing and RGM, that is often missed by many professionals in the field. If interest rates are low, as they have been in the years up to 2021, then profits further in the future have a higher present value and it is reasonable for many companies to favor growth over profits. Pricing can support growth with lower prices. This typically leads to a focus on higher market shares and revenues. If interest rates increase, future profits become less valuable, and the pricing

---

[24] European Commission (2023); Statista (2025) for monthly inflation data.
[25] COGS: costs of goods sold. These are the variable unit costs.
[26] UK Government (2025), restricting promotions of HFSS products.

focus needs to shift toward higher profits in the present. Therefore, capital market requirements directly affect the central strategic RGM tradeoff between profit and revenue described in Section 2.2.2.

To systematically analyze how a specific macro trend affects pricing and RGM, it is helpful to visualize them in terms of supply and demand, and how this affects profit and revenue optimization. In Figure 2.22, we show this for the trends listed in Figure 2.21. For example, inflation increases COGS, but also competitor prices, and this shifts the demand curve up – as with higher competitor prices, sales are higher at every price point. This reduces price elasticities, and it results in new revenue and profit-optimal prices. We strongly recommend going through this visualization exercise when faced with a new macro trend to understand the nuances of how it affects pricing and RGM.

Figure 2.22   Macro trends have a direct RGM impact

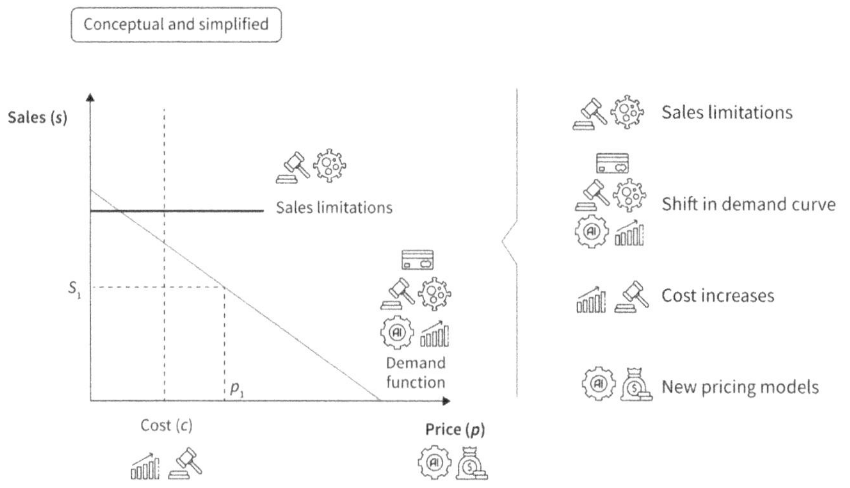

2.4 PRICING AND RGM IN PRACTICE

Over the past decades, first pricing and then more broadly RGM have become established professions with their own set of solutions. They include a set of pricing, PPA, and other RGM research methods, tools, and heuristics. These are being spread among professionals via word of mouth, internal company trainings, consultants, textbooks, and professional societies. In this section, we will provide an overview of these and provide sources for further study.

2.4.1 Pricing Research

There is a large collection of different research methods to support pricing and RGM decisions. These are focused on assessing shoppers' or customers' price sensitivity or their willingness to pay for products or specific product attributes. We will discuss the most important methods in this section. It is interesting to note that research on competitors is much less established than research on buyers. There are different reasons for this. Most important of all, there are typically many more customers than competitors – particularly in B2C markets. Therefore, it is both more difficult to assess the competitor behavior – for example via surveys – and to predict it, because pricing and RGM decisions by competitors often depend on a small number of decision-makers. Further, in many cases – particularly in B2B – competitor offers are nontransparent. In cases where pricing or RGM teams have full visibility on competitor offers (i.e., portfolios, promotions, prices, and so on) they can recognize patterns in previous decisions (e.g., competitor A always follows my previous price changes, competitor B always increases in line with inflation, etc.). Frequently, such patterns persist and are helpful in identifying relevant scenarios of future competitor offer changes.

Figure 2.23 shows an overview on the key research methods. These can be summarized in the three categories of market data assessment, surveys, and expert judgment. Please note that the selection of the research methods presented here is based on our practical experience, not some theoretical classification. We include what we see most in working with our customers.

2.4.1.1 Market Data Assessment

When possible, it is always best to use real market data, because it best shows how price or product choices actually affect sales and what customers actually value. Different techniques are available. The three most important ones are regression analysis, AB testing, and more recently pattern recognition using machine learning (ML), for example to understand promotion effectiveness.

Regression Analysis

Price elasticities are widely used in practical pricing, because they reduce the complexities of market dynamics into a single number, the price elasticity, that can easily be used to assess the effects of a price change. The most

Figure 2.23 **Overview of pricing research methods**

Market data assessment	Surveys	Expert judgment

• Regression analysis
   • Price elasticities
   • Value driver/attribute
• AB tests
• Machine learning (ML) based pattern recognition
• …
	• Van Westendorp
	• Gabor-Granger
	• MaxDiff
	• Conjoint analysis
	• …
		• Value driver/attribute assessment
		• Price elasticity assessment
		• …

Table 2.2 Example data linear regression

Week	Price	Sales
1	€2.59	176
2	€2.79	133
3	€2.59	261
4	€2.49	275
5	€2.69	125
6	€2.59	225
7	€2.19	482
8	€2.29	373
9	€2.39	284
10	€2.29	262

common way to determine price elasticities is via a regression model, that identifies the linear relationship between price (p) and sales volume (s) as described in Section 2.3.2 using historical sales data.[27] To outline the procedure, consider the example weekly sales numbers in Table 2.2. In this simple example, sales only depend on price with some noise, because not every week does the same number of shoppers show up who come to the same buying decision. However, there is no seasonality, no trend, or other factors such as the weather affecting sales in this example.

The objective of the linear regression analysis is to find the linear relationship that best captures the relationship between price and sales. The standard method to find the linear relationship is called ordinary least square (OLS) analysis.[28] The idea is to find a model of the weekly sales volumes that is closest to the actual sales over the weeks. This is achieved by

---
[27] Alternatively, the linear regression can be modeled on a log-log scale, which often provides a better fit, especially across larger price ranges and isoelastic demand.
[28] Wooldridge (2020).

minimizing the sum of the squared distances between all actual sales (s_i) and the modeled sales (s_i^*) for all periods i:

$$s_i^* = a + bp_i + e_i,$$

where p_i is the actual price in period i, and e_i is an error term. It can be shown that the total sum of the squared distances is minimized if:

$$b = \frac{\sum_{i=1}^{n}(p_i - \bar{p})(s_i - \bar{s})}{\sum_{i=1}^{n}(p_i - \bar{p})^2} \text{ and } a = \bar{s} - b\bar{p},$$

where $\bar{p}$ is the average price and $\bar{s}$ is the average sales volume. To determine how good the price versus sales relationship is represented by the linear model, the coefficient of determination (R^2) is often used. It is defined as the ratio of the explained variance in sales (EVS) and the total variance in sales (TVS):

$$R^2 = \frac{\sum_{i=1}^{n}(s_i^* - \bar{s})^2}{\sum_{i=1}^{n}(s_i - \bar{s})^2} = 1 - \frac{EVS}{TVS}.$$

R^2 ranges from 0, the model does not explain the data at all, to 1, the model fully explains the data and all sales are on a line in the price-sales graph.

Figure 2.24 shows the regression analysis that is based on the data in Table 2.2. The parameters $a = 1{,}495$, $b = -496$, and $R^2 = 0.79$ mean that at a price of €0, 1,495 units will be sold and with every €1 of price increase, 496 units are lost. The R^2 suggests that the model explains 79% of the total variance in weekly sales. By looking at the graph, it is easy to confirm that the relationship between price and sales is not perfect but well represented by the linear model. Now, computing price elasticities is a bit more tricky, as the price elasticity in a linear model is different at each price point. For example, using the formula from Section 2.3.1 the price elasticity is −6.1 at a price of €2.59, and at a price of €2.39 it is −3.8. So, it would be overly

Figure 2.24 Linear regression example

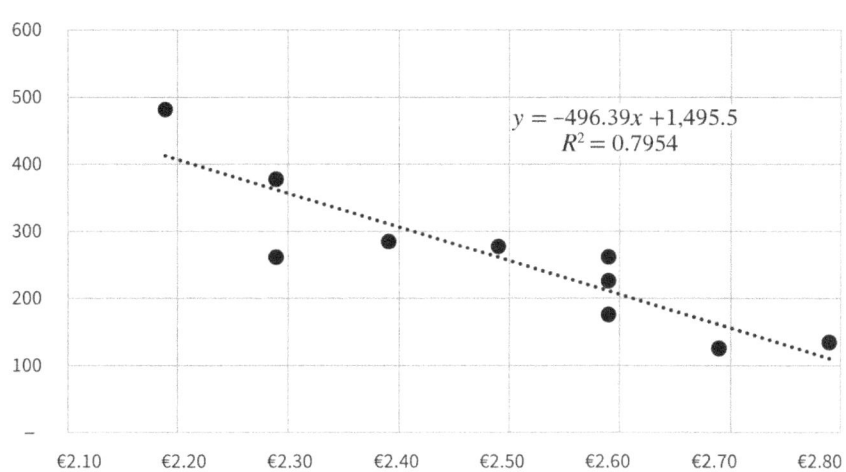

simplistic to attribute a single price elasticity to this product. Rather, the price elasticity needs to be specific to each price point – particularly in a case with high price elasticity as in this example.

In practice, most (linear) regression analyses produce R^2 values around 0.3, so the relationship is generally much weaker. Further, real sales data is affected by additional factors such as seasonality, weather, or competitor pricing and promotions. Analysts need to correct for these confounding factors before the price elasticity can be computed.[29] Also, in practice, such regression analyses are typically conducted by specialized agencies or dedicated data science teams within organizations. Here, we only want to provide a short introduction into the topic and highlight the general idea of determining price elasticities via regression analysis. In addition, alternative demand functions can be a better representation of the data. For example, the isoelastic or normal demand functions discussed in Section 2.3.1 are candidates.

There are some important caveats to measuring price elasticities via regression analysis. First, the choice of the demand function (e.g., linear or

---
[29] Kennedy (2008); Wooldridge (2020).

isoelastic) has significant impact on the result. In the case of linear demand, the price elasticity is different for each price point, while for isoelastic demand, it is the same for all price points. Second, regression analyses can easily be gamed by excluding "outliers" until the expected relationship between price and sales is identified. Third, such models do not capture well the interaction between products – either from within the own portfolio or from competitors. Therefore, if the change in demand for a product is also significantly affected by the price changes in other products, then the price versus sales relationship is not as straightforward as the regression analysis above suggests. Rather, the historical sales figures will already be affected by other products' price changes, and the regression analysis identifies the specific price elasticity for this historical combination of price changes across products.

Multivariate Regression Analysis for Promotion Analysis

The multivariate regression is an important extension of the univariate regression, which only looks at price changes to explain sales changes, that considers potential further sales drivers. These include external factors such as seasonality or long-term trends that increase or decrease sales of a product category. An example of seasonal changes is ice cream – today, summer sales in the United States are about 50% above winter sales (compared to 500% 100 years ago).[30] An example for a long-term trend is bottled water, where US producer revenues more than doubled from about $13.8 billion in 2014 to $28.2 billion in 2024, resulting in an average annual growth rate of about 7%.[31]

In practice, the most important drivers of sales in addition to price are promotions. To analyze the effect of promotions, we extend the previous univariate model to

$$s_i^* = a + bp_i + c_j \delta_{i,j} + e_i.$$

---

[30] FRED Blog (2024).
[31] Beverage Marketing (2025).

Here, the predicted sales s_i^* in week i depend on the price p_i in week i and the sales uplift c_j coming from promotion j ($\delta_{i,j}$ takes the value 1 if promotion j is run during week i and 0 otherwise). The uplift c_j is the additional uplift that comes in addition to the uplift attributable to a promotional price decrease. This might be caused by additional awareness because a product is promoted in an advertisement or a flyer – or because it is positioned more prominently on a shelf or on a website.[32] Also, behavioral effects can play an important role. For example, a 2-for-1 promotion can be perceived very differently than a 50% discount. These differences between promotions can be picked up via different promotion types (j) in a multivariate regression analysis. Again, e_i is an error term that captures the unexplained effects. To keep the example simple, we only included the price and the promotion effects. A more detailed model can also include season and trend effects outlined before, competitive offers, or interaction terms – for example, between price and promotion, if promotions show a different effectiveness at different price levels.

Figure 2.25 shows the example from the previous section with the addition of a promotion in weeks 7 and 10, which on average increases sales by about 800 units. Here, it looks like the regression does not fully pick up the difference in the promotion strength in the two weeks. This might have different causes that can, to some extent, be identified by an analyst. For example, promotions or price changes of other products affect sales differently in weeks 7 and 10, or the promotion effect is not additive but multiplicative, or it interacts with the price (i.e., the promotion effect is stronger if price is reduced more).

To sum up, measuring price elasticities via regression analysis is one of the most frequently performed exercises in pricing. They provide a good rough estimate of how price and promotions affect sales, particularly in

---

[32] Here, we are showing the simplest form of adding promotions. An extension might be the inclusion of an interaction $d_j p_i \delta_{i,j}$ between price and promotion i,j, as a promotion might work differently well at different prices.

Figure 2.25 Actual and estimated sales with promotions in weeks 7 and 10

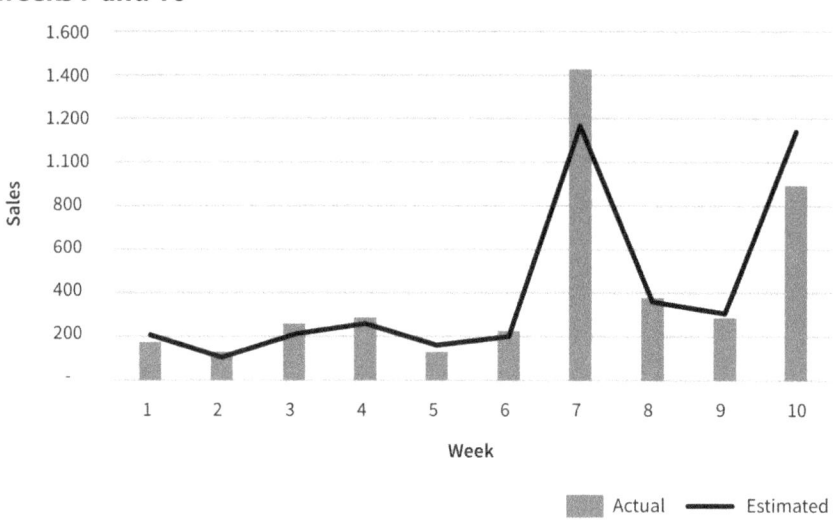

stable markets where, for example, competitors change their price in the same way as they did in the previous years. However, they do not work very well in markets with interdependence between products and competitors and a dynamic macro environment with, for example, inflation and demand changes over time.

AB Tests

One way to mitigate some of the challenges of regression analyses are AB tests. Specifically, these address the potential effects of other changes that are going on in a market, such as competitor price changes or macro effects such as a rise in inflation that are affecting the sales in some of the weeks that are used for the regression analysis.

The basic idea of an AB is to randomly split a group of potential buyers into two subgroups, A and B, and to then show them the two variations of an offer.[33] An important feature of AB tests is that they are conducted with

---

[33] For an introduction on AB testing, see Kohavi et al. (2020).

real customers in the real environment. For example, subgroups A and B are shown different offers on an online shop – and when a shopper goes through the full buying process, this constitutes an actual purchase of the product.

In the example of Figure 2.26, 2,000 randomly selected potential buyers are shown the offer A (buy an apple for the price of €1.00), and 2,000 randomly selected potential buyers are shown the offer B (buy an apple for the price of €1.10). The resulting sales are 1,000 apples in group A, and 900 in group B. The price elasticity between €1.00 and €1.10 is then computed as $\frac{-10\%}{10\%} = -1$. The advantages of this method are obvious. First, because potential buyers were assigned to the two groups randomly, all other effects (such as inflation or the price of peaches) affect buyers' decisions in both groups equally. Further, AB tests can also be used to test all other properties of an offer, not only price changes for a single offer.

Figure 2.26 Simple AB test

Figure 2.27 provides a selection of features that can be tested. These include price changes within a portfolio of a single or multiple products, changes in product features, or behavioral effects such as price thresholds or highlighting specific options. Note that only properties of the own offer can be tested. To assess the effect of competitors' offer changes, pricing analysts need to resort to other sources such as regression analysis.

AB tests are widespread in online channels, where potential buyers can be split into different groups. For offline channels such as physical retail stores, conducting AB tests is more difficult and thus much less widespread, because buyers cannot easily be split into random groups. All shoppers within a store see the same offer, and if complete shops need to be assigned to subgroups A and B, then it is typically difficult to ensure that the test groups are unbiased (i.e., they include the same number of small and large stores, urban and rural stores, etc.).

Further, AB tests can be extended to ABC... tests depending on how many variants need to be compared. Testing many variants – for example, many different price points and not only two – is often desired to gain broad insights, but this is typically limited by the costs of conducting the test and by the number of potential buyers that are available for testing to ensure that test results are statistically significant. For smaller businesses or long-tail products that are sold less frequently, AB tests on pricing often need to run for months, until results are statistically significant.

Determining the required sample size is always an important topic before conducting an AB test. Tools that support AB testing typically compute sample sizes,[34] but it is useful to understand how they are determined. In AB testing, required sample sizes depend on the effect size (p_1 vs. p_2, for the success rates in groups), the significance level (α) – typically $\alpha = 0.05$ – and the statistical power ($1 - \beta$). Statistical power is the probability of correctly detecting a true effect. A power of 0.8 means there is an 80%

---

[34] For example: https://www.surveymonkey.com/mp/ab-testing-significance-calculator/

Figure 2.27   Example of effects for AB testing

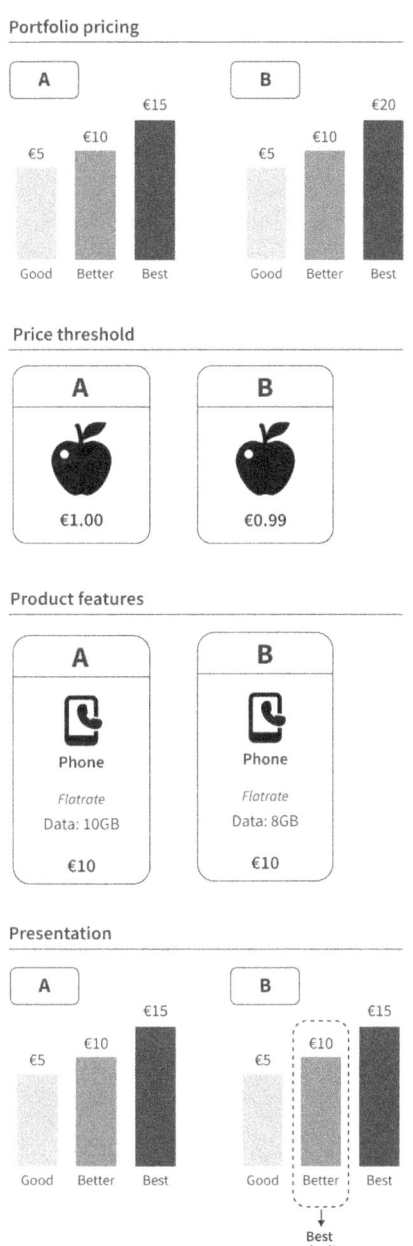

chance of finding a real difference if it exists. Higher power requires larger samples.[35]

The sample size (n) formula for comparing two ratios in an AB test is:

$$n = \frac{\left(z_{1-\alpha/2}\sqrt{2p(1-p)} + z_{1-\beta}\sqrt{p_1(1-p_1) + p_2(1-p_2)}\right)^2}{(p_1 - p_2)^2},$$

where p_1 and p_2 are the expected success probabilities (e.g., conversion rates) in the control and the treatment groups, and $p = \frac{(p_1 + p_2)}{2}$ is the pooled average.[36] Here, n is the sample size for each subgroup A and B. The total sample size for both subgroups together is $2n$.

For example, if the baseline conversion rate is $p_1 = 0.05$ (5%) and the expected conversion rate after some measure (e.g., a price reduction) is $p_2 = 0.06$ (6%), with $\alpha = 0.05$ ($z_{1-\alpha/2} = 1.96$) and power = 0.8 ($z_{1-\beta} = 0.84$), then the formula yields approximately $n \approx 7{,}450$ observations per group. This illustrates that detecting a one-percentage-point increase requires several thousand users per variant. Therefore, computing reliable price elasticity values using AB tests can only be done in cases with significant sales volumes. This is particularly the case because for reliable measurements, more than two price points should be tested.

2.4.1.2 Surveys

Surveys are the first choice if direct customer data from actual sales to answer a specific question is unavailable. For example, if an RGM team needs to understand how shoppers value a potential new brand or product feature before it has been introduced into the market, they typically revert

---

[35] Cohen (1988); Zhou et al. (2023), on sample size calculations in AB testing.
[36] Chow et al. (2017), on sample size calculations in clinical research.

to surveys. Here, we will introduce the most relevant survey types based on our daily work in the field.

Van Westendorp

The Van Westendorp method or Price Sensitivity Meter (PSM) was first introduced by Van Westendorp in 1976.[37] The objective of the method is to measure the price sensitivity of a product by surveying potential buyers of that product. This method is primarily used for innovations where it is difficult to get an understanding of buyers' willingness to pay from actual sales data. The results of the survey are used as a rough estimate of the relevant price range for a new product. Specifically, participants are asked (see Figure 2.28) to name the price points at which they consider a product so cheap that they would question its quality (**too cheap**), the price point at which the product is a bargain (**cheap**), the price point at which the product is expensive, but they would still consider buying it (**expensive**), and

Figure 2.28 Van Westendorp questionnaire

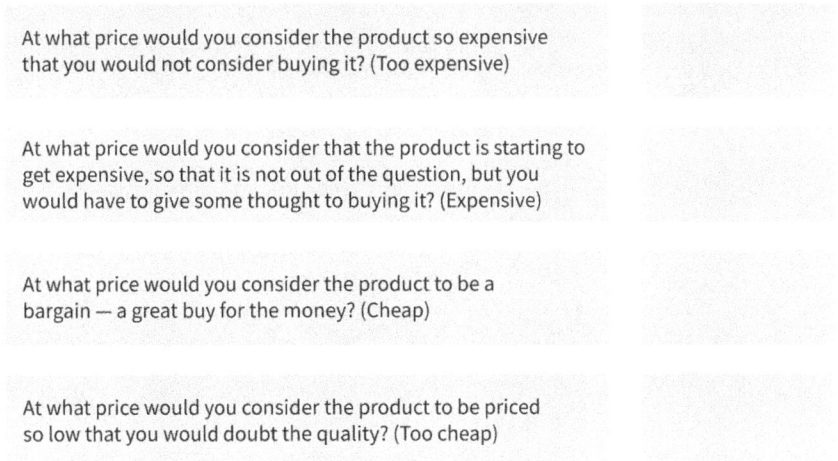

---
[37] Van Westendorp (1976).

the price point at which the product is so expensive, that they would not buy it any more (**too expensive**).

The results of the questionnaire are then plotted in the typical Van Westendorp graph as illustrated in Figure 2.29. The four plots show the share of respondents who consider the prices within the price range too cheap, cheap, expensive, and too expensive. The plots for cheap and too cheap are decreasing with increasing price and the plots for expensive and too expensive are increasing with price. The graph includes two important intersections. First, the intersection between the "cheap" and "expensive" plots is called the indifference price point (IPP). Here, the same number of respondents consider the product expensive and cheap. This price is considered the typical market price level. The second important intersection is the one between the "too expensive" and "too cheap" plots. It is called the optimal price point (OPP). Here, the same number

Figure 2.29 Van Westendorp Price Sensitivity Meter

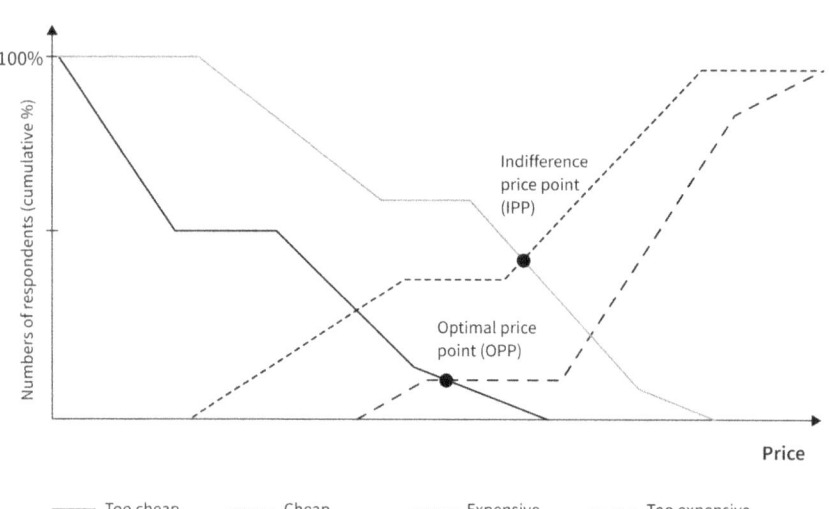

of respondents consider the product too expensive and too cheap. According to the Van Westendorp analysis, here the resistance to buy is lowest, and the price is considered optimal. There are many other interpretations of the graph among professionals. Most of these should be taken with a grain of salt. The common theme is that the intersections of the four plots mark the relevant price range for the product. However, for most of these claims it is difficult to find support in empirical evidence. Therefore, the Van Westendorp analysis is typically seen more as directional and one element of a larger RGM exercise that also includes other analyses.

In our work, we find another use of the Van Westendorp results. The too-expensive curve is closely related to the demand curve. If a respondent labels a price as too-expensive, then this is their maximum willingness to pay. For example, if a price is too expensive for 100% of respondents, demand is 0. If a price is too expensive for 50% of respondents, then demand is 50% of the total demand, etc. Figure 2.30 shows how the demand function can be generated from the too expensive plot.

Figure 2.30   From the too-expensive plot to the demand function

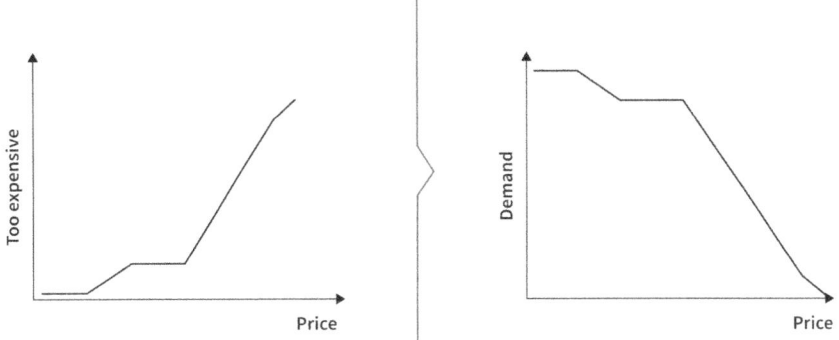

The advantage of the Van Westendorp analysis is that it typically provides robust results and can be run with limited effort and low costs. However, it only provides a price range, and not an optimal price. Also, it focuses on a single product, and it does not inform the analyst about the importance of product attributes or the competitive price position, or the interdependencies within a product portfolio.

Gabor–Granger

The Gabor–Granger method was introduced by André Gabor and Clive W.J. Granger,[38] and its objective is to determine the demand function for a product. This is achieved by asking respondents how likely they are to buy a product at specific price points.

Figure 2.31 shows a typical questionnaire with predefined price points. Alternatively, respondents can be asked – starting with the highest price point of the test range – if they would buy the product at that price point and then reducing the price if they say "no" until they say "yes." The result

Figure 2.31 Gabor–Granger questionnaire (excerpt)

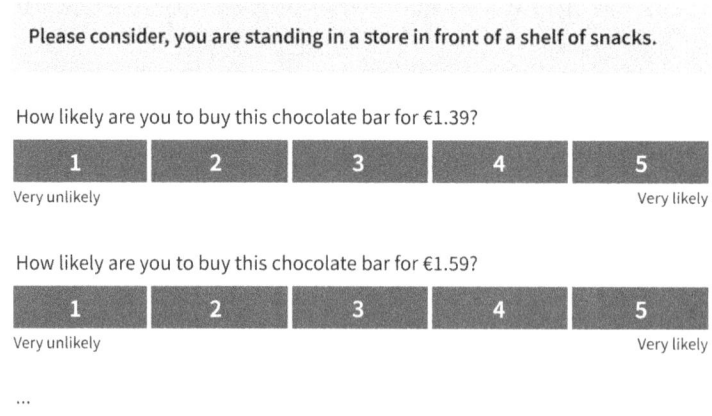

---

[38] Gabor and Granger (1979).

of these different techniques across a number of survey participants is a demand function as shown in Figure 2.32.

Comparable to the Van Westendorp method, the Gabor–Granger analysis can be conducted quickly and with a low investment. It also has similar disadvantages to the Van Westendorp method in that it focuses on a single product and does not inform the analyst about how the product performs against competition or the dynamics within their own portfolio. For example, where do the lost sales go? Do they go to a competitor or to a different product within their own portfolio? Further, results of such a direct price query can often be biased, as respondents might provide strategic answers (e.g., they report a willingness to pay below their actual value).

Some of the disadvantages of these survey methods can be mitigated by performing, for example, a Van Westendorp and a Grabor–Granger survey to see if they produce consistent results, or by comparing results to a

Figure 2.32   Gabor–Granger results (example)

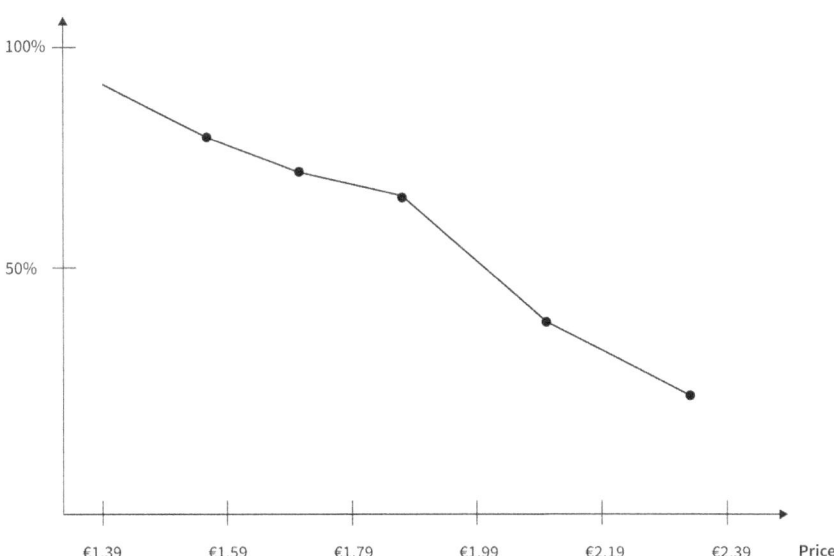

sales-data-based analysis of price elasticity for existing products to understand a potential bias in the survey.

Maximum Difference (MaxDiff)

The next survey method is the Maximum Difference – or simply MaxDiff – method.[39] The objective of the method differs from the two previous survey methods in that it is not used to measure the willingness to pay distribution for a product or service, but to assess the importance of different value drivers or features for potential buyers. Figure 2.33 shows a typical MaxDiff survey question, where respondents are repeatedly asked to identify the most and least important feature from a subset of all potential product features.

The selection of features on the screens presented to respondents is typically prepared dynamically by the survey software based on previous

Figure 2.33   MaxDiff survey example

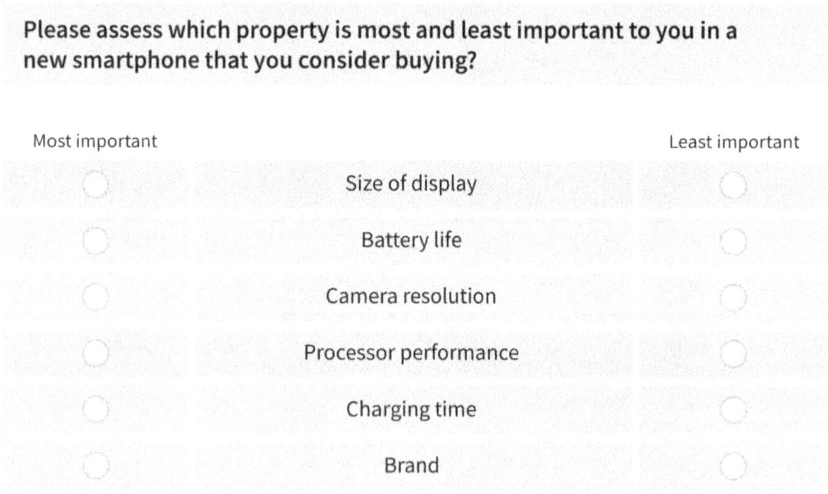

Please assess which property is most and least important to you in a new smartphone that you consider buying?

Most important		Least important
○	Size of display	○
○	Battery life	○
○	Camera resolution	○
○	Processor performance	○
○	Charging time	○
○	Brand	○

---

[39] For an overview, see Louviere et al. (2015) and Chrzan and Orme (2019).

answers of a respondent to best determine their importance rank-order. Because the method asks many simple questions in each case (to identify the most and least important from a list), the result is more robust than directly asking participants to rank-order features.

Figure 2.34 shows a typical output from a MaxDiff analysis. In the example, all features are ranked by their preference share. The preference share measures the probability that a value driver is chosen over all others if a random respondent is asked to select from the list. Here, value for money is most important and camera resolution least important. It often makes sense to perform this analysis for different segments, such as different countries or existing and potential new buyers to understand key differences.

Figure 2.34 Output MaxDiff survey – importance ranking

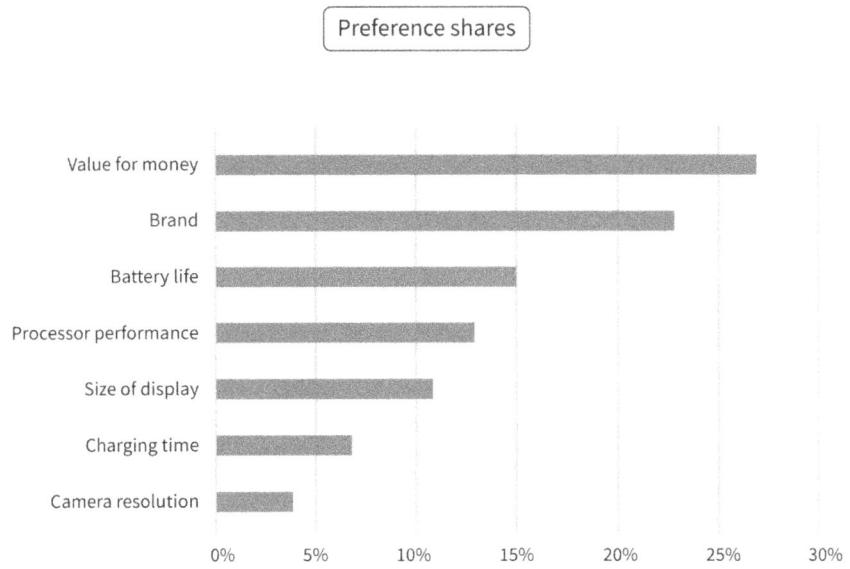

MaxDiff is a popular survey among pricing and RGM professionals because it provides cost-efficient and fast insights into buyers' preferences, and it often serves as a complement to other analyses such as the Van Westendorp and Gabor–Granger surveys discussed before, which focus more on willingness to pay for a complete product or service and not its features. MaxDiff is also often performed in combination with a conjoint analysis (discussed next) or other solutions that build on value drivers and attributes to identify the relevant number and selection of value drivers to be considered further. Typically, five to seven value drivers are needed to capture most of the variation in value, as it is difficult for buyers to consider more features when deciding.

Conjoint Analysis

Conjoint analysis is the most comprehensive of the survey methods discussed here. It attempts to present to the participant a decision situation that is as close as possible to the actual purchasing decision. The method is rooted in psychology and emerged with the growing importance of branded products and the need for companies to understand how to build and price their brands.[40]

It is the core idea of the method to always let the participant choose between alternative – and often fictional – products. The products are composed of a predefined selection of relevant value drivers (e.g., selected via the MaxDiff method), such as brand or size, and a set of attributes within each value driver to be tested – for example, Apple, Samsung, or Sony as potential smartphone brands. To make the decision situation as realistic as possible, different options are available, from which participants need to choose. Surveys range from simple online questionnaires to inviting prospects to an event where they see and use the actual

---
[40] Green and Srinivasan (1975).

products – including those not yet on the market. In the automotive industry, for example, it is not uncommon to show prototypes of new vehicles together with the relevant competitor vehicles to survey participants before they answer the conjoint questions to ensure that they understand the differences between designs and specific features.

Figure 2.35 shows a typical screen that is shown to survey participants who need to choose between different products composed of different attribute levels and the option to buy none of the products. In an actual survey, respondents are shown multiple screens (typically around 10 to 30) where in each case the previous answers can be considered by the algorithm to compose the next screen such that the utility differences of the different options become smaller. For example, if a respondent has a high preference for brand A, the other options (with alternative brands) will be made successively more attractive by lowering the price or adding more valuable features until the respondent switches. This allows the most precise assessment of the value of brand A.

The respondents' answers are then transformed into utility values for all attribute levels including the tested price levels, which in turn can be used to determine the importance of the different value drivers and attribute levels.

Figure 2.35   Example of conjoint analysis (for TVs)

	Option 1	Option 2	Option 3	Option 4 (None)
Brand	A	B	C	*I will not purchase any of these TVs*
Type	Plasma	LCD	LED	
Size	40 inch	50 inch	60 inch	
WiFi connectivity	Smart TV	Non Smart TV	Non Smart TV	
Price	€699	€799	€899	

Figure 2.36 shows an example output of the importance of the different value drivers. The importance of each value driver is determined by taking the difference between the value of the most highly valued attribute level and the least highly valued attribute level of that value driver. For example, the relative importance of the value driver "brand" of 25% is computed by taking the difference between the relative value of the most valuable and the least valuable brand tested.

Figure 2.37 shows the values of all tested attribute levels across value drivers. These outputs show analysts how valuable specific attribute levels are. Particularly, the relative brand values are of high interest for marketers and losing or winning a rank in brand value can ruin or light up the day.

The outputs of a conjoint study can also be used to build what is called a market simulation that allows pricing and RGM professionals to model how feature or price changes in a portfolio affect market shares, revenue, and profit. This modeling is highly useful for decision-making but must often be taken with a grain of salt, because such market simulations can be

Figure 2.36   Conjoint output – relative importance of value drivers

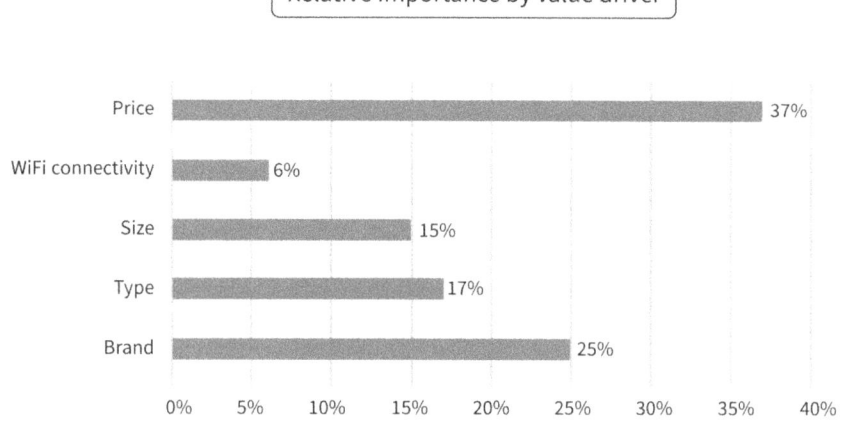

Figure 2.37 Conjoint output – relative importance of attribute levels

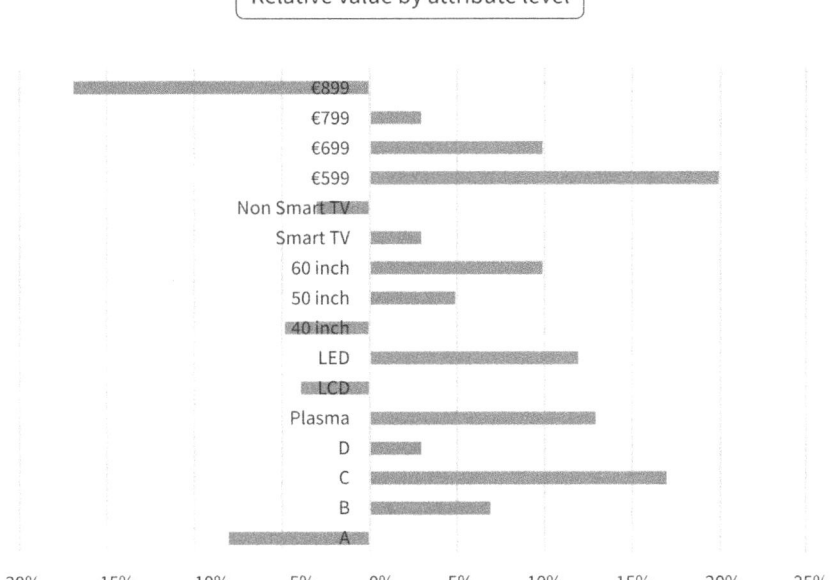

very inaccurate if compared to actual market share and often require substantial adjustments that then limit their precision when making predictions on the effects of feature changes. Such differences arise from differences between the survey and the actual buying decisions, where decisions are influenced by many other factors including promotions, marketing, and product placement. Further, such market simulations often run in Excel and take a market across channels and weeks as a monolith and ignore the actual market dynamics, where offers differ from week to week and between channels. We will discuss in Chapter 4 how to address these challenges.

Furthermore, to determine market responses such as price elasticities, it is necessary to always include a "buy nothing" option in the survey (as in

Figure 2.35). Otherwise, the survey will only be able to determine relative market shares of products but not total market sizes. For example, if all prices are increased by 100%, this might not affect relative market shares, but it might cut the total market by 50%. To determine the latter, the "buy nothing" option is required so that analysts can see when shoppers leave the market.

The above version of the conjoint study is typically called a choice-based conjoint (CBC). It is the most common study type used in practice. It is often combined with other elements such as the MaxDiff analysis where respondents can first indicate which value drivers and attributes are relevant to them. There are many great resources available on the details of conjoint analysis.[41]

Other Survey Methods

There are further survey methods that can be applied but they are less common in RGM practice. For example, simulated auctions can be used to determine participants' willingness to pay (WTP) for a product. This is because auctions are incentive-compatible: participants have a financial motivation to reveal their true (maximum) WTP, if the mechanism is chosen well. For example, in a Vickrey auction the highest bidder wins but pays second-highest bid. In this case, it is best for each participant to bid their true WTP. While such a mechanism is clever in theory, it is very rare in practice.

Another survey type that is more common is the focus group. Here, a group (often selected by customer segment) of about 10 participants are put in a room together with a moderator to discuss their preferences, product needs, issues they have with current options, and new product ideas – often actual prototypes. The idea here is to gather mostly qualitative information on potential new value drivers or attributes and product

---

[41] For more details on theory and history see Green and Srinivasan (1990), for a practical industry-focused overview see Orme (2014), and for modern methodological and applied insights see Vriens (2014).

ideas – as well as a rough idea on price and competitive positioning. Focus groups can be a useful tool to get a quick and typically less costly market validation of ideas at an early stage in the product development process. In my experience, I have seen a case where the product team was fighting over whether a new product ideal would do well in the market if introduced. The question was quickly decided after an afternoon of focus groups, where 0 out of 30 participants liked the new product variant.

2.4.1.3 Expert Judgment

Having access to real market data is obviously always to be preferred. However, it is often unavailable. For example, in most B2B pricing cases insights on competitor offers such as the price for an offer are unavailable. In other cases, specific insights – for example, the value of a CPG's new brand – can be gathered via an appropriate survey.[42] However, this can require a considerable investment and several weeks until an answer is available. In those situations, an expert judgment by someone sufficiently familiar with the field can be very useful – in the former case because of a lack of alternatives; in the latter case, to gain a quick assessment whether an idea generally makes sense and the investment in empirical research is warranted. Furthermore, for all empirical analyses it is always useful to cross-check the results using the team's expertise.

Different techniques are available to systematically gather expert judgment either from within the own team or external experts. For example, consultants or industry experts from company intelligence platforms such as Tegus, AlphaSights, or GLG (Gerson Lehrman Group) can be a great resource to gain expert inputs.[43] Here, we will introduce the two most important research techniques based on our experience.

---

[42] CPG: consumer packaged goods.
[43] See Tegus, AlphaSights, and GLG Insights websites.

Price Elasticity Assessment

A very straightforward way to gather expert insights on price sensitivity is via a direct survey. In this, all relevant team members with insights into customers' price sensitivity should participate and fill in the demand-response for relevant price changes.

Figure 2.38 shows this for one participant and one product. In actual exercises, around 5 to 10 participants should fill in the demand reaction for up to 20 products. It is useful, as in the example here, to ask for two demand responses – with and without a competitor reaction – as the demand reaction typically depends substantially on whether others follow a price change. For example, a market and price leader can always expect that others follow their price changes – to some extent. On the other hand, price changes of smaller players often do not cause others to follow.

The results across all experts need to be aggregated. Different experts or departments may be weighted differently. The results can be weighted, for example, if sales have a better understanding of customer preferences than marketing or product – or vice versa. Here, it is important to note that experts can be expected to answer more complex or direct questions than the people who participate in the previously discussed conjoint studies or other surveys directed at a larger group of potential buyers. However, it is also important to know that the answers of experts are typically aimed at the average or typical customer of a segment rather than the full distribution. So, their answers might be biased, and they typically lack some of the nuance of real-customer data.

Figure 2.38   Input price elasticity assessment

Expected sales	Price change				
	-20%	-10%	0%	10%	20%
Without competitive reaction	135	115	100	86	68
With competitive reaction	112	105	100	95	88

With the expert estimate of demand, key outputs can be produced. For example, the price elasticities for different price changes with and without competitor reaction are shown in Figure 2.39. Two observations are noteworthy. First, experts typically judge that the price elasticity of small price changes is lower (closer to 0) than for large price changes. This is based on the assumption that customers will not notice small changes. This can be the case but should be validated. Second, if competitors follow a price change, the price elasticity is always lower than without a competitor reaction.

In a next step, revenue and profit curves can directly be derived from the data, as shown in Figure 2.40. This helps teams assess – based on the expert judgment – what price change is beneficial.

Overall, this method has several clear advantages. These include the fast results if experts are available, and differences in the assessment between people or departments can trigger a useful discussion to better understand customers' price sensitivity. Also, while experts very often get differences in price sensitivity rights – that means they are very often correct in assessing if one product, customer segment, or channel is more

Figure 2.39   Output price elasticity assessment

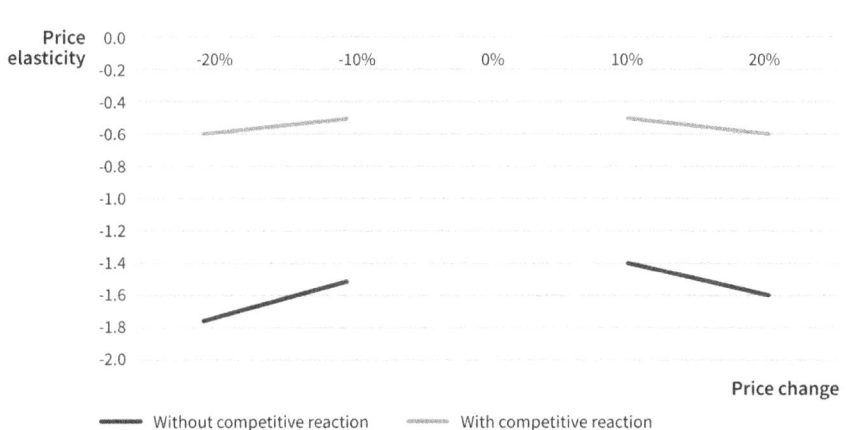

Figure 2.40 Profit and revenue curves based on expert judgment

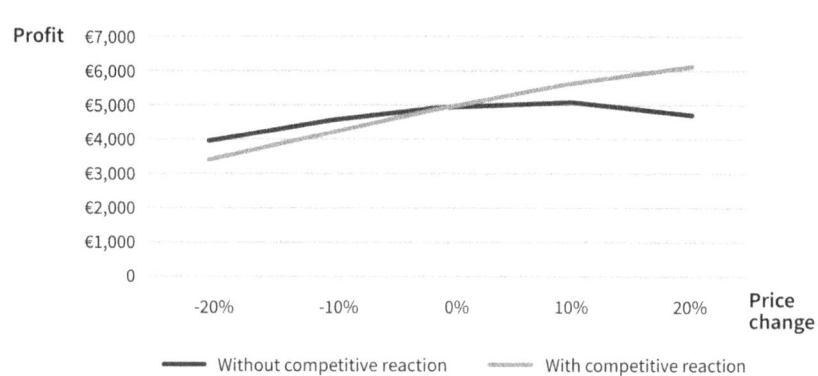

price sensitive – they cannot provide the precision of real, large-scale customer data. Therefore, if the difference between a price elasticity of −1.6 and −1.7 is important, an analysis of real sales or transaction data should be preferred.

Value Driver/Attribute Assessment

It is also possible to torture experts a bit more to gain insights into the relevance of different value drivers and customers' preferences for individual attribute levels. Specifically, we want to produce Figures 2.36 and 2.37 from the conjoint analysis using expert judgment instead. An established approach for this is the following two-step expert survey.

First, experts are asked to assess the **importance** of relevant value drivers on a scale of 1 to 10. Figure 2.41 shows an expert rating for the conjoint TV example from Figure 2.38. As in the previous expert judgment exercise, results can be collected from a single expert or a group of experts. Second, the experts rate the **performance** of key products (products 1, 2, and 3 in the example) for the relevant value drivers – again on a scale from 1 to 10. Here, the ratings are based on the specific attributes for the three products 1, 2, and 3. Then, the rating shares shown in Figure 2.42 directly show the importance of each value driver – this corresponds to the results in Figure 2.36 based on survey respondents.

Further, the performance ratings of the three products for the value drivers can be used to derive the relative values of the corresponding attribute levels. These are shown in Figure 2.43 not only for the attribute levels of the three products, but for all attribute levels also tested in the conjoint survey (Figure 2.37).

The values (x) in Figure 2.43 are computed from the performance ratings via the formula $x = \dfrac{p - \text{MP}}{\text{max} - \text{min}} \cdot share$, where p is the performance

Figure 2.41 Importance and performance rating

Value driver	Importance		Performance rating by product		
	Rating	Share	1	2	3
Brand	8.0	26%	2.0	5.0	9.0
Type	7.0	23%	8.0	3.0	7.0
Size	5.0	16%	2.0	5.0	8.0
WiFi connectivity	2.0	6%	10.0	1.0	1.0
Price	9.0	29%	7.0	4.0	1.0
Sum	31.0	100%			

Figure 2.42 Value driver assessment from expert judgment

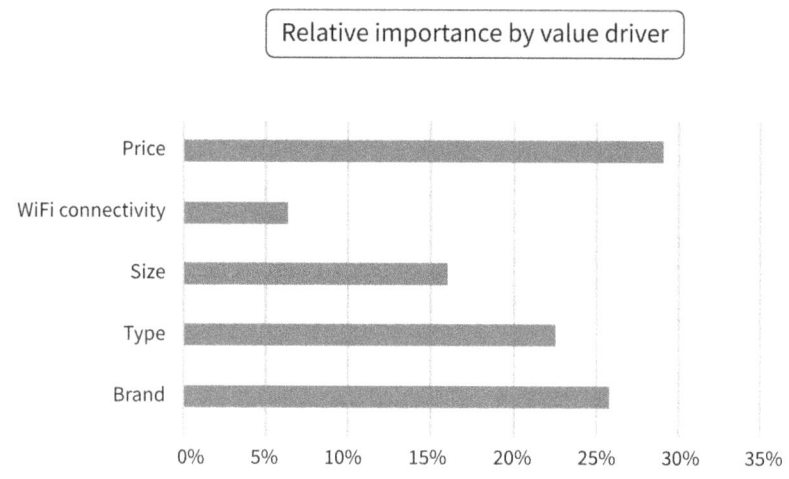

Figure 2.43 Attribute level output based on expert judgment

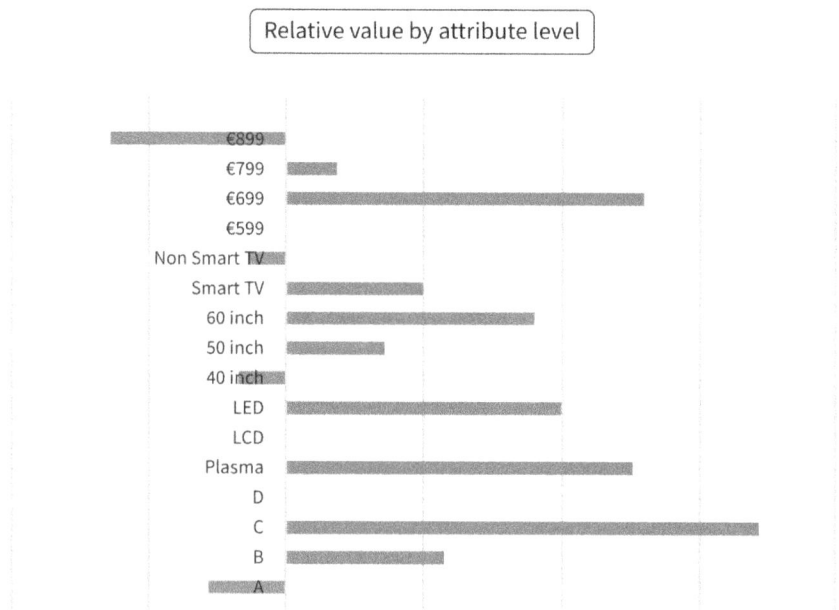

rating (e.g., 2.0 for brand in product 1), min is the minimum value (1), max is the maximum value (10), *share* the value driver's importance share, and MP is the mid point. This defines the rating that corresponds to a value of 0%. This mid point can be set arbitrarily, but to produce an outcome similar to the conjoint study, a mid point value of 3 should be used in the example. Note, that for each value driver the difference between the minimum and maximum values is equivalent to the importance share of that value driver.

The results of this expert judgment exercise can also be used to better understand the value proposition of the own products against those of key competitors. Two representations are commonly used: (1) the matrix of competitive advantages and (2) the value map.

1. **Matrix of competitive advantages:** The idea of the matrix of competitive advantages is to map the importance of each value driver against the performance of the own products. Figure 2.44 shows this for product 1 of the example. In general, products must perform well in important value drivers and do not need to perform well in less important value drivers. If importance and performance are aligned, then a product's values should be close to the main diagonal (highlighted in gray). For product 1, this is the case for all value drivers except the WiFi connectivity, which it offers although it is not considered important (section "overperform"), and the two more expensive products (products 2 and 3) do not offer it either. Here, the team should consider removing the feature from the product. Likewise, if the product performed poorly in an important category, the team should consider improving here (section "competitive disadvantage").

2. **Value map:** Aggregating the importance-weighted performance of each product over all dimensions except price yields the perceived value index of the products. The value map shows this index against the price performance index of each product. Figure 2.45 shows

Figure 2.44 Attribute level output based on expert judgment (example: Product 1)

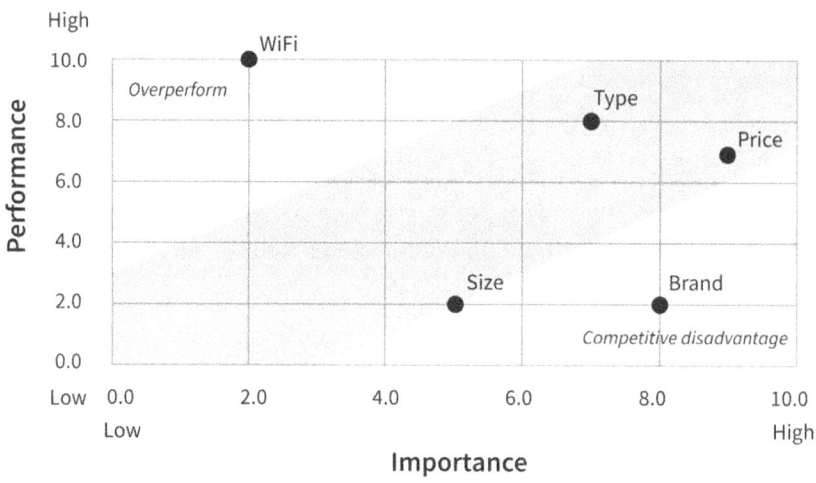

Figure 2.45 Value map

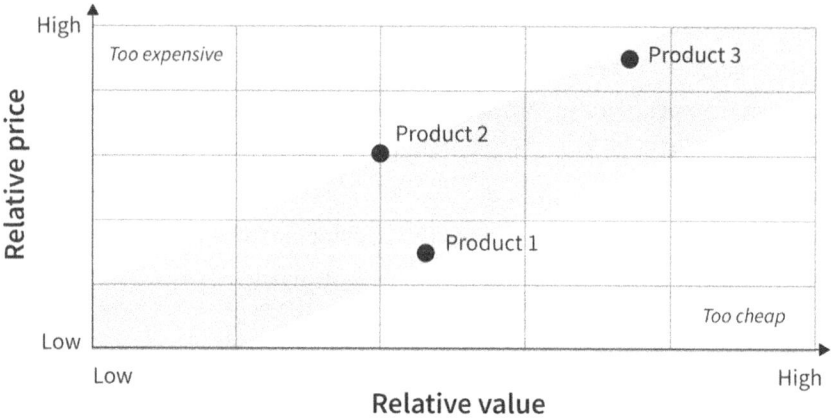

this for the three products (products 1, 2, and 3). Products that are on the main diagonal (gray area) are considered correctly priced, whereas products below the main diagonal are considered too cheap and products above too expensive.

It is often useful to differentiate these assessments by, for example, customer segment and channel, or analyze the differences between the assessment of different teams (e.g., sales vs. marketing vs. product) or to compare the internal and the external (e.g., via a focus group) view. The latter often helps teams understand where their own and their customers' views on their and their competitors' products differ.

It should be clear that these techniques must always be taken with a grain of salt. They produce fast results with limited resource requirements – particularly if the surveys can be performed with internal experts – and they are also available in cases with limited access to market data, as in many B2B scenarios. However, they can only provide a rough assessment. Particularly in data-rich industries, expert judgments should primarily be used to identify areas to dig deeper using real-customer data to make decisions.

2.4.1.4 Further Considerations

In this section, we have provided an overview of the most relevant research approaches for pricing and product assessments in pricing and RGM today. In addition, there are further analyses that are relevant to completing the picture but are much less commonly performed in our experience. This is also an area where software tools that add efficiency can be of much support. Here is a brief overview of the further areas to analyze in RGM.

Competitor Analysis

There are two relevant levels of competitor analysis. First, gaining transparency on what competitors do: What prices do they set, how do they change their portfolios, what promotions do they run? This is what most companies do to some extent and which is the basis for all forms of competitive pricing – for example, pricing with a mark up or down against a competitor or staying within a competitive price corridor (e.g., within ±10 compared to the market average). There are some technical challenges here – for example, matching the right products – but otherwise this a straightforward exercise.

The second – and conceptually more difficult exercise – is using competitor information such as historical price changes to understand the competitor's behavior. For example, does the competitor follow someone else's price changes or do they always change prices roughly in line with inflation, regardless of what others do – or does the competitor work with many innovations or promotion changes? These are important insights that can be used to better understand the effects of own RGM changes.

Cost Analysis

Cost analysis is typically not performed by pricing or RGM teams and is used as an input by these. However, cost changes are a crucial input for pricing decisions and need to be understood. This is particularly the case for interactions between RGM and costs – for example, if larger packs or multipacks reduce costs and this favors a different price-pack architecture. Also, costs may differ between channels, which can affect pricing, portfolio, and promotion selection by channel.

Differences Between Industries

In this chapter, we mostly focused on FMCG. While there are many commonalities in pricing and RGM across different industries, there are also some important differences that need to be considered. Here, we will not be able to describe all of these and their implications. However, we will point out the key ones for a selection of industries.

FMCG operates in high-volume, often low-margin, and promotion-driven markets. Pricing is often mass-market and data-rich, relying on sell-in and sell-out data, shopper panels, surveys, and a range of other inputs. RGM focuses on the levers pricing, price-pack architecture, promotions, mix, and trade terms optimization. Decisions are fast, mostly incremental, and heavily influenced by retailers' power and shopper behavior.

In telecommunications companies (telco), pricing is subscription-based with a strong focus on ARPU (average revenue per user), churn reduction, and lifetime value. Data is individualized and transactional, enabling personalized, dynamic pricing and segment-level price elasticity modeling. Promotions target retention and upselling rather than mass discounts. While providers have detailed insights on their own customers, they often have much less transparency on their competitors beyond their overall market shares. Therefore, they frequently rely on surveys for their competitor insights rather than actual sales data.

Consumer electronics features medium-volume, innovation-driven pricing. Lifecycle pricing (launch, growth, decline) is crucial, as is channel management between online and offline retailers. RGM focuses on launch price setting, markdown optimization, and product bundling. Data combines sales analytics with market share tracking and online sentiment. Because of the frequent product innovations, many products are subject to technical inflation that needs to be managed – for example, the value of a product attribute, such as 128 GB for a USB flash drive memory stick, has a fairly short half-life.

Automotive pricing is high-ticket and highly configurable, with RGM centered on option pricing, financing terms, residual value management, and service and after-sales pricing. Data comes from dealership transactions, market benchmarking, and macroeconomic indicators rather than daily sales feeds. Pricing cycles are long and strategic.

B2B industries rely on relationship-based, negotiated pricing with complex discount structures. RGM emphasizes customer profitability, deal scoring, and value-based pricing. Data is less frequent but deeper – spanning contracts, service levels, and cost-to-serve analytics. Competitor insights are very limited. For many deals, sales reps do not know which other competitors submitted an offer – and if they did, what products and services were offered at what price. Because of that, RGM is often much more heuristic in nature, rather than scientific.

Customer Differentiation

Differentiation between shoppers is mostly important, when identified differences can also be addressed – for example, with specific prices and offers. In FMCG, this is often difficult for manufacturers without direct contact with their shoppers. Here, manufacturers and retailers rely on shopper cards to send individualized offers. In other industries such as telco or B2B, individual relationships and with that individualized offers are more the norm than the exception.

For individualized offers to be better than general undifferentiated offers, companies rely on a wide range of research methods and statistical tools to identify differences in preferences, willingness to pay, or price sensitivity of different shoppers. Only when these are large enough, and they can be identified reliably, does it make sense to differentiate. In our experience, we see more often companies that differentiate offers and prices in situations where a general offer for all would be better than when we see companies that are too undifferentiated in their offers and pricing.

2.4.2 Traditional RGM Methods

There is a wide range of traditional methods and heuristics to deal with pricing and RGM challenges. These are mostly based on the theoretical foundations presented before in this chapter. Here, we will outline the most relevant of the traditional methods that are used in RGM. These are closely related to the five key challenges of RGM as shown in Figure 2.46.

Figure 2.46   RGM levers

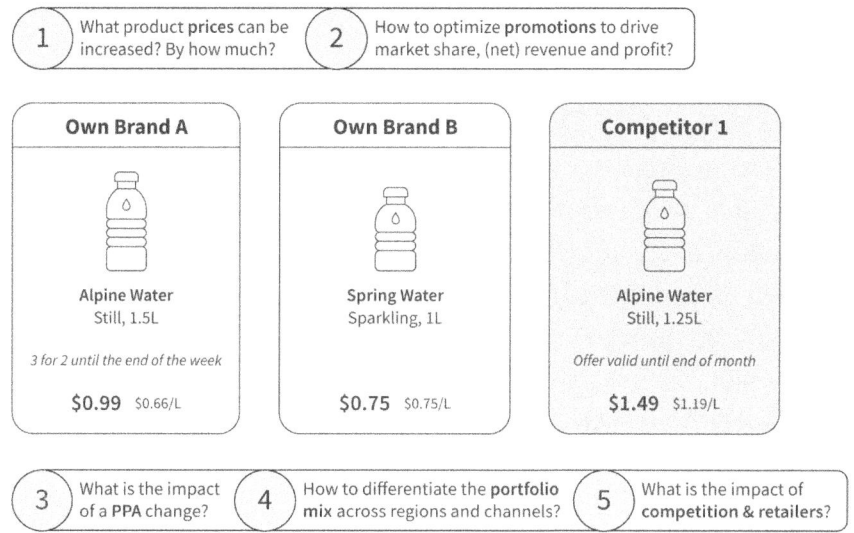

After discussing each lever in detail, we will also show how they can be integrated to form the basis of a coherent pricing and RGM strategy.

2.4.2.1   Pricing

The first lever to discuss is pricing.[44] It is the one decision every pricing or revenue manager must make, even if they only manage a single product and cannot use promotions or other forms of offer differentiation. It is also by far the one that is most discussed in the literature and among professionals, which has produced the widest range of methods among the levers. Here, we will discuss the key pricing methods that are used in the field and show how they can be used in combination, as they often differ in their implications. Some of these methods, such as value pricing, can also be used for the other levers.

---

[44] Note that pricing is at the sole discretion of the retailer.

Cost-Plus Pricing

As everyone who has ever priced a product knows, finding the right price is not easy. A very simple way to set a price is cost-plus pricing. It describes the practice of setting the price based on the marginal cost of producing a good or service and adding a markup (see Figure 2.47). The markup is often based on what is considered usual in the industry, and it assures that the resulting price is comparable to competitor offers. Also, it allows, to some extent, to account for differences in the quality of inputs, as these are often reflected in different costs. For example, a larger product variant uses more material, therefore costs more and is sold at a higher price. A prominent example is food pricing by restaurants that widely apply a 300% markup on their wholesale costs, which implies a 75% margin before rent, labor, and other fixed costs.

Figure 2.47   Cost-plus pricing

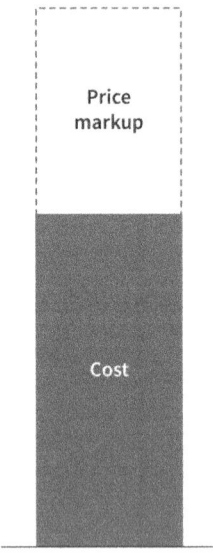

Cost-plus pricing is often unjustly mocked for only looking at cost and not at competition or value to the customer.[45] However, it is arguably in line with a traditional – pre-neoclassical optimization – view on pricing that focuses on fairness and often works well in established and stable markets. Further, price increases triggered by cost increases are automatically passed on and they are often more accepted by customers. However, it does not work well in dynamic markets with many price changes or promotions by competitors, or for products with high capital and low marginal costs such as software, telco, or hospitality.

Competitive Pricing

Competitive pricing is similar to cost-plus pricing in that the price is based on a reference price point – the competitor price (see Figure 2.48). In practice, this might either be the average price of key competitors or the price of a market leader. The latter is often called the price leader – for example, the firm that sets the industry's price and most of the others follow. The obvious advantage of competitive pricing is that it saves a lot of effort, because once the reference competitor price is identified, only the markup or -down needs to be decided. In most practical cases, firms decide on the markup or -down based on their assessment of how premium their brand and products are versus the benchmark. For smaller companies that operate in a market with transparent competitor prices and clear price leadership by some dominant competitor, this can be a good approach. The core challenges with this approach are determining the right reference products and the markup or -down. In practice, most companies that use competitor pricing use a single competitor or a basket of two to three competitors and a 5% or 10% markup or -down depending on how strong they feel versus the benchmark.

---

[45] Dholakia (2017).

Figure 2.48   Competitive pricing

This method also has several problems. First, it ignores how a change in reference price or markup affects margins, sales, revenues, and profit. Therefore, this approach is passive and the results depend largely on the actions of others – the competitors. Further, we must not underestimate the risk involved, if competitors reference price each other without considering constraints relative to cost or value to the customer. Figure 2.49 demonstrates this in the example of an obscure biology book on Amazon (*The Making of a Fly*), which was offered by two sellers that had automatically and continually reset their price relative to the other. This had gone on unnoticed until the price of the book had reached $23.7 million.[46]

Finally, in cases where competitor offers and prices are not available, competitor pricing is not possible. This is predominantly the case in B2B

---

[46] Eisen (2011).

Figure 2.49 Example of competitive pricing getting out of control

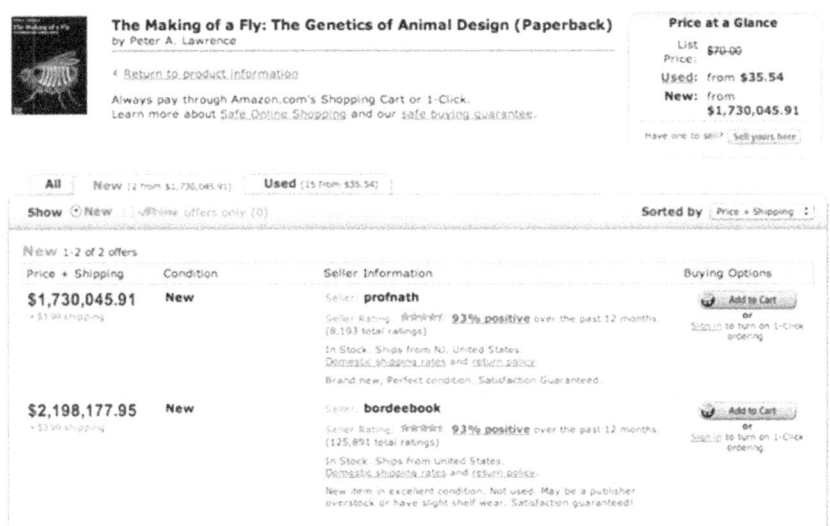

pricing, where own and competitor prices are almost always deal-specific. In that case, even if a competitor has published a price list for all offers, these can typically not be relied upon as the customer-specific variations from the list prices are unknown.

Price Elasticity-based Pricing

We discussed price elasticities previously and their application to optimize pricing in Section 2.3. In practice, the use of price elasticities is straightforward. Pricing managers use price elasticity tables such as the example shown in Figure 2.50 to determine how sales volumes, revenues, and profits change after a price change. Such tables can simply include a single price elasticity value per product, or they can also provide different price elasticities for different situations. In the example table, it also shows different price elasticities for different promotion types. Sometimes, tables also

Figure 2.50 Example price elasticity table

	Base price	Promotion elasticities		
Product	elasticity	Shelf	Flyer	Extra display
A	-1.8	-2.3	-2.1	-2.3
B	-1.4	-1.7	-1.4	-2.1
C	-1.3	-1.6	-1.4	-1.9
D	-1.2	-1.7	-1.3	-1.9
E	-1.9	-2.1	-2.0	-2.4
F	-1.5	-1.8	-1.6	-2.2
G	-1.4	-1.8	-1.5	-1.9
H	-1.6	-2.1	-1.9	-2.2

include a different price elasticity that is to be used if a price threshold (e.g., €0.99) is crossed. In our experience, teams seldomly use the condition $\varepsilon \cdot m = -1$ to identify the profit optimum but rather test the effects of different price changes.

Many of the limitations of using price elasticities have already been discussed in Section 2.3. These include the fact that a product's price elasticity typically changes if the price is changed, which is not captured in the table. Also, price elasticity tables generally ignore cross-effects between products, and do not, for example, capture the difference in price elasticity if only a single price is changed versus a change in the price of all products in a portfolio. Also, the effect of promotions is not well captured in price elasticity. Rather, a promotion – by increasing attention and demand for a product – shifts a demand curve, which can result in an increase in sales even without a promotion price reduction. In Chapter 4, we will discuss a more advanced solution for considering price and promotion responses in decision-making.

Value-based Pricing

The core idea of value-based pricing is to price products based on their value to customers.[47] If there is only one customer who has a maximum willingness to pay of €10 for a certain product – and that is known to us – then value pricing suggests that we ask for €10. Further, if we add a feature to that product that is worth €5 to that customer, then the total value-based price is €15. In value-based pricing, the total value of a product is often determined by aggregating the individual values assigned to a product's attributes across the value drivers. This can also be used to define a product architecture for a range of products. Figure 2.51 shows an example of value pricing for ski jackets. Here, the base price for a ski jacket is $100, the markup for down filling is $50, and the markup for water column >15,000 mm is also $50. This results in a price for the waterproof jacket with down filling of $100 + $50 + $50 = $200.

There can be variations in how attribute values are computed, but the additive model shown here is most common. An alternative is multiplicative aggregation. In the above example, the price might be determined as: $100 \cdot (1 + 0.5) \cdot (1 + 0.5) = $225, with a markup of 50% instead of $50. The multiplicative aggregation leads to a wider spread of prices in a portfolio. In the example, with additive markup, prices range from $100 to $200; in the multiplicative case from $100 to $225.

It is typically difficult to determine which aggregation method of the two is better in a given situation. For a good answer, a conjoint study might be consulted, or the advanced AI methods described in Chapter 4 provide a precise answer. Without this, a good heuristic is the following: Features such as down filling in the above example are additive, while metric value drivers such as a product's weight, size, or number of units are multiplicative.

In most cases, there will be more than one customer. Each customer then potentially has different preferences and a different willingness to pay.

---

[47] Dholakia (2017).

Figure 2.51   Value-based pricing

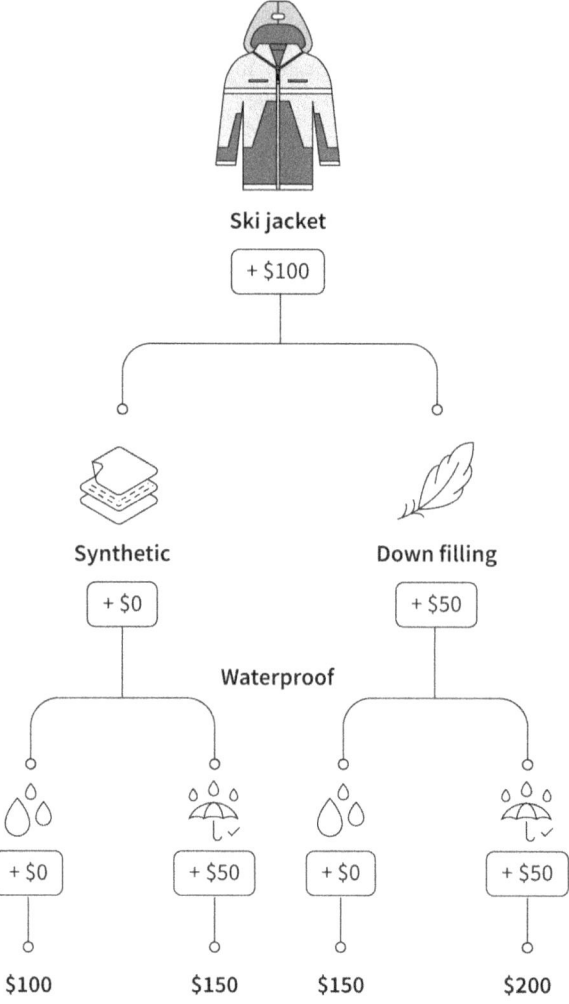

Then value-based pricing becomes a bit more difficult. When selling to a mass market as in the ski jacket case, practitioners often work with averages across the market or within subsegments to determine the markup or -down for specific features. For example, after conducting a market study, a pricing manager might conclude that the overall average willingness to pay for down versus synthetic filling is €50, or that within the segment of customers who prefer down to synthetic, their willingness to pay for down is €50.

This example already shows that while the basic idea of value-based pricing is simple, its application is not and leaves room for different approaches. Herein we already find a key problem with value-based pricing. Where price elasticity-based pricing makes a prediction on how sales will react to price changes that can be tested in practice, value-based pricing makes no such prediction, and it is now straightforward to test if a value-based price was successful or not. In general, there is a very broad range of approaches that are called value-based pricing, which differ in how values are determined and aggregated.

It is noteworthy that value-based pricing is not limited to B2C applications, but it is also used for B2B pricing. In the latter case, it is often used to determine customer-specific prices, rather than market prices as in the B2C case. This requires that pricing managers can determine if, for example, customers from industry A are willing to pay more or less than customers from industry B. In some cases, this can be easy. For example, if a machine saves a customer €100 in energy over a competitive product, this is the value add, and it should be considered in determining the value-based price. However, in many cases we see it is much more difficult to quantify the benefit.

Behavioral Pricing

In Section 2.3.2 we already discussed the conceptual basics of behavioral economics and behavioral pricing. Here, we will now provide an overview of the most important effects in practice based on our daily work. Unlike the other methods, behavioral pricing does not offer a full and autonomous recommendation, but rather it is used in combination with other methods such as value-based pricing. For example, a price computed via value-based pricing is adjusted to the nearest price threshold using behavioral insights. There are many behavioral effects that have been identified in the literature that can be used for pricing.[48]

Figure 2.52 provides an overview of the seven most relevant ones based on our practical experience. Here are the details on each:

1. **Default nudge:** Nudging is the predictable altering of shopper behavior through positive reinforcement. When you create a default nudge you suggest, for instance, that the default option is the most commonly chosen one. This tends to sway your customers to choose the default product. It also includes highlighting a product on your website as a "preferred option" or using naming conventions like "standard product" versus "plus product." Default nudges can have substantial effects on choices. Famously, Johnson and Goldstein found that opt-out systems consistently exceed 90% consent rates for organ donations, compared to 4–28% in opt-in systems.[49] Effects in pricing are not as extreme, but also meaningful. For example, in our work we see that in a four-product portfolio (good, better, best, excellent), up to 10–15% points of penetration rate can be shifted up from mostly the better to the best option with the right nudge, compared to no nudges. This can have a substantial financial impact.

2. **Power of free:** The so-called zero price effect describes the phenomenon that shoppers tend to choose a free product more often than its inherent utility suggests. In his book *Predictably Irrational*, Dan Ariely describes a chocolate experiment, in which participants chose a free Hershey's Kiss over a Lindt truffle at 13 cents substantially more often than they should with the preferences they revealed

---

[48] The following sources together provide a more comprehensive collection: Ariely (2009); Ariely and Kreisler (2017); Husemann-Kopetzky (2017); Kahneman (2011); Lindstrom (2008); Shotton (2018).
[49] Johnson and Goldstein (2003); Thaler and Sunstein (2008).

Figure 2.52 Overview of behavioral pricing effects

previously when given the option between the two products with the Hershey's Kiss priced at 1 cent and above.[50] In practice, it is often sufficient to give some elements of an offer for free. For example, customers frequently overvalue "free shipping" above some minimum purchase. The same is true for free hotel upgrades.

3. **Price anchor:** A price anchor can help set a buyer's expectations about a price at a desired level.[51] For example, if a potential buyer walks into a car dealership with a plan to spend about $50,000 on a

---
[50] Ariely (2008).
[51] Tversky and Kahneman (1974).

new car and the salesperson first shows a $120,000 car with everything the customer wants in it, the next vehicle they show at $70,000 looks like a much more reasonable choice. Price anchors are most often used to make the sticker price look comparatively cheaper. For example: "Was $100, now only $50!" This approach is often used in discounting but also when referencing a hypothetical price recommendation. Price anchors are most effective when tied to real discounts. Credibility is too valuable to risk with artificial pricing.

4. **Price thresholds:** One of the most relevant behavioral pricing effects is the price threshold. Buyers tend to behave irrationally when they see, for example, $5.99 instead of $6.00. This is especially true when a threshold moves by a decimal, such as $0.99 versus $1.00 or $9.99 versus $10.00. These subtle differences matter because consumers anchor their judgments on the left-most digit, creating a perception of greater value even when the economic difference is negligible.[52] In practice, crossing a price threshold can trigger a disproportionate change in demand, which makes identifying and respecting these psychological boundaries a central concern in pricing strategy.[53] The strength of price threshold can depend on many factors, as we will show in an example at the end of this section.

5. **Time-limited offers:** Time-limited offers, also known as urgency-based pricing or limited-time promotions, are a behavioral pricing technique that leverages the psychological principle of scarcity and the fear of missing out (FOMO).[54] Using limited-time discounts or promotions can create a sense of urgency, encouraging customers

---
[52] Monroe (2003).
[53] Nagle et al. (2016).
[54] Broeder and Wentink (2022).

to make quicker purchasing decisions to take advantage of special pricing.

6. **Reference pricing:** This refers to the practice of evaluating a product's price relative to other price points that act as benchmarks in consumers' minds. These reference points may come from competing products, different items within the same brand portfolio, or even shoppers' past experiences and expectations. By managing reference prices carefully, firms can influence whether a product is perceived as a bargain, fairly priced, or overpriced, thereby shaping purchase decisions.[55] Unlike anchor pricing, which introduces a salient price to steer perceptions, reference pricing relies on comparisons to existing or remembered benchmarks.

7. **Endowment effect:** The endowment effect refers to consumers' tendency to assign greater value to a product once they own it, compared to when they did not. This bias suggests that ownership itself increases perceived value. In pricing strategy, firms often exploit this effect through free trials or limited subscription periods. For instance, a streaming service might offer a 30-day free trial. Once consumers have integrated the service into their daily routines, they are more inclined to pay for continued access because they now view the service as something they "own" and would incur a loss by giving it up.[56]

The key practical problem of behavioral pricing as it is applied today is that it is not a consistent method but rather a selection of anecdotes and specific cases. For example, the previously mentioned wine decoy example (in Section 2.3.2) cannot easily be transferred into other product categories. If customers have a clear understanding of their own needs and priorities, they are far less susceptible to being swayed by a decoy option. Also, it

---

[55] Monroe (2003); Winer (1986).
[56] Kahneman et al. (1990); Thaler (1980).

is often difficult to derive specific business implications from an example like the wine decoy. For example, should the decoy wine be priced at €40, €50, or €60?

Further, the strength of effects can depend on many context-specific parameters, and measured values often vary heavily with the research method. Here is a practical (and anonymized) example from our work at Buynomics. In a Gabor–Granger price study, consumers were asked if they would buy a chocolate snack at a price of 60, 70, 80 cents, etc. The results are shown in Figure 2.53. Here, the line shows the percentage share of customers who would buy the snack based on the survey results. Noticeably, there is a significant price threshold with a loss of about 35% of sales as the price increases from 90 cents to €1.00. In contrast, the dots show the actual weekly sales and average prices across retailers in the country that was surveyed. They do not show the same strength of the price threshold. There is still a threshold, but it is substantially weaker.

Figure 2.53   Survey results vs. actual sales

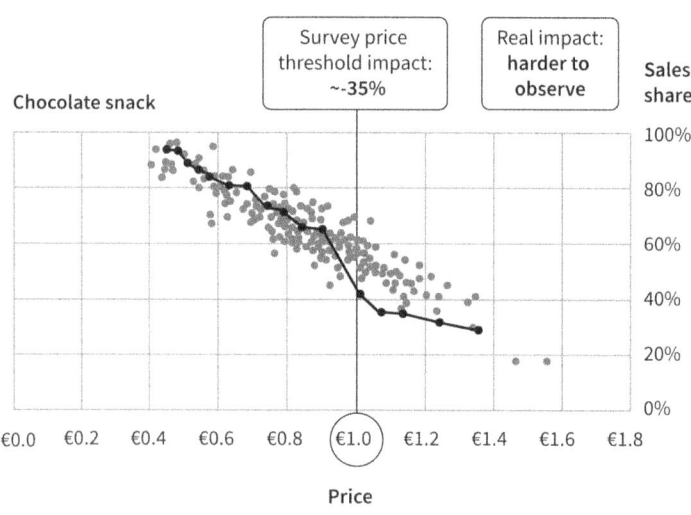

Data anonymized.

The difference here is that in the experiment consumers only had to say if they would buy this specific chocolate snack and they were not offered an alternative product. However, in stores the choice for shoppers is not between buying or not buying the product but rather between buying this specific product or buying something else from the shelf. As a result, the effect is dampened when shoppers are faced with many options. Therefore, RGM managers need to be careful when they use such survey results, because the strong price thresholds identified in surveys almost never show up in actual sales data.

In sum, many behavioral pricing effects are available, but there is often no consistent guidance on how to best use them. In Chapter 4, we will show how to better integrate behavioral insights from different sources into one coherent model.

Integration of Pricing Methods

Most practitioners use the above pricing methods in combination. For example, the base price in a portfolio is determined via price elasticity analysis, and the product variants are then differentiated using value pricing – and the price is finalized using some behavioral pricing cosmetics (e.g., €9.99 instead of €10.00).

The problem with this approach is that the different methods are based on different assumptions, which makes it difficult to combine their results. For example, value-based pricing looks at "the" customer to assess the value of a product. Price elasticities imply that the value of a product differs between customers, as only some – and not all – will not buy a product anymore if the price is increased. Further, price elasticities with their roots in classical economics assume that customers make rational decisions based on their preferences. Behavioral pricing on the other hand starts with the acknowledgment that customers are – to varying degrees – irrational. One common difficulty that arises from this conflict is the way price elasticities are used at price thresholds. Often, the price elasticity is simply increased if a price change crosses a price threshold – for example, from −2 to −3 – so that in the calculation the effect of the threshold depends on the magnitude of the price change. In reality, a certain percentage of customers is lost at the price threshold, independent of how large the total price change is.

In sum, the different pricing methods cannot be integrated into a consistent method that is more than just the average of the results of incompatible methods. One of the companies that now uses Buynomics has previously worked with a consulting firm that had produced recommendations using cost-plus, competitive, value-based, and price elasticity-based pricing. For an example product, the recommendations from the different methods were: €8, €12, €17, and €25. The consultants recommended to just take the average (see Figure 2.54).

A more sophisticated method to integrate the different pricing methods is to use them in sequence, as shown in Figure 2.55. For a single product or the anchor product of a product group, you first define a base margin – for example, a minimum margin that needs to be achieved – that together

Figure 2.54 Price recommendations from different pricing methods

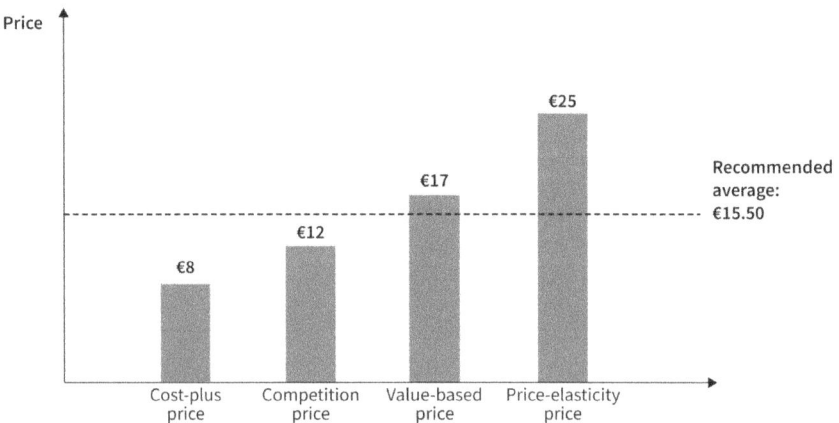

Figure 2.55 Step-by-step price build up

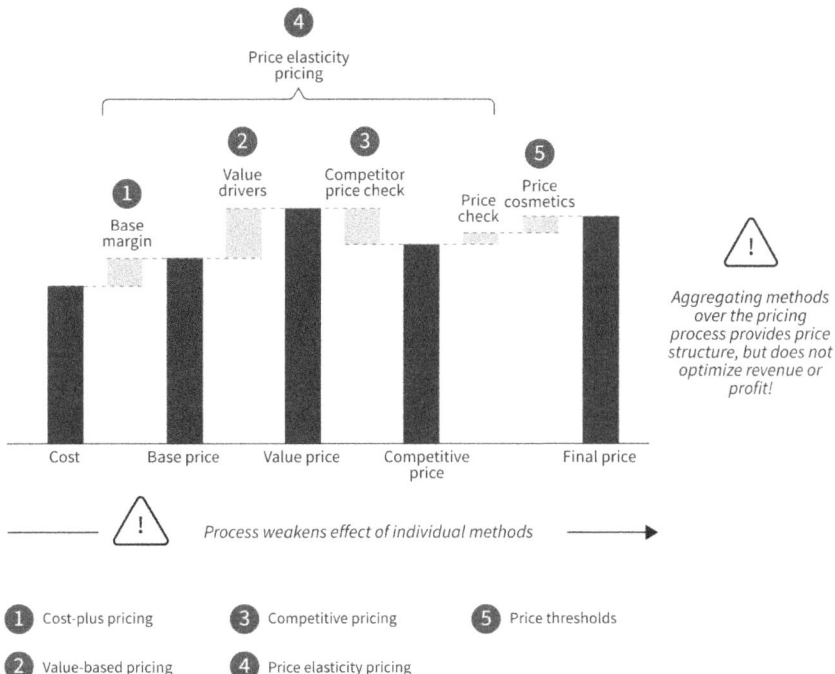

with the cost basis results in a (cost-plus) base price. Then value drivers are applied as in the previous ski jacket example. These can be applied to a single product or to differentiate the different product variants within a product group. Then, the resulting "value prices" are compared to relevant competitor prices. This is often done by defining competitor price corridors. For example, prices up to 10% below or above the competitor prices are allowed. After a potential adjustment based on the competitor price comparisons, it may be required to again adjust some prices to maintain the internal (value-based) price structure, that is typically preferable to external consistency (against competition). In the final step, it often makes sense to apply behavioral pricing cosmetics. For example, adjusting the computed price of €9.87 or €10.12 to the nearest price threshold of €9.99 (step 5 in Figure 2.55).

At Buynomics, we find that these traditional methods are of great importance to learn about pricing, to understand the principal market mechanics using simplified case studies, and to produce a rough price recommendation. However, they should no longer be used for actual and high-impact pricing decisions.

2.4.2.2 Price-Pack Architecture

The price-pack architecture (PPA) or portfolio architecture addresses the challenge of mapping products with relevant shopper segments and needs. A common tool for this is the OBPPC framework (occasion, brand, package, price, channel). It was popularized by McKinsey & Company to help companies align offerings with real consumption moments and shopper choices.[57] Figure 2.56 shows the first step of this framework (occasion)

Figure 2.56 Alignment of consumption occasion and product size

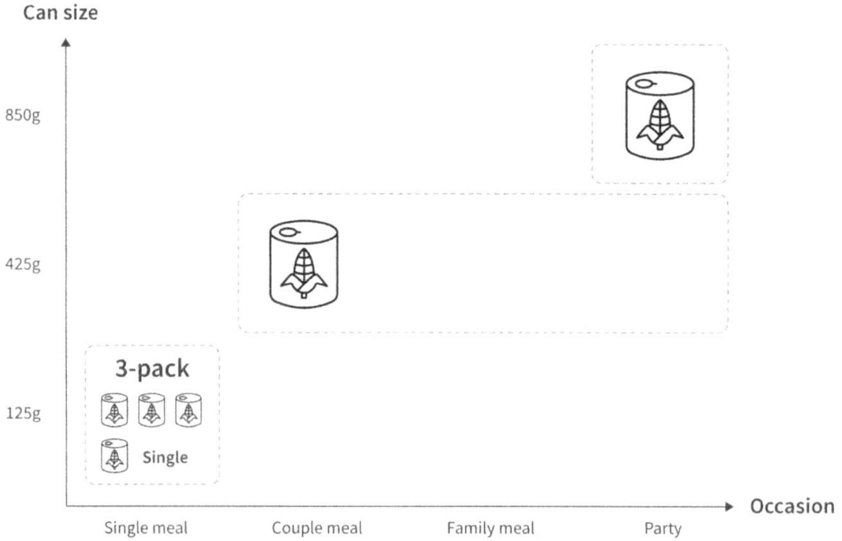

---

[57] McKinsey & Company (2019b); Kotler and Keller (2022).

for a simple example – the other steps are addressed subsequently. In Germany, the standard size of canned corn is 425 g (15 oz). Canned corn is primarily used for salads, and the corn in a standard sized can fits well with the needs of couples, families, and larger events such as parties, where also many cans can be used. However, for a single meal, a full can is usually too much. This opens a niche for a smaller can, and a 150 g can was introduced a few years ago, that is sold in single and multipacks at a significant premium. It is only 35% of the size of the 425 g can, but it is sold at only a 20–30% discount.

Matching products with needs or target shoppers can be performed along different dimensions. The most common dimensions are brand and product size. Multi-brand manufacturers need to target different segments with their different brands. Figure 2.57 shows a brand ladder across the

Figure 2.57   Brand ladder

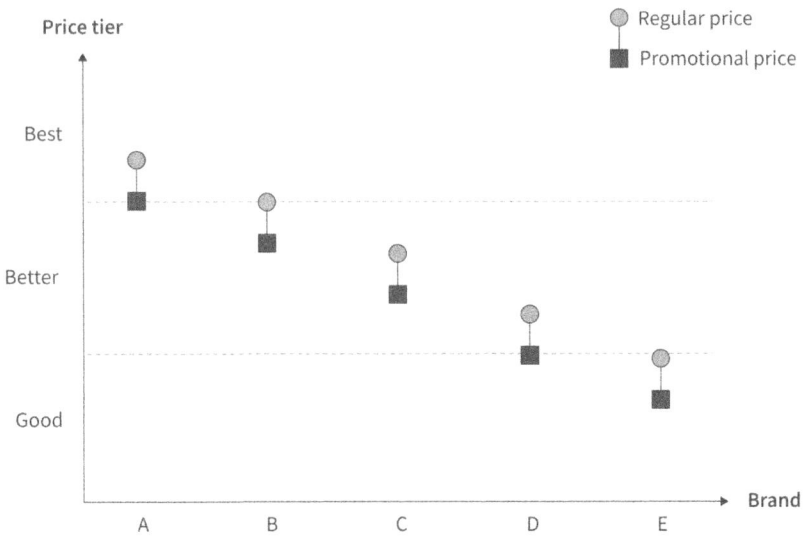

price tiers good, better, and best. The idea is to assign all brands to defined price bands. This results in a brand hierarchy. Within this framework, RGM teams can define strategic guardrails for specific pricing decisions. For example, is a brand allowed to be promoted at a price below the regular price of a strategically lower positioned brand?

Another key dimension that needs to be structured is the pack size of products. This is the core of PPA analysis. It answers the question of what product sizes should be offered at what price points. As in the canned corn example, the relevant pack sizes need to be selected based on shopper needs, competitor offers, and potential logistical constraints. The result of such a PPA exercise is typically a curve to describe the price versus pack size relationship, on which the different pack sizes are priced. One way to represent this relationship is by mapping the pack size against the price per unit, where the unit can be kilogram, liter, or number of pieces in a box. In most cases, shoppers expect the price per unit to go down as the pack size increases. They want a better deal if they must store a larger pack at home and they expect the cost per unit to go down with pack size for manufacturer and retailer – and that they pass a share of their savings on to the shopper.

Figure 2.58 shows an example of different product sizes and the price per 1,000 g, which is decreasing with size, while the price for the pack itself increases with size. For example, the 1,000 g pack is more expensive than the 750 g pack. A commonly used heuristic is to reduce the price per size unit by 10–15% with every size step (e.g., from 500 g to 750 g in the example). Note that this heuristic is often difficult to reconcile with the pricing tools outlined in the previous section. In the example of Figure 2.58, the 750 g pack is too expensive compared to the hierarchy suggested by the three other pack sizes, because its price per 1,000 g is above the line of the other three pack sizes. However, at a price elasticity of -0.9, its revenue and profit both decrease if its price is reduced. Also, the price-pack heuristic

Figure 2.58 Price-pack architecture

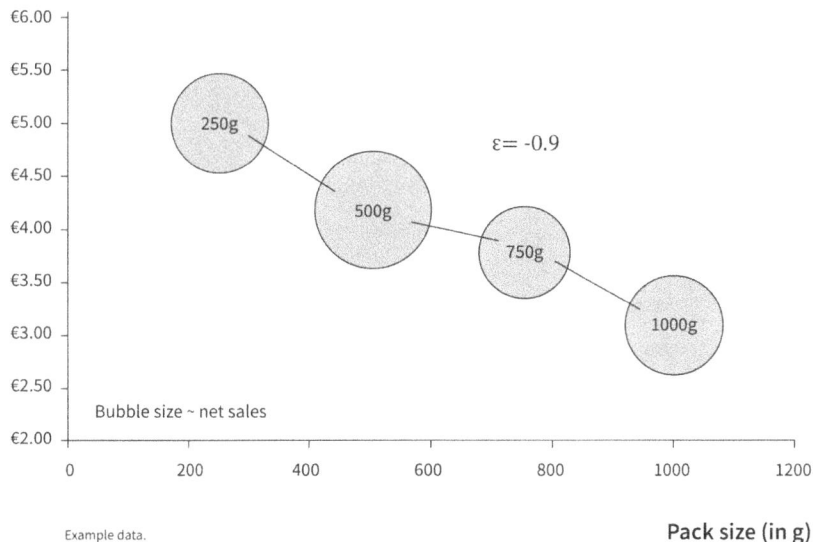

Example data.

outlined here ignores cross-effects between the sales of the different pack sizes if the price of one of them is changed. This will be discussed in Chapter 4.

The combination of brand and pack size is shown in Figure 2.59. This type of graph is widely used to make the portfolio structure transparent and to identify inconsistencies or missing or superfluous products in the portfolio. The graph can also include competitor products to highlight the competitive landscape or other product attributes such as packaging (e.g., can or glass). Particularly, the comparison with competitors in this graph helps identify white spots in the own portfolio. These are areas in the graph where products are missing – for example, when competitors have high sales in some sizes that are missing from the own portfolio.

Figure 2.59 Brand- and pack-size-architecture

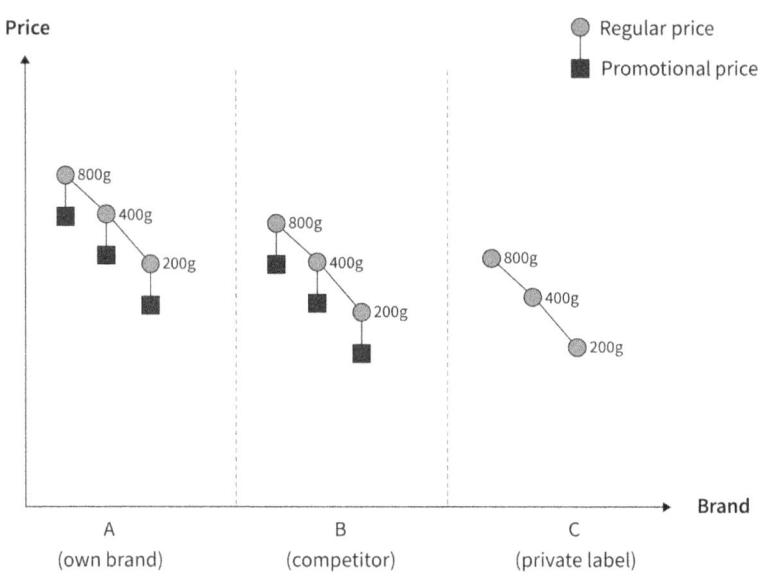

2.4.2.3 Promotions

Promotions are a key instrument in the arsenal of any pricing and RGM manager. Compared to the other levers discussed here, its use is often more tactical. For example, promotions can be used to help achieve a revenue goal or to correct a too optimistic price increase, both by increasing the number and depth of promotions run. Here, we will briefly describe promotion mechanics, objectives, and promotion types.

The uplift in sales during a promotion comes from two effects shown in Figure 2.60. First, a shift in the demand curve that is caused by attracting more demand via a more prominent placement at the point of sale (PoS), increased advertising, or increasing the product value (e.g., by increasing the product size). From this, the sales volume increases from (I) to (II). Second, the price reduction during a promotion leads to a movement along

Figure 2.60 Promotion dynamics

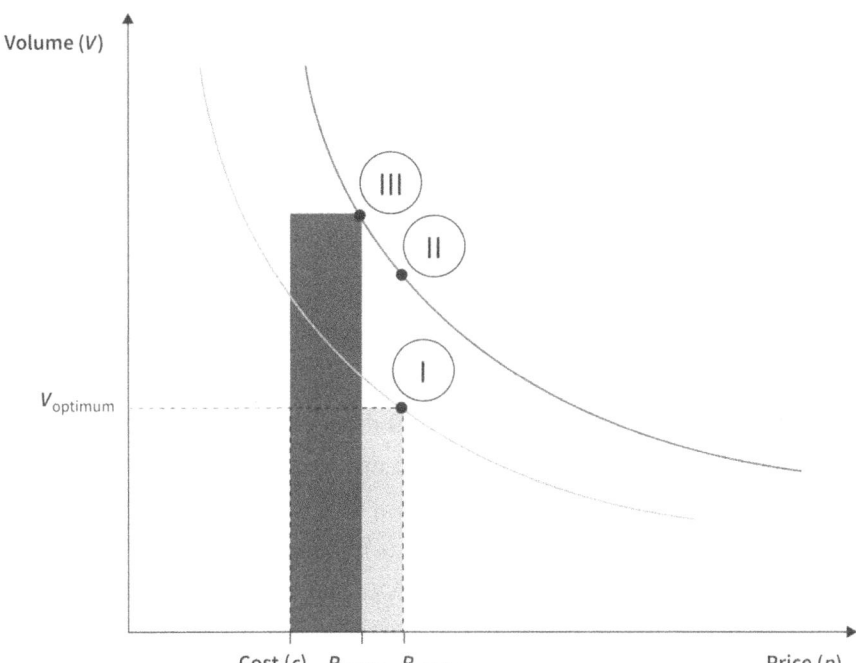

the promotion demand curve from right to left resulting in an increased demand. This leads to a sales volume increase from (II) to (III). Simplifying this two-step mechanism with a single promotion price elasticity often leads to difficulties, for example in promotions without a price change, or it leads to inaccuracies because the shift in the demand curve results in strong price elasticity differences depending on the level of promotion discount. Instead of using a promotion price elasticity, it is usually better to compound the separate effects of the promotional sales volume uplift specific to the promotion type and the sales volume uplift from a price reduction.

To assess the effectiveness of a promotion, the investment into the promotion and the benefits must be compared. This is often done by computing the promotion return on investment (Promotion ROI). It is defined as the ratio of the net profit impact and the promotion investment:

$$\text{Promotion ROI} = \frac{\text{Net profit impact}}{\text{Promotion investment}}.$$

Let's look at an example. During a specific week, you would sell 1,000,000 units at the regular price with a profit of €0.10 per unit for a total net profit of €100,000. Now, you invest €40,000 during that week into a promotion and sell 3,000,000 units at a unit profit of €0.05 for a total net profit of €150,000. Then, the net profit impact for this week is €150,000 − €100,000 − €40,000 = €10,000. At a promotion invest of €40,000, this results in a Promotion ROI of €10,000 / €40,000 = 25%. This is the direct effect of the promotion on the promoted product during the promoted week. Here, a promotion is profitable if the Promotion ROI is positive.

A more advanced way of determining the effectiveness of a promotion is by looking at the different levels outlined in Figure 2.61. Here, we differentiate between immediate and long-term effects. Immediate effects take place while the promotion runs. These include the direct effect on the promoted products and the indirect effects on unpromoted products

Figure 2.61 Promotion effectiveness

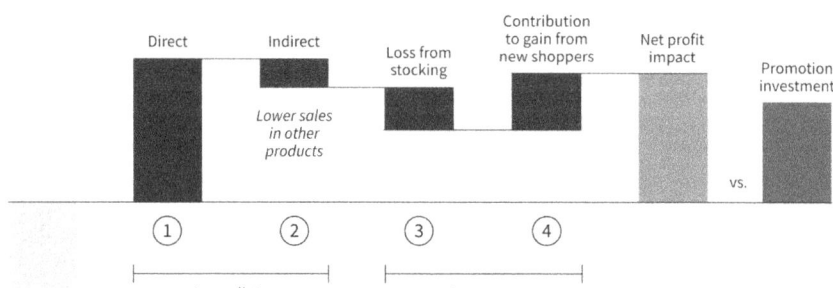

from the own portfolio. (1) The former is described in the above example, and (2) the latter typically affects sales, revenue, and profit negatively, as the promoted sales cannibalize the unpromoted products. Therefore, promotions that are profitable when looking at the promoted products only can also be negative, when considering the negative effects across the portfolio. Further, (3) promotions also frequently – particularly for nonperishable goods – draw sales from other periods or other channels, as shoppers might anticipate a future promotion and delay a purchase, buy in a different channel, or they stock up on products (e.g., pasta or detergents) reducing sales in subsequent weeks. This reduces total promotion ROI. Finally, (4) one of the key objectives of a promotion is increasing long-term sales of a product by getting new shopper segments to test the product at a promoted price and then sticking with it after they have been convinced by its quality. This would lead to higher long-term sales and a positive effect on promotion ROI. Therefore, RGM teams should look at four types of promotion ROI by subsequently adding the four different profit impact buckets shown in Figure 2.61 and comparing the result with the promotion investment. Instead of comparing net profit impact with promotion investment, teams may also choose to look at net revenue impact resulting from a promotion investment. It is important to note here that it is typically difficult for teams to precisely measure these different promotion ROI levels – and even more difficult to predict these different levels when planning a promotion. Today, different software tools are available to support teams: we are discussing some of these in Chapter 4.

To design promotions, teams have a vast array of levers at their disposal. These include the selection of the promotion type, the selection of promoted products, the frequency of promotions, and the mix of these levers. Figure 2.62 provides some examples of the different levers. Working with these in practice is crucial for pricing and RGM performance, and finding the best promotional approach requires deep insights into the

Figure 2.62 Promotion levers

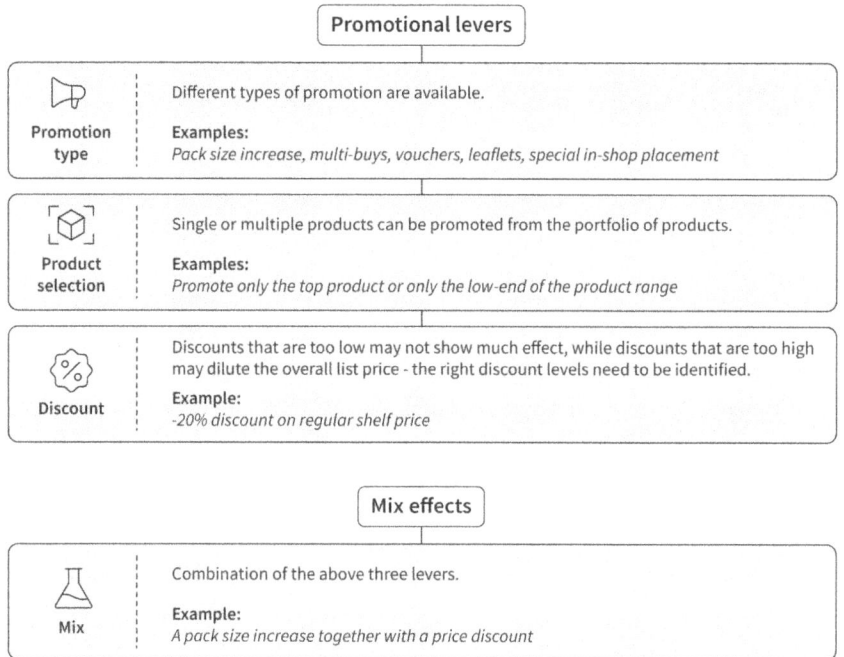

specific market dynamics. Here, we can only provide a brief overview, but many resources are available for more details on promotional mechanics.[58]

2.4.2.4 Trade Terms

The trade terms determine how margins are divided between manufacturer and retailer – or other parties such as wholesalers if they are involved. Here, we are looking at this relationship from a manufacturer's perspective. However, the overviews and insights presented here are relevant for all parties. The starting point for analyzing trade terms that then result in the trade spend is the price waterfall as shown in Figure 2.63. It depicts the

---
[58] Malik (2010); Singh and Sharma (2019); Promotion Optimization Institute and Deloitte (2023).

Figure 2.63   Price waterfall (example)

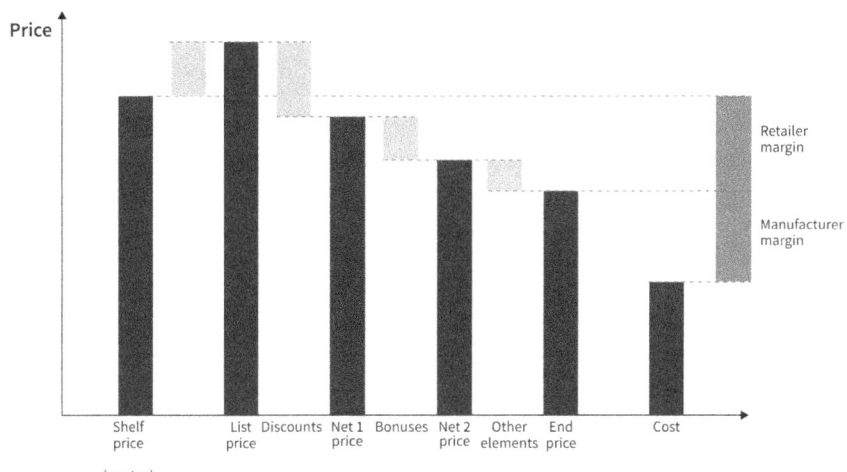

different price levels from shelf price (what shoppers actually pay), list price (the manufacturer's or supplier's standard selling price for a product before any discounts or other deductions), the different net price levels, to finally the end price.

This price waterfall is the standard tool for analyzing trade terms and with that trade spend. The key dimensions are:[59]

- **Width:** Refers to the number of trade term elements.
- **Depth:** Refers to the total sum of discounts from list price to end price, typically used as a percentage of the list price.
- **Rules:** These determine if and how much a retailer receives from a specific term's element. For example, some elements such as a base discount may be unconditional, whereas others are tied to sales, availability of products, display, or other agreed targets.

---

[59] See Baker et al. (2010), Nagle and Müller (2018), Simon-Kucher & Partners (2019), and Simon and Fassnacht (2019).

The structure – that is the combination of these three elements – determines the effectiveness of a trade terms system. Width and depth can differ largely between industries, countries, and companies, but the number of trade spend buckets (width) is typically in the range of 5–10 and the total spend around 15–30% (depth) in Europe and North America.[60] The critical part for making a trade terms structure performant are the rules that determine the amount of spend per element. For this, a useful distinction is that between discounts and bonuses as in Table 2.3. Discounts are usually applied on-invoice and they reduce the amount to be paid on invoices directly. Bonuses, on the other hand, are typically paid off-invoice. These are additional payments or credits given by the manufacturer to the retailer – for example, quarterly or annually – often based on performance achievement. Most performance-based elements are in the bonus category. Notable exceptions include cash discounts if the invoice is paid within a defined time frame (e.g., 14 days) or discounts for bulk orders. This is because it is easier to track performance over longer periods of time rather than on individual invoices. Table 2.3 provides an overview of typical discount and bonus elements.[61]

The selection of elements depends on several factors. The most important are the objectives of the manufacturer, its strength in the market – as stronger brands can more easily ask for a larger share of performance-based elements – and its historical trade systems, as it is difficult to implement large changes if those increase uncertainty for retailers. One very common phenomenon is that over time many trade terms elements that started as conditional incentives become unconditional entitlements over time. For example, if a retailer does not reach the target required for a 5% bonus because of some external factor (e.g., a strike or pandemic) and the manufacturer still pays the bonus to protect the relationship, then it will be

---

[60] On the share of gross revenues, see Deloitte (2025) and Strategy&/PwC (2017).
[61] See Nagle and Müller (2018), Simon and Fassnacht (2019), Shipley and Jobber (2012), and Monroe (2003).

Foundations

Table 2.3 Overview of typical discount and bonus elements

Type	Element	Typical treatment	Purpose	Performance sensitivity level
Discounts (on invoice)	Trade discount	Immediate deduction from list price	Adjusts price by channel or customer type	Low
	Functional discount	Reduction for services (e.g., warehousing, logistics)	Compensates intermediaries for functions	Medium
	Order volume discount	Reduction on large single orders	Rewards bulk orders	Medium
	Cash discount	Deduction for early payment	Encourages prompt cash collection	Medium
	Promotional discount	Temporary price cut during promo period	Stimulates short-term demand	Medium
	Free goods/Bonus packs	Additional units for purchase or promo	Boosts sales volume	Medium
	Introductory discount	Launch discount for limited time	Encourages initial distribution	Low
	Seasonal discount	Offered off-season or pre-season	Balances demand over time	Low
	Regional/Channel discount	Price variation by geography or channel	Adjusts for cost and competition	Low

Type	Element	Typical treatment	Purpose	Performance sensitivity level
Bonuses (off invoice)	Volume bonus	Bonus based on sales thresholds (e.g., quarterly/annual)	Rewards cumulative volume	High
	Growth or performance bonus	Payment for exceeding growth or share targets	Aligns distributor goals with manufacturer growth	High
	Listing bonus	Payment or goods for shelf placement	Secures product presence in stores	Medium
	Display bonus	Payment for display or visibility execution	Enhances in-store presence	Medium
	Marketing support	Shared funding for retailer media	Promotes brand awareness	Medium
	Bill-back allowance	Credit after verified promotion or sell-out	Ensures incentive follows results	Medium
	Lump-sum/Annual support payment	Fixed negotiated payment	Simplifies annual trade investment	Low

very difficult to reinstate the conditionality. This is sometimes referred to as *term creep*, and it often requires a trade terms reset every 5–10 years to reinstate a performance-based trade terms system.

To close this section, we note that there are other elements beyond discounts and bonuses as shown in Table 2.3 that can exist, such as penalties, fees, allowances, or accruals. But these most often play a much less central role and are not used to manage the trade terms system.

2.4.2.5 Channel Mix

In FMCG, channel mix refers to the deliberate allocation of products, activities, and trade spend across different routes to market – such as modern trade, traditional retail, e-commerce, wholesale, convenience, and out-of-home. As one of the five core RGM levers, it determines not only where a brand competes, but also how profitably it does so.

A channel mix approach must balance reach, margin, and brand equity considering specific channel needs and differences. Typically, each channel serves distinct shopper missions: supermarkets drive planned purchases and visibility, convenience stores win impulse moments, e-commerce offers assortment and convenience, and traditional trade is important for penetration in emerging markets. The goal is not to be everywhere with the same offer, but to be in the right place with the right mix of RGM levers.

1. **Understand shopper behavior by channel:** Effective RGM begins with insight. Shopper needs, trip frequencies, and price sensitivities differ widely across channels. For example, e-commerce shoppers respond to bundle offers and delivery convenience, while traditional trade shoppers prioritize affordability and trust. Granular understanding of these behaviors enables tailored assortment, price-pack architectures, and promotions that resonate with each shopper segment.

2. **Manage profitability and cost-to-serve:** Not all channels are created equal in terms of their cost structure. Modern trade often demands higher trade spend and compliance costs, while small stores can carry higher logistics expenses. Optimizing channel mix requires clear visibility on net revenue and margin contribution by channel, not just topline growth. RGM leaders allocate investment where incremental profit and (net) revenue are maximized.
3. **Align channel strategy with brand positioning:** Channel choices send brand signals. Premium brands may lose equity if overexposed in discount or wholesale environments, while mass brands may miss reach if absent from them. A disciplined channel strategy ensures consistent brand experience and price integrity across touchpoints.
4. **Orchestrate portfolio and execution:** Winning in channel mix also demands differentiated portfolios and tailored execution plans. This may include channel-exclusive SKUs (stock-keeping units), customized packaging, or digital activations aligned with platform algorithms. Excellence lies in harmonizing national brand strategies with localized commercial realities.
5. **Use data and analytics to optimize continuously:** Many leading FMCG companies use advanced analytics to monitor performance at the intersection of channel, region, and shopper type. Predictive models can identify profit pools, cannibalization risks, and white-space opportunities, allowing agile optimization of channel investments.

In essence, channel mix is the art and science of putting your brands in the right places, at the right prices, with the right propositions – optimizing profit and (net) revenue across every route to market. When executed well, it transforms distribution into a driver of profitable growth.

2.4.2.6 Bringing It All Together

So far, we have discussed every RGM lever in isolation. The question is now: How to integrate these different methods? There is no straightforward answer within the traditional methods framework discussed here – and this has been the motivation for us to develop a new technology that can integrate these levers naturally. We will discuss this RGM native technology – the Virtual Shoppers – in Chapter 4. Therefore, in practice these different levers are today mostly analyzed and decided in sequence and with the (often implicit) assumption that everything else stays essentially the same – often by different teams. Also in Chapter 4, we will discuss the challenges with this integrated approach in more detail.

2.4.3 Beyond Pay-Per-Unit: Pricing Models

We can define a pricing model as the way a company monetizes its products and services. This includes four key elements:

- **Object of monetization:** For example, product, user, transaction, hour, outcome.
- **Metric of monetization:** For example, per unit, per mile, per gigabyte, per click.
- **Timing of payment:** For example, upfront, subscription, after use, after results.
- **Mechanics of charging:** For example, fixed, variable, dynamic, or hybrid methods.

In FMCG, the dominant model toward the shopper is pay-per-unit – with some degree of variation for the price. For example, prices may vary for promotions or the number of products bought together. Other variations such as subscriptions or dynamic pricing in stores are occasionally tested but are currently not playing a major role.

In other industries, alternative pricing models have been introduced more successfully. The aerospace industry offers one of the most cited examples: Rolls-Royce's "Power by the Hour" model, which charges airlines per engine hour, transformed the traditional product sale into a service contract. By monetizing uptime and reliability, Rolls-Royce turned what was once a capital purchase into a continuous revenue relationship.[62] In telecommunications, service providers are using a series of different pricing models ranging from fixed bundles to usage-based charging, billing per gigabyte data volume, megabyte data speed, or per active user. The variation allows providers to align offers with actual consumption and customer value rather than arbitrary metrics.[63] Software companies have undergone a similar transformation. Instead of selling perpetual licenses, Adobe, Microsoft, and countless SaaS (software-as-a-service) firms rely on subscription-based pricing, monetizing ongoing access, updates, and cloud integration.[64] The automotive sector is following suit. Carmakers such as Porsche and Volvo have launched flexible subscription programs, while Tesla and BMW experiment with feature-based micro-transactions – charging monthly for software-activated capabilities like driver assistance or heated seats.[65] These cases illustrate that today, the structure of how companies charge is becoming more important in many industries.[66] However, because such pricing model variations are less important in FMCG, we refer to the cited references for further details.

---

[62] Ng et al. (2013).
[63] Osterwalder and Pigneur (2010).
[64] Klein (2020).
[65] Automotive World (2023).
[66] Zatta (2022).

2.4.4 Current Technology Solutions

In practice, the above pricing methods are primarily used within an Excel environment. Figure 2.64 shows an example of a pricing logic using both a price elasticity- and value-based approach. Based on our experience, that is true across industries and companies. Excel spreadsheets have been around since the 1980s. Their benefits are clear: Flexible modeling, low cost of use, easy access, and fast when making rough calculations. However, 40 years later, they seem like ancient tools closer to the paper and pencil era. They are typically not integrated with any other data models, they are impossible to scale across an organization, they lack predictive capacity, they are limited by the laptop's computing power, and, most of all, they frequently cannot be understood or maintained by anyone other than the original developer.

For the past decade, rule-based pricing software has been developed by numerous providers that basically employ Excel-logic with a nicer

Figure 2.64 Example Excel pricing tool

Price elasticity based pricing

Price elasticity - 2,0

				Current				Target				
Product	Current Price	Cost	Price elasticity	Units	Revenue	Profit	Margin	Margin	Price	Units	Revenue	Profit
Own Peanut Brand 1000g	16,99 €	9,00 €	- 2,0	2.655	45.108 €	21.213 €	47%	50%	18,00 €	2.365	42.577 €	21.289 €
Own Peanut Brand 750g	12,99 €	6,00 €	- 2,0	725	9.418 €	5.068 €	54%	50%	12,00 €	850	10.195 €	5.097 €
Own Peanut Brand 500g	9,99 €	4,50 €	- 2,0	575	5.744 €	3.157 €	55%	50%	9,00 €	708	6.376 €	3.188 €
Own Peanut Brand 250g	6,99 €	2,50 €	- 2,0	3.400	23.766 €	15.266 €	64%	50%	5,00 €	6.645	33.225 €	16.612 €
Competitor A 1000g	12,05 €		- 2,0	1.855					12,05 €	1.855		
Competitor A 500g	9,62 €		- 2,0	15					9,62 €	15		
Competitor B 1000g	12,49 €		- 2,0	1.510					12,49 €	1.510		
				7.355	**84.036 €**	**44.704 €**				**10.568**	**92.373 €**	**46.187 €**

Value based pricing						Price decision			
							Weight		
							50%	50%	
Brand	Size	Base	Brand	Size	Price	Current	Elasticity	Value	Price Decision
Own	1000g	6,00 €	5,00 €	5,00 €	16,00 €	16,99 €	18,00 €	16,00 €	**16,99 €**
Own	750g	6,00 €	5,00 €	3,00 €	14,00 €	12,99 €	12,00 €	14,00 €	**12,99 €**
Own	500g	6,00 €	5,00 €	2,00 €	13,00 €	9,99 €	9,00 €	13,00 €	**10,99 €**
Own	250g	6,00 €	5,00 €	1,00 €	12,00 €	6,99 €	5,00 €	12,00 €	**8,49 €**
A	1000g	6,00 €	3,00 €	5,00 €	14,00 €	12,05 €			
A	500g	6,00 €	3,00 €	2,00 €	11,00 €	9,62 €			
B	1000g	6,00 €	2,00 €	5,00 €	13,00 €	12,49 €			

interface – and are often cloud-based. Such tools come with most benefits of Excel while making usability and computing power less of a concern. But the fundamental framework of thinking about pricing remains the same. They lack predictive capacity and do not consider the customer view sufficiently. Mostly, they use the traditional methods described above and automate these based on simple rules like "if the price of competitor product A rises by X%, raise the price of my own product B by Y%." A similar system was responsible for the previous Amazon book example (see Figure 2.49). More recently, automated price elasticity engines have emerged, that claim to employ machine learning algorithms to automate and improve the process of elasticity-based pricing. Given sales data, these solutions constantly calculate price elasticities and make automatic price changes. However, being based on price elasticities, they typically ignore both the interaction between products stemming from buyers' switching, and they are unable to properly include other important factors such as promotions, pack sizes, and product features. All in all, these tools simply automate the use of a flawed concept, price elasticity. However, speed alone does not achieve sustainable profitability. Further, these price elasticity-based tools only focus on assessing price changes, and they cannot evaluate the effects of portfolio changes such as changes in product features, delisting of products, or the introduction of innovations. Given this status quo of most pricing tools, it is obvious that a fundamental change is needed. This will be discussed in Chapter 4.

The Excel tools to help set prices are at the center of the pricing and RGM challenge. However, there are other important tools. Table 2.4 shows an overview of the most relevant categories. In this context, the pricing tools are part of the RGM platforms. Other important categories for FMCG include trade promotion management (TPM) and optimization (TPO), which is often split into two solutions, where the TPM helps users manage promotions and the TPO supports in identifying the best promotion plans. Further, price, promotion, and assortment management systems for

Table 2.4 Overview of pricing and RGM tool categories

Category	Definition
Revenue growth management (RGM) platforms	Integrate pricing, promotion, portfolio, trade terms, and mix optimization across functions to drive profitable growth
Trade promotion management (TPM) and optimization (TPO)	Enables planning, budgeting, execution, and post-event analysis of trade promotions to improve ROI and manage channel spend effectively
Retail price, promotion and markdown optimization	Provides analytics to optimize list prices, markdowns, and promotions using both internal and competitor data
Price monitoring and competitor intelligence tools	Track competitor prices and product availability across offline and online channels and deliver data to pricing tools
B2B profit and price optimization software	Tools that use analytics to set price recommendations, discounts, and rebates across segments and channels
Configure-price-quote (CPQ) applications	Automate product configuration, pricing logic, and quote generation to ensure accurate and profitable deal execution
Subscription and recurring billing/ Monetization	Manage recurring, usage-based, or hybrid billing models. Automate invoicing, renewals, and revenue recognition to support scalable SaaS and digital business models

retailers are an important category. Particularly for larger players with larger portfolios and dynamic price changes, these are required. Another important category is price and competitor monitoring. Here, crawlers collect information on competitor websites.

To conclude, in B2B pricing CPQ solutions and offer optimizers are important. For software and other subscription businesses, billing and monetization systems are available.[67]

---

[67] For further details, including overviews of providers, see the more detailed overviews in Gartner (2024, 2025a, 2025b); Forrester (2025); IDC (2024); and Mordor Intelligence (2025).

2.4.5 Pricing Myths

When you google "pricing myths," you will find many lists of pricing myths. Many agencies and consultants have compiled these lists – mainly to sell their ideas. We will do the same here, but from a different angle. Typical lists of pricing myths include the following[68]:

- **Myth:** Costs are the basis for pricing – **Presented reality:** Costs are not important for pricing. Only value to the customer counts.
- **Myth:** Customers are highly price sensitive – **Presented reality:** Most customers are not price sensitive, particularly if price changes are small.
- **Myth:** Products are difficult to differentiate – **Presented reality:** Differentiation is important and not difficult.

While there is some truth in some of these – for example, some customers are price sensitive, and some are not – as a result, some products have a high and some have a low price elasticity. However, the first "myth," that costs are important for pricing, is almost certainly not a myth – as the analyses in Chapter 2 showed. In fact, the real – and dangerous – myth is that costs are not important for pricing. There are many such myths circulating in the pricing field. Therefore, we will discuss the most important ones here, so you can recognize them when you see them.

2.4.5.1 Myth: Costs Do Not Matter in Pricing

The rise of value-based pricing is based on the recognition that value to the customer is key to determining the price of a product or service. Only pricing based on costs will ignore this basic fact. However, the truth is that both the market side, including customers and competitors, reflected in

---

[68] E.g., Hinterhuber (2016).

demand function and price elasticity, as well as variable costs need to be considered to optimize profits.

To demonstrate this relationship, consider the following simple example based on the microeconomics outlined in this chapter (see Figure 2.65): A product costs €100 to produce and demand is linear with a price elasticity of −2 at a price of €200. Then the €200 is the profit-optimal price, because margin (here, 50%) multiplied by the price elasticity (−2) is −1. As margin and price elasticity determine the optimal price, it becomes clear that costs do matter – together with value-to-the-customer reflected in the demand curve. This is further highlighted when costs increase, and the new profit-optimal price needs to be identified. If in the example costs increase by €10 from €100 to €110, then the new profit-optimal price is €105 – a €5 price increase. The formula to determine the profit-optimal price shown in Figure 2.65 indicates that half of a cost increase needs to be passed on (the term $\frac{c}{2}$) in the case of linear demand if the price before the cost increase was also profit optimal. Also if demand is not linear, the

Figure 2.65 Costs matter for profit optimization!

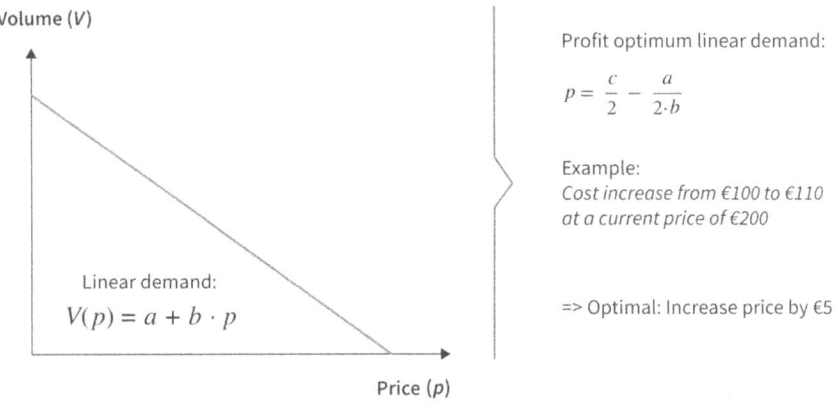

Profit optimum linear demand:

$$p = \frac{c}{2} - \frac{a}{2 \cdot b}$$

Example:
Cost increase from €100 to €110 at a current price of €200

=> Optimal: Increase price by €5

Linear demand:
$V(p) = a + b \cdot p$

Assumption: the price before the cost increase is optimal.

condition "price elasticity times margin is −1 in the profit optimum" ensures that costs always need to be considered for profit optimization.

To close this section, we add two comments: First, fixed costs do not matter for pricing, only variable costs. Fixed costs only need to be considered to assess if it makes sense at all to enter a market to sell products. Second, (variable) costs do not matter for revenue optimization. In some industries such as telco, software, or the hotel industry variable costs are so low that they can be neglected. In those cases, the same price (i.e., where price elasticity is −1) optimizes both revenue and profit. Then, costs do not matter for pricing – but only because they are negligible to start with.

2.4.5.2 Myth: Pricing Is All About Value to "the Customer"

In value-based pricing, prices are set according to the value perceived by the customer, rather than production cost or competitor pricing. This approach can lead to higher profitability, as it allows companies to capture more of the customer's willingness to pay. When executed well, it aligns price with the benefits and outcomes that customers experience from a product or service.

However, implementing value-based pricing is far from straightforward. The central challenge lies in identifying which customer to optimize for. Customers differ widely in terms of needs, preferences, and value perceptions. Thus, a single "value-based price" often does not exist, because there is not "the customer." Rather, all customers differ in how they value a product, which is reflected in the demand curve (see Figure 2.66). It shows all (potential) customers sorted by their willingness to pay. Note that here we could argue that price elasticity pricing is simply a more mathematical representation of value-based pricing.

Proponents of value-based pricing often suggest grouping similar customers into customer segments and representing those by buyer personas. While visualizing buyer personas is useful for helping professionals think

Figure 2.66   Pricing is all about value to the customer!

"Pricing is all about value to the customer"
Example of value-based pricing

Value pricing optimizes for value to *the* customer… | …but which customer are we talking about?

Typical definition:

Value pricing is customer-focused pricing, meaning companies base their pricing on how much *the* customer believes a product is worth.

Volume (V)

This one..?
…this one..?
…or this one?

Price (p)

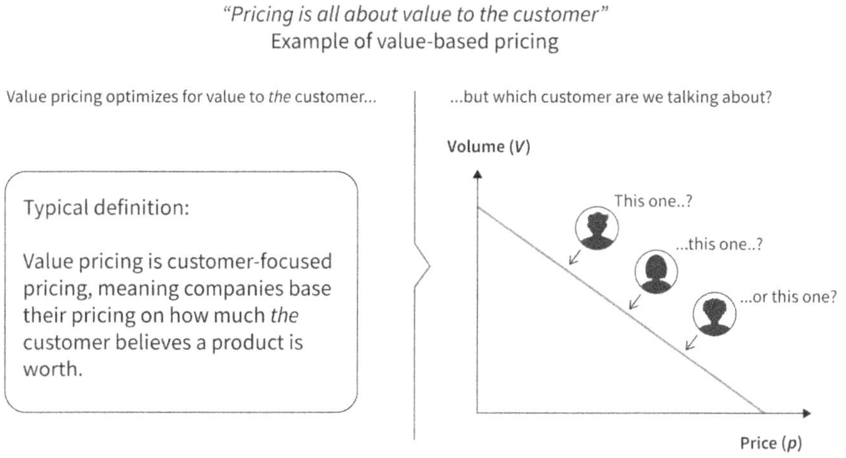

about their customers, it must also be clear that a real market is not well represented by four or five buyer profiles. Everyone who has seen real-customer data across a large customer pool is certainly aware that real preferences look like the graph on the left side in Figure 2.67 – and not like the graph on the right side. That means preferences are distributed more smoothly among customers as represented by demand functions with most of the mass in the center, rather than lumped together as assumed by customer segmentations or representative buyer personas, which typically impose artificial groupings on data sets.

Another problem arises when value to the customer is applied to differentiate products as in the ski jacket example in Figure 2.51. Here, different values are assigned to different product attributes based on how "the customer" values them – for example, the difference between synthetic and down filling. Again, while this approach is convenient and straightforward to implement, it is problematic for the following reason. Customers do not neatly split into subgroups of those with the same preferences for specific attributes. In the ski jacket example, customers do not split into subgroups

Figure 2.67 Customer segmentation and personas

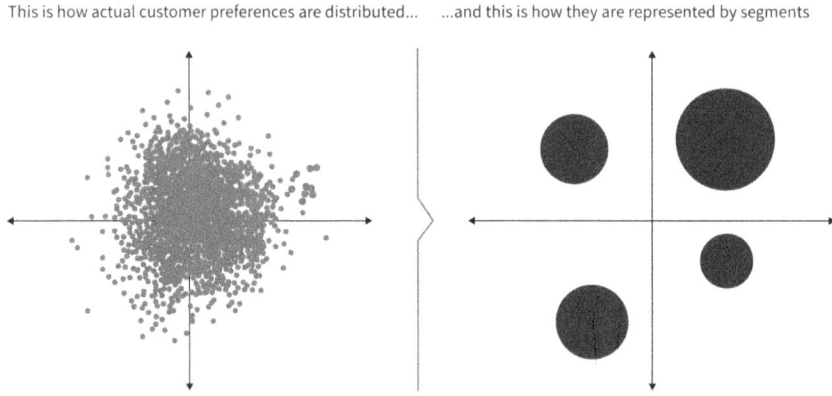

of those who would pay $50 more for the down filling and those who do not. Rather, the extra willingness to pay for the down filling will likely follow some continuous (e.g., linear) distribution across all potential customers. That means that depending on the price difference between down and synthetic fillings, customers will switch between the two, resulting in some optimal price difference that also depends on how preferences between the two fillings correlate with other preferences. In summary, all potential customers have different preferences for product features – the average of "the customer" is less relevant than understanding the distribution of preferences and how they affect decisions between alternatives.

2.4.5.3 A Corollary Myth: It Is Always Better to Differentiate Prices Between Customers

There is one important addition to the previous myth about "the customer," that results essentially in the exact opposite problem. That is, in cases where prices can be differentiated between customers, it is often argued that pricing should aim to maximize profit by charging every customer their maximum willingness to pay. This is typically justified by the analysis shown in Figure 2.68. The left side shows the profit optimum if the product is sold at a single (optimal) price to all with a willingness to pay above that price. In the example, the overall maximum willingness to pay is $150, demand is linear, maximum market size is 3,000, and unit costs are $50. Then, the (single) profit-optimal price is $100 with resulting sales of 1,000 units and a profit of $50,000 (indicated by the square). However, if each customer pays his maximum willingness to pay (right side of the graph), then the achieved profit is $100,000 (the full triangle under the demand curve) – twice that of the single-price optimum.

While this is certainly tempting, it also requires a very precise understanding of each customer's exact willingness to pay. If only a single price is optimized, only the distribution needs to be known, as it does not matter who buys the product, only how many are sold. If everyone is charged their estimated (maximum) willingness to pay, then each overestimated

Figure 2.68 Price differentiation

willingness to pay results in a lost sale. A simulation study of the relationship between the accuracy of the WTP estimation and the resulting profit, indicates that estimated and actual WTP need to correlate with more than 0.95 for this full price differentiation (right side) to be more profitable than a single optimal price for all (left side).

There are certainly ways to increase profit with (typically some less extreme) form of price differentiation. However, this myth is important because it shows that pricing professionals need to be careful with price differentiation.

2.4.5.4 Myth: Price Elasticity Is a Single Number

At a conference I once witnessed the following discussion between two pricing experts.

> **Expert 1**: "What do you think? What is the price elasticity of bananas?"
>
> **Expert 2**, while stroking his stomach: "Hmm, it should be around -1.4 ... but shoppers have become more price sensitive lately, so maybe -1.5 to -1.6!"

I do not recall why they were discussing bananas, but the conversation highlights a common misconception in pricing. That is the – often implicit – assumption that products can be associated with a specific price elasticity value. Based on what we discussed in this chapter, this is theoretically only possible in the case of isoelastic demand (i.e., a constant price elasticity) and no alternative products in the market that can affect demand. In practice, this is almost never the case. Hence, it is a common myth that a product has a price elasticity. A product has a price elasticity at a specific price and a specific pricing action such as a 5% price increase across the portfolio and a competitor price increase of 3%. Price elasticities can differ greatly depending on what other changes happen at the same time (see also Figure 2.17 on this).

We often see that companies work with static price elasticity tables, typically provided by agencies – sometimes with some mild differentiation, such as price elasticity values for regular price changes, crossing price thresholds, or for promotions. Such price elasticity tables have limited value, as price elasticities depend on the specific situation and can change substantially. In practice, these static price elasticities are often not used to better understand a category and identify the best action, but to justify a preconceived price change. This use reminds us of Andrew Lang's famous quote: "He uses statistics as a drunken man uses lampposts – for support rather than illumination."[69] Do not be like this!

2.4.5.5 Myth: Identified Behavioral Effects Can Be Applied Directly

Applying insights from behavioral pricing in real-world contexts requires careful consideration of how shoppers make actual purchasing decisions outside controlled settings. Behavioral pricing research – often conducted in laboratory or online experimental environments – provides valuable insights into how psychological factors such as price thresholds, reference products, or prices affect buying decisions. However, applying these findings is often not straightforward and demands attention to the complexities of real buying situations.

In laboratory studies, participants typically face simplified choices and limited contextual details. For example, they choose between three or four products and not between dozens, as in a real store. Further, in surveys researchers often try to isolate a single effect, such as the decoy effect discussed earlier in the context of the famous two versus three wine bottles experiment. In a real store, many things are going on at the same time, making it more difficult for each single effect to fully affect decisions. One known

---

[69] Lang, quoted in *The Oxford Dictionary of Quotations* (2014).

effect is shown in Figure 2.53, which compares price threshold survey research with real sales data. Here the difference is particularly strong – both in the difference of research and real buying situation (one product alternative vs. dozens in a shelf) and the outcome: a strong price threshold versus a minimal effect.

For practitioners, this means that behavioral pricing insights should be used with caution. In the context of the traditional pricing methods discussed in this chapter, this often means that field experiments, AB testing, and pilot implementations are essential to validate behavioral pricing interventions in the actual market context. Behavioral effects may perform differently depending on product category, channel, and shopper group. Successful application therefore requires an iterative approach: integrating behavioral insights into pricing design, testing their real-world impact, and refining strategies based on observed consumer responses. A more advanced approach to integrate behavioral effects directly will be described in Chapter 4, where we introduce the Virtual Shoppers technology, which can be trained with specific behavioral effects and is able to integrate the insights into the real-world setting.

2.5 FURTHER READING

In this chapter, we aim to provide an introduction on pricing and RGM. However, there is a rich ecosystem of different sources that are available including books, societies, and conferences for more detail. Here, we will provide an overview of these sources and recommend further study into the specific areas of interest, for example behavioral pricing, B2B pricing, or innovation pricing.

2.5.1 Books

Here is a list of 10 books on pricing and RGM with different focus from practical to academic and across different industries and use cases.[70]

1. Thomas T. Nagle, Georg Müller, and Evert Gruyaert, *The Strategy and Tactics of Pricing: A Guide to Growing More Profitably* **(2023)**

A classic reference for value-based pricing. It links customer segmentation, perceived value, and price structures to profitable growth and provides several examples of CPGs facing inflation and retailer pressure.

2. Hermann Simon and Martin Fassnacht, *Price Management: Strategy, Analysis, Decision, Implementation* **(2019)**

An academically rigorous framework integrating economics, psychology, and strategy to manage price from design through execution. The book is particularly strong on competitive positioning and behavioral insights.

3. Robert L. Phillips, *Pricing and Revenue Optimization* **(2021)**

A technical foundation for RGM analytics, covering demand estimation, elasticity modeling, and dynamic pricing. Ideal for FMCG analysts who need to integrate data-driven methods into price-pack architecture and promotion strategy using traditional tools.

4. Walter L. Baker, Michael V. Marn, and Craig C. Zawada, *The Price Advantage* **(2010)**

A McKinsey-based manual on operationalizing pricing excellence – pocket price waterfalls, discount governance, and performance tracking, aimed at commercial and RGM teams who need to translate strategy into action.

---

[70] Portions of this text were drafted with assistance from ChatGPT5 by OpenAI. This AI tool supported initial research for this sub-chapter. All AI-generated content was carefully reviewed, edited, and approved. The final analysis, conclusions, and interpretations represent my views and expertise. I take full responsibility for the content and accuracy of this work.

5. Stephan M. Liozu, *The Pricing Journey: Leading and Transforming Your Pricing Function* (2020)

Focuses on organizational change and capability building in pricing – the "soft side" of RGM maturity. Offers frameworks for governance, culture, and leadership needed to embed pricing excellence in large organizations.

6. Tim J. Smith, *Pricing: The Third Business Skill: Principles of Price Management* (2013)

Positions pricing as a managerial discipline equal to marketing and finance, emphasizing structured decision-making and cross-functional coordination. Aimed at general managers or category leads in companies navigating pricing complexity.

7. Danilo Zatta and Maciej Kraus, *Pricing Decoded: How Leading Pricing Practitioners Manage Price to Boost Profits* (2022)

A practitioners' guide with many corporate case studies across industries, including consumer goods. Explains how to professionalize pricing processes and implement profit-driving RGM systems.

8. Rafi Mohammed, *The Art of Pricing: How to Find the Hidden Profits to Grow Your Business* (2013)

A concise, practical introduction to designing pricing models around customer value and willingness to pay. It answers the question of how to use price to uncover hidden profits and find new opportunities for growth.

9. Greg Thain and John Bradley, *FMCG: The Power of Fast-Moving Consumer Goods* (2016)

Provides an industry-wide look at how brand, trade, and pricing dynamics interact in FMCG markets. It focuses on RGM strategies within real-world retailer negotiations and consumer behavior trends.

10. Madhavan Ramanujam and Georg Tacke, *Monetizing Innovation: How Smart Companies Design the Product Around the Price* (2016)

Shows how leading companies start with customers' willingness to pay to design the right offer, avoiding costly product misfires. An important book for RGM professionals seeking to embed value thinking into innovation pipeline decisions.

2.5.2 Professional Societies and Conferences

A global ecosystem now supports the disciplines of pricing and RGM. This ecosystem connects academics, practitioners, and commercial leaders who share a commitment to improving how businesses create, communicate, and capture value. Here, we highlight five organizations as key organizers and thought leaders shaping this community.

2.5.2.1 Societies and Professional Organizers

The Professional Pricing Society (PPS) is the cornerstone of the global pricing profession. Headquartered in the United States, it has built the most extensive network of pricing practitioners worldwide. PPS provides the Certified Pricing Professional (CPP) credential, executive education, and specialized events that define industry best practice. Over the past three decades, the society has helped formalize pricing as a corporate function, establishing the benchmarks and professional standards that underpin the field today.

Europe's most influential organization is the EPP, the Pricing and RGM Platform, based in Belgium. EPP serves as a global network for professionals working at the intersection of pricing, revenue growth, and commercial excellence. It combines capability development, benchmarking, and peer learning with an explicit focus on RGM maturity. EPP's mission goes beyond pricing in isolation. It connects pricing to broader business transformation – linking it with promotion management, trade spending, and value creation across industries.

Within the academic and analytical community, the Revenue Management and Pricing Section of INFORMS provides intellectual leadership. As part of the Institute for Operations Research and the Management Sciences, this section focuses on the quantitative and data-driven aspects of pricing – revenue optimization, demand forecasting, and analytical modeling. Its members form a bridge between academic research and applied business practice, ensuring that the discipline remains grounded in rigorous, evidence-based insights.

In Germany, Ardensi has emerged as a dynamic organizer of global events that position pricing as a central theme of digital transformation. Its Pricing Strategy Summits, hosted in Europe and North America, unite senior executives and strategists around the question of how monetization models evolve in digital commerce and technology-enabled environments. Ardensi's approach highlights pricing as both a strategic and a cultural capability, reflecting its growing role in enterprise transformation.

Finally, the Promotion Optimization Institute (POI) stands as the leading global forum for professionals in consumer goods and retail who manage trade promotion, shopper activation, and revenue growth management. Based in the United States, POI's mission is to elevate commercial collaboration between manufacturers and retailers by improving promotional ROI, trade efficiency, and digital shelf execution. For many in fast-moving consumer goods, POI is the nexus of thought leadership in modern trade and promotion optimization.

The collective influence of these and other organizations in the field is most visible in the annual rhythm of conferences and forums that punctuate the pricing and RGM calendar.

2.5.2.2 Conferences for Pricing and RGM

The global pricing community gathers several times each year across North America and Europe, following a well-established seasonal cadence. Each event has a distinct identity, audience, and learning purpose.

The year typically begins with the profitABLE Conferences organized by the Professional Pricing Society. Held in spring and again in autumn, these events bring together practitioners from around the world for workshops, case studies, and networking. They are practical and built around professional development – ideal for those refining pricing capabilities or seeking certification through PPS's CPP program.

As summer approaches, the INFORMS Revenue Management and Pricing Section Conference convenes academics and data-driven practitioners. For many, it is the intellectual high point of the year, where cutting-edge research on demand modeling, optimization, and price analytics is presented and debated. The conference blends quantitative sophistication with applied insight, making it particularly valuable for companies that build pricing algorithms or manage large analytical teams.

Autumn belongs to Europe, when the EPP Global Pricing and Revenue Management Forum takes center stage. This event unites senior pricing, RGM, and commercial excellence leaders from industries as diverse as manufacturing, life sciences, and consumer goods. The discussions move beyond technical models to the broader transformation of pricing functions – organizational design, capability building, governance, and change management. It is less about formulas and more about leadership.

Running parallel to these established institutions, Ardensi's Pricing Strategy Summits have become a modern bridge between pricing and digital strategy. The European edition, typically held in spring, attracts executives exploring monetization in digital commerce, SaaS, and platform business models. Its North American counterpart follows in autumn, reflecting the growing importance of pricing as a driver of digital business growth and innovation.

In the same seasonal rhythm, the Promotion Optimization Institute (POI) Summits convene commercial and RGM professionals from consumer goods and retail. The spring summit often focuses on trade promotion optimization and data integration, while the autumn edition emphasizes retail collaboration and execution. POI's events are less theoretical and more applied – where practitioners share lessons on balancing promotional effectiveness with long-term profitability.

Throughout the year, EPP also hosts a series of industry-specific forums covering sectors such as FMCG, Life Sciences, Chemicals, and Industrial Manufacturing. These gatherings dive deeply into industry-specific pricing challenges, regulatory environments, and value-based pricing models.

There is a pattern across all these events: spring and autumn are the social seasons of pricing and RGM, summer provides academic reflection, and winter serves as the planning cycle for capability development. Together, these societies and conferences form the living infrastructure for a profession that sits at the heart of modern commercial excellence, where pricing and RGM are taking the center stage.

CHAPTER THREE
BUILDING THE RGM PLAYBOOK

In this chapter we will now apply the ideas and concepts presented previously to build an RGM Playbook for practical use. Of course, every company's playbook will be different, but there are many commonalities and frameworks that can be used to structure the work and serve as a starting point for your RGM playbook. In Section 3.1, we will discuss pricing strategy. This will be the starting point for the RGM framework presented in Section 3.2. We conclude the chapter with discussing international considerations (Section 3.3) and a practical guide on how to build your own RGM playbook (Section 3.4).

3.1 PRICING AND RGM STRATEGY

Good strategy is like great art. It is difficult to define what it is, but you immediately recognize it when you see it. Here is a classic example:[71] In the tale of David and Goliath, David knew of his slingshot capabilities and likely also of Goliath's weakness. Therefore, it was good strategy to take the risk of the challenge and to reject the protection that was offered to him and would only have made him slower.

Unfortunately, good strategy is rare, and most of the time, the adjective "strategic" has no meaning when added to any business function such as strategic marketing, strategic finance, or strategic pricing. Yet, strategy workshops and the practice of defining a pricing strategy are well-established rituals in the corporate world that frequently result in a conclusion that is a variation of this: "We aim for profitable growth!" It is not always clear what that means but it is flexible enough to justify any pricing goal including both profit and revenue maximization – depending on who you talk to. Upper management and marketing typically prefer profit, while sales favor revenue.

Because bad pricing strategy is so common, most pricing professionals have never experienced how powerful a good pricing strategy can be. So, let us see if we can change that. In the following, we first explain what pricing strategy is all about, then we outline a concept of how to develop a good pricing strategy, and finally we look at some examples.

Strategy in general and pricing strategy in particular are all about choice – that is, deciding to do one thing and not the other. If a company decides it is fully committed to profit, it must accept that it will likely lose some customers in the process. If it aims for revenue, it will keep more

---
[71] See details in Section 3.1.2.1.

customers, but stockholders tend to be less happy and bonuses slimmer. There is no escape from such fundamental trade offs in deciding on the right pricing strategy. They need to be addressed, discussed, decided – and then result in coherent action.

The key objective of pricing is to support the overall strategy of the company. The pricing and RGM strategy is the pricing manager's theory of how to best achieve this. If the company's objective is immediate profit maximization, then the pricing strategy needs to focus on how to extract the largest possible share of the value the company creates. A good pricing strategy does this very effectively.

3.1.1 Pricing Strategy Framework

One of the most useful practical books on strategy is certainly Richard Rumelt's (2011) *Good Strategy, Bad Strategy*. In addition to the many entertaining strategy examples, the book also provides a very concise and useful framework for developing a good strategy. Here, we apply the three steps of the framework – diagnosis, guiding policy, and coherent action – to pricing strategy (see Figure 3.1).

Figure 3.1   Strategy framework – the kernel of good strategy

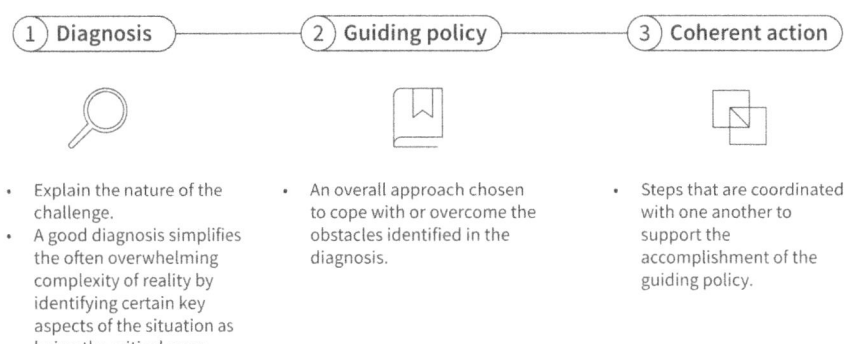

Diagnosis: Based on the understanding of the overall strategy and how pricing can support it, the diagnosis needs to provide an explanation of the nature of the pricing challenge. A good diagnosis simplifies the complexity of reality by identifying those aspects of the situation that are critical for pricing success. For example:

- Does it make sense to simply follow the pricing of key competitors with an established product?
- Should you price an innovation at a low price to keep competitors out of the market or at a high price to skim off the high willingness to pay of early adopters?

Guiding policy: This is the overall approach to master the pricing challenges identified in the diagnosis. The guiding policy needs to specify the core pricing objectives, the key performance indicators (KPIs) to measure success, and guidelines on pricing methods, tools, and processes to achieve it. A good guiding policy can be summarized in no more than one page.

Coherent action: This includes the coordinated implementation of the guiding policy in the pricing methods, tools, and processes. The complexity of this task depends on the industry's pricing requirements (e.g., number of products, differentiation between customers) and the role of the company (e.g., price leader or follower).

Figure 3.2 shows the framework adapted to pricing and RGM.

3.1.2 Simple Examples

The following examples highlight how the three steps can be applied in practice. We start with a non-pricing example – that we already mentioned at the beginning of this chapter – which everyone should be familiar with.

Figure 3.2   Pricing strategy framework

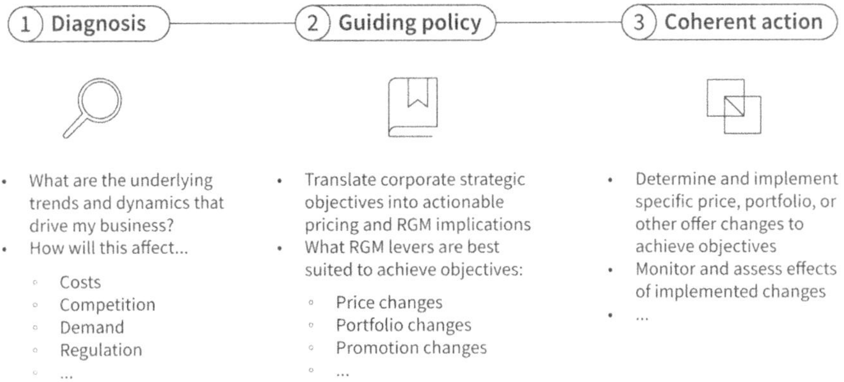

① Diagnosis ── **② Guiding policy** ── **③ Coherent action**

- What are the underlying trends and dynamics that drive my business?
- How will this affect...
  ○ Costs
  ○ Competition
  ○ Demand
  ○ Regulation
  ○ ...

- Translate corporate strategic objectives into actionable pricing and RGM implications
- What RGM levers are best suited to achieve objectives:
  ○ Price changes
  ○ Portfolio changes
  ○ Promotion changes
  ○ ...

- Determine and implement specific price, portfolio, or other offer changes to achieve objectives
- Monitor and assess effects of implemented changes
- ...

3.1.2.1 David and Goliath

To analyze the strategic situation in the diagnosis, we use the well-known SWOT framework, which structures the strategic analysis into four areas: **S**trength, **W**eaknesses, **O**pportunities, **T**hreats.[72] Here is David's assessment in the tale of David and Goliath[73]:

- **Diagnosis:** Goliath is the strongest man in the world and considered undefeatable (Threat). I'm weak (Weakness), but I'm pretty good with the slingshot – and no one knows about this (Strength). Also, I've detected a spot in Goliath's armor, where he is unprotected – right between his eyes (Opportunity).
- **Guiding policy:** I can beat him, if I can hit him with my slingshot before he comes too close. Therefore, I need to be agile to get one good shot at him. That is my only chance.

---
[72] For more details see Kotler and Armstrong (2020).
[73] See Rumelt (2011).

- **Coherent action:** Reject armor that was offered to me. It would only make me slower and does not offer relevant protection if Goliath hits me. Focus all attention on my first – and probably only – shot.

There are two take aways from this example, which are common for good strategy: (1) Good strategy is very clear and straightforward; (2) Don't expect others to understand it before they have seen its success.

Next, we discuss two examples where we apply the framework pricing strategy. Both cases focus on the core elements and highlight what makes a good pricing strategy.

3.1.2.2 AOL

AOL was the internet giant of the 1990s that introduced the internet via dial-up to the public and merged as the larger partner with Time Warner in 2001. With the advent of broadband internet, it became clear that AOL's dial-up business was dead.

- **Diagnosis:** With its 56 kilobits per second, AOL had a much inferior technology compared to broadband's 16+ megabits per second. But, with a multimillion-user base and slow churn in many segments, there was still some money to be made.
- **Guiding policy:** There was no benefit in pricing on value and substantially reducing prices to compete directly. Therefore, all focus needs to be on broadly maintaining prices and reducing churn.
- **Coherent action:** Maintain prices at $20 per month and fight to win back each lost customer by offering free months or reduced rates.

Result: In 2015, AOL had still more than two million paying customers and was sold to Verizon Communications for $4.4 billion.[74]

---

[74] Later in 2021, AOL – together with Yahoo – was sold to Apollo Global Management for $5 billion.

3.1.2.3 Oil Lamps

Oil lamps are a classical example of good pricing strategy. Oil producers gave away lamps for free, so people soon had a need to buy oil to fuel their lamps.

- **Diagnosis:** When oil became readily available, there wasn't enough demand for it, as many people saw the high cost of lamps rather than the benefit of having easy access to light all day and night.
- **Guiding policy:** Take away the initial high barrier of having to buy an expensive lamp to make it easy for people to get used to consuming oil. The many recurring payments for the oil are each small steps for the customers but add to a major improvement for the seller.
- **Coherent action:** Give away the lamps for (near) free and then sell the oil.

Result: The oil baron John D. Rockefeller became the first dollar billionaire.

This model has been widely adapted by manufacturers of a variety of products ranging from razor blades to coffee tabs. In modern times, manufacturers of electric vehicles are attempting a variation of this model. In the traditional automotive business model, many manufacturers sold their vehicles with close to zero margins and then earned their living by later selling spare parts and services at a better margin. Electric vehicles are also sold at cost or below, but later on they do not require many service parts such as oil filters. If then autonomous driving also takes away a large share of accident-related parts, then it is very unclear how to ever make money with e-mobility. The industry is still lacking a good pricing strategy.

These examples highlight that pricing strategy matters. If it is well developed and executed, the pricing and RGM strategy is well aligned with the overall corporate strategy and supports profitable growth on a path toward optimal long-term value capture. There is not always an inspiring story as in the three previous examples, but there is always a chance to diagnose the key pricing challenges, develop a coherent guiding policy to address the identified challenges and address them with coherent action. In the next chapter, we will discuss the role of AI for pricing and RGM. However, we can already reveal that for the foreseeable future, the key strategic questions need to be answered by the commercial, pricing, and RGM leadership. AI will play a decisive role in the execution and tactics – but for now, it will not be a substitute for strategy. If employed correctly, it will be a very capable enabler.

3.2 INTEGRATING INTO A PRICING FRAMEWORK

The previous examples are useful to convey the general idea of how to set up and implement a pricing strategy, but to really make the concepts applicable for pricing and RGM professionals, a more detailed framework is required. Figure 3.3 shows the framework we have developed at Buynomics to help our customers structure their RGM work, develop their specific playbooks, assess and benchmark their RGM maturity, and structure our RGM trainings. In this playbook, we will use this framework to structure the RGM process and setup.

The RGM framework consists of three main steps: (1) the RGM process, (2) people, and (3) technology. The RGM process is further divided into three parts, and each part then consists of one to three substeps – for example, within Strategy (Step 1.1), there are the substeps Strategy, Differentiation, and RGM Levers. Each substep is not equally important. Particularly in smaller organizations, not all substeps must receive the

Figure 3.3 Pricing framework

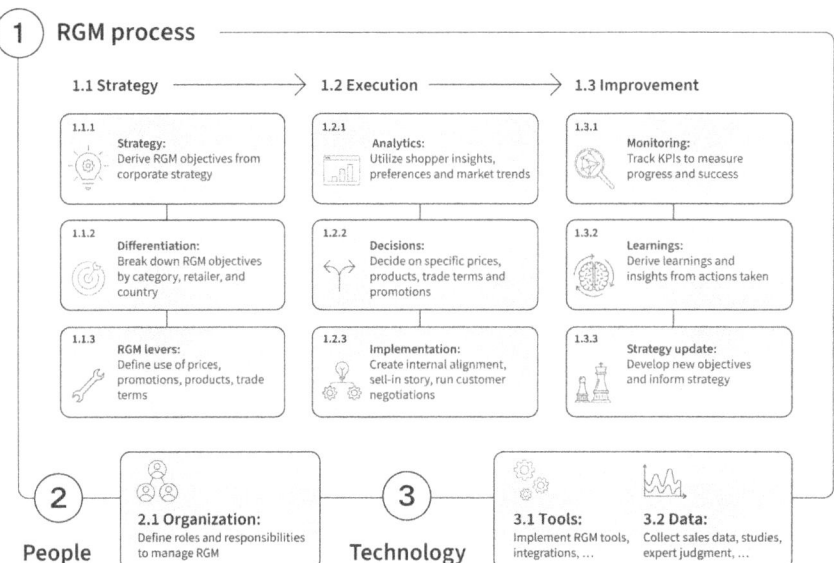

same high level of attention from the start. When building their own RGM playbook, teams often focus on their most important elements. However, for RGM to be effective, the key parts need to be well orchestrated.

At the end of this section, we will discuss some approaches to building a playbook and what subsections to focus on when getting started. Before we do this, we will first lay out the basics of the framework. To make this exercise more practical and provide some ideas for templates that can be used for a playbook, we will discuss the principles using an example dairy company. This exemplary dairy company operates in a mid-sized market, with net sales of around $500m across five categories (milk, butter, cheese, yoghurt, and other) and sells through three retailers.

3.2.1 Step 1 – RGM Process

The RGM process is the central element of the framework. It includes all the moving parts of the RGM function: the development of the RGM strategy (Step 1.1 in Figure 3.3), its execution (Step 1.2), and its improvement (Step 1.3).

3.2.1.1 Step 1.1 – Strategy

The RGM strategy is the starting point of the RGM process. Here it is important to understand that RMG does not exist in isolation but is an integral and important part of the overall strategy of the corporation. As we discussed in Chapter 2, a company has two core tasks: value creation and value capture. RGM is the team exclusively focused on the latter, and it needs to implement the company's theory of how to manage the relationship between the two tasks – particularly the tradeoffs between markets, products, and over time. For example, if the overall strategy is focused on growth, then RGM teams should likely not aim for profit maximization. Therefore, the RGM strategy first needs to be derived from the overall corporate strategy. Specifically, it needs to determine the RGM objectives (Step 1.1.1), break them down by, for example, region, country, channel, and category (Step 1.1.2) – and then select the right RGM levers to address the objectives (Step 1.1.3).

Step 1.1.1 – From Corporate to RGM Strategy

The term corporate strategy was popularized by H. Igor Ansoff.[75] It refers to the overarching plan of a company and the framework through which the organization defines its long-term vision and objectives, makes high-level decisions, and allocates resources. To maximize overall value across its businesses, the corporation needs to address the question of what businesses it should be in, how to structure the corporate portfolio, and how to create and capture value across the different business units.

---

[75] Ansoff (1965).

The first part of this list – the question of what businesses to be in – is currently in 2025/26 gaining more attention as many large CPG (consumer packaged goods) companies are reshaping their portfolios. Recent examples include moves by Kraft Heinz and Mars. In splitting into two stand-alone companies, Kraft Heinz is effectively using divestiture to respond to the market's verdict that its mega-conglomerate model was underperforming. By creating Global Taste Elevation Co. and North American Grocery Co., it signals that separately managed units can attract more focused capital and leadership attention, and potentially higher valuations. Mars, by contrast, is pursuing the opposite path by using its acquisition of Kellanova (the former Kellogg's snacks and international cereal unit) to consolidate control of high-growth snack categories and strengthening bargaining power across retail channels. Taken together, these moves illustrate how corporate control transactions – whether spinoffs or acquisitions – serve as disciplinary tools in realigning firms toward segments where they can achieve superior growth, efficiency, and investor appeal.[76]

While the management of the business units is carried out by the C-level executives, steering the details of value capture within business units is a core RGM task. Most corporations aim for some combination of (net) revenue and profit improvement that they want to achieve each year and over time. This reflects the tradeoff between growth and profitability. Figure 3.4 shows this in a stylized graph. To achieve this goal, RGM has two important tasks:

- **First,** identify and execute offer changes that achieve an optimal (net) revenue and profit improvement combination. Optimal combinations are those where it is not possible to further improve in one dimension without losing in the other dimension (efficient boundary).
- **Second,** select the combination on the efficient boundary that is best in line with the overall corporate strategy.

---

[76] Wall Street Journal (2025); Reuters (2025); Mars (2024); Barron's (2025).

Figure 3.4   Strategic trade off between profit and revenue

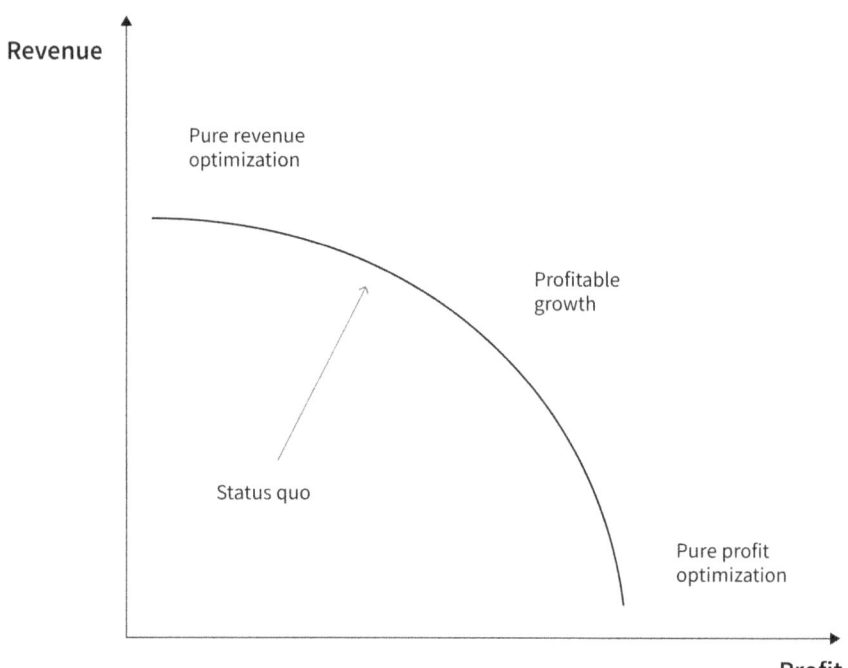

The importance of the role of RGM for achieving this task is increasingly often recognized by top management, as is exemplified by the C-level quote in Figure 3.5. What makes this task difficult is not only that strategic objectives are changing frequently, as they are largely driven by capital market needs. For example, if interest rates are low, then most corporations favor growth over profitability as later profits are less discounted and are therefore now more valuable. Likewise, if interest rates are high, profitability becomes more important.

RGM is also difficult because of a range of often frequently changing trends and uncertainties that RGM needs to consider and react to. Figure 3.6 lists some of the key trends that were identified by RGM teams

Figure 3.5   Examples of statements of corporate objectives

> "Two key pillars of our [...] strategy lie in **enhanced capabilities in data and analytics, and revenue growth management**."
>
> (Steve Cahillane, Chairman and CEO of Kellogg's, 2023)

> "Revenue growth management is one important aspect of the **sustainable growth** of KraftHeinz's revenue."
>
> (Miguel Patricio, CEO and Chairman of the Board at KraftHeinz)

> "Our company was struggling with the inflation and wants to rebuild to a **sustainable and consistent growth rate**."
>
> (Linda Rendle, CEO of The Clorox Company)

as most important in the second half of 2025.[77] For example, commodity price volatility always poses a challenge to RGM teams as cost changes often necessitate a price adjustment or some other reaction (e.g., a pack size or promotion change) as was discussed in Section 2.3. When cocoa prices rose from a level of $2,000 in 2022 to more than $12,000 in 2024 and then back down to $7,000 in the same year,[78] chocolate manufacturers were faced with a real challenge, particularly as products with cocoa contents ranging from 15% to more than 90% required very different price changes as a reaction to the cocoa cost changes.

Another example is the uncertainty about tariff levels in the United States in 2025, as different competitors were faced with very different impacts depending on the country from where they imported their products. Finding the right response to such a dynamic competitive situation

---
[77] Buynomics webinar surveys (2025a).
[78] Trading Economics (n.d.).

Figure 3.6   Key trends relevant for RGM in the second half of 2025

Global supply chain disruptions

Disruptions as in the Red Sea shipping lanes can drive intermittent shortages and variable costs.

Discounters and private label

Discounters and value retailers expand assortments and intensify private label competition across categories.

AI maturity curve

AI adoption is progressing from pilots to enterprise-wide deployments, raising expectations for speed, accuracy, and integration in RGM decisions.

ESG investor fatigue vs. regulatory tightening

While investor focus on ESG has softened, regulatory requirements on transparency and compliance have intensified.

Tariffs

New tariffs between the US, EU, China, and other regions are increasing landed costs on key inputs and requiring market-specific pricing adjustments.

Commodity price volatility

Prices for cocoa, sugar, grains, dairy inputs, vegetable oils, and energy, among others, remain highly volatile, complicating price setting.

using all RGM levers is very difficult but can have a substantial impact on profit and (net) revenue outcomes.

To start the RGM strategy process, teams must gather all key insights on the current strategic situation. Figure 3.7 shows this for the example dairy producer. Here, the diagnosis of the current challenges is performed at the corporate level. From this, the objectives for RGM are derived. They instruct the team to aim for profitable growth with a focus more on net revenue rather than profit growth in the next year. Furthermore, the specific key developments such as a faster changing portfolio landscape across categories and challenges such as increasing fixed costs need to be considered to derive the strategic implication for RGM. In the example, this

Figure 3.7 General strategy

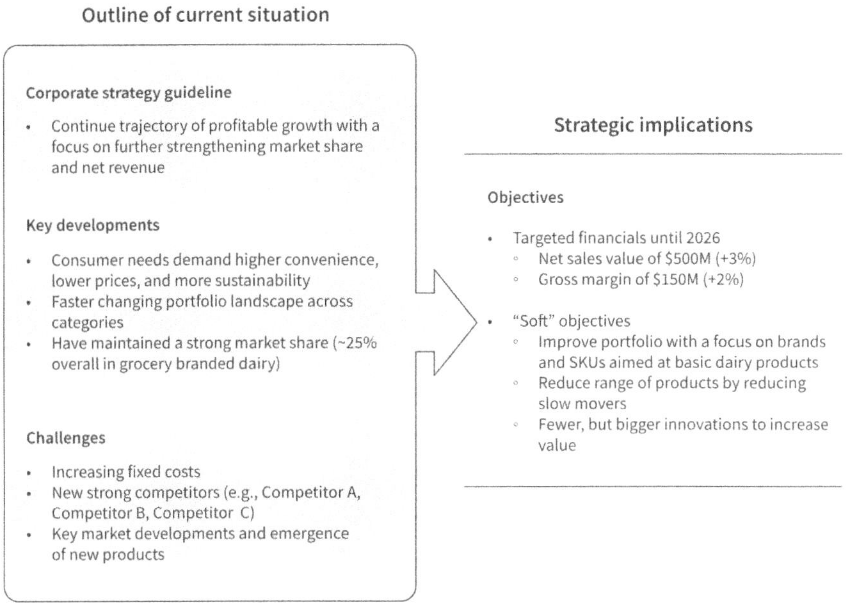

Outline of current situation

Corporate strategy guideline
- Continue trajectory of profitable growth with a focus on further strengthening market share and net revenue

Key developments
- Consumer needs demand higher convenience, lower prices, and more sustainability
- Faster changing portfolio landscape across categories
- Have maintained a strong market share (~25% overall in grocery branded dairy)

Challenges
- Increasing fixed costs
- New strong competitors (e.g., Competitor A, Competitor B, Competitor C)
- Key market developments and emergence of new products

Strategic implications

Objectives
- Targeted financials until 2026
  - Net sales value of $500M (+3%)
  - Gross margin of $150M (+2%)
- "Soft" objectives
  - Improve portfolio with a focus on brands and SKUs aimed at basic dairy products
  - Reduce range of products by reducing slow movers
  - Fewer, but bigger innovations to increase value

---

results in specific net revenue and gross margin growth targets together with a set of "soft" objectives such as reducing the product range.

We see in many companies we work with that top management dictates specific net revenue and profit growth targets that are either unachievable or too unambitious – without prior consultation with the RGM team. RGM teams with strong analytics should try to avoid this and provide early insights into what net revenue and profit growth combinations are achievable.

The other key strategic input is a set of RGM guidelines that codify the rules of how a company structures its commercial offer. Every company we have seen has these guidelines – explicitly written down or implicit in how teams identify relevant options or take decisions. Figure 3.8 shows the set

Figure 3.8 RGM guidelines

	Pricing boundaries	Implications
Brand positioning	Brand positioning within own portfolio	• Pricing must follow brand's position within category • Portfolio diversification must be aligned with category and brand strategy
	Brand positions toward competition	• Pricing and portfolio diversification must follow the brand's position toward competition
Retailer	Positioning (e.g., low-price strategy at Retailer I)	• Shelf price levels must be aligned with the retailers' market positions
	Margin objectives	• Shelf prices, list prices and trade terms must consider retailers' margin objectives
	Established practices (e.g., promotion standards)	• Relevance and rigidity of established standard practices must be considered in pricing, promotion and portfolio optimization
Competition	Pricing practices	• Anticipated price changes by competitors must be considered for pricing decisions
	Portfolio coverage	• Competitors' portfolio structure and performance must be considered to evaluate changes to own portfolio
	Promotions practices	• Anticipated promotions by competitors must be considered for promotion planning • Evaluation of ad hoc promotions
Minimum Prices	Costs	• All relevant variable costs must be considered to guarantee profitability
	Market share boundaries	• Market share targets must be considered in pricing, promotion and portfolio optimization
Production	Production capabilities and financing	• Minimum/maximum production capabilities constrain volumes and must be adhered to

of pricing guidelines for the example dairy company. These typically include some competitive positioning – for example, a target price difference against the market leader of some average category price. This is reflected in statements such as: "We have the strongest brand, we need to price 10% above the market average," or "Brand A is the market leader, and we should stay 5% below them."

Further, most teams apply minimum prices that are, for example, derived from their COGS and a defined minimum margin. While this rule is very straightforward in theory, it can become difficult to compute in practice. This is particularly true for differentiated prices such as during a promotion or if different customer segments have different discount schemes. Also, international price consistency is becoming more and more important to manage gray markets and negotiations with international retailers who can compare prices across countries. We will discuss the key aspects relevant for international pricing in Section 3.3.

Here is an important reminder in the context of RGM guidelines. The complexity of a pricing or RGM system increases exponentially with the number of guidelines – and the implicit rules are in practice often even more problematic than the explicit rules. As a result, teams then resort to simple flat price increases as anything more differentiated would violate some of the guidelines. This is not the intention of RGM. Also, teams should always try to formulate all their implicit pricing and RGM rules so they are transparent and can be challenged if needed or checked for consistency.

Step 1.1. 2 – Differentiation

When it comes to achieving the top-level objectives, not all categories and channels are equal. Some categories and channels offer better opportunities than others. This needs to be considered by RGM teams. Specifically, the net revenue and profit objectives defined in the previous step need to be broken down – typically by country, channel, and category. The differentiation between countries is often steered by global teams who identify the specific opportunity of each country. Here, we will focus on the differentiation within countries. The techniques shown can also be applied – with adjustments – to the global level.

To differentiate net revenue and profit contribution by category or product against channel or retailer, two types of input need to be considered. First, the more strategic portfolio considerations. These include the long-term roles of products and categories. Questions include: Where does the company expect growth in the future, what are the relevant trends and shopper needs that must be addressed to drive growth? Which channels and retailers will become more and which less important in the future? Many frameworks and tools have been developed to support a systematic answer to these questions. The most prominent is the BCG Growth-Market Share Matrix (see Figure 3.9).[79] It is a strategic tool that evaluates a company's products[80] based on market growth rate and relative market share by classifying them into four categories. **Stars** represent products with high growth and high market share, often requiring significant investment but offering strong future potential. **Cash Cows** are low-growth, high-share products that generate steady profits and fund other areas of the business. **Question Marks** are high-growth but low-share products that need careful consideration on whether to invest heavily or divest. Finally, **Poor Dogs** are low-growth, low-share products that typically underperform and may be phased out. In an ideal world, products move through the matrix from Question Mark to Star to Cash Cow and eventually end up as Poor Dog. Along this journey the focus generally shifts from net revenue or market share to profit. This way of looking at products helps companies prioritize resources, balance their portfolio, and align short-term profit generation with long-term growth opportunities.

---

[79] Henderson (1970).
[80] It is also used to analyze whole business units, but this is less relevant here.

Figure 3.9 BCG growth-market share matrix

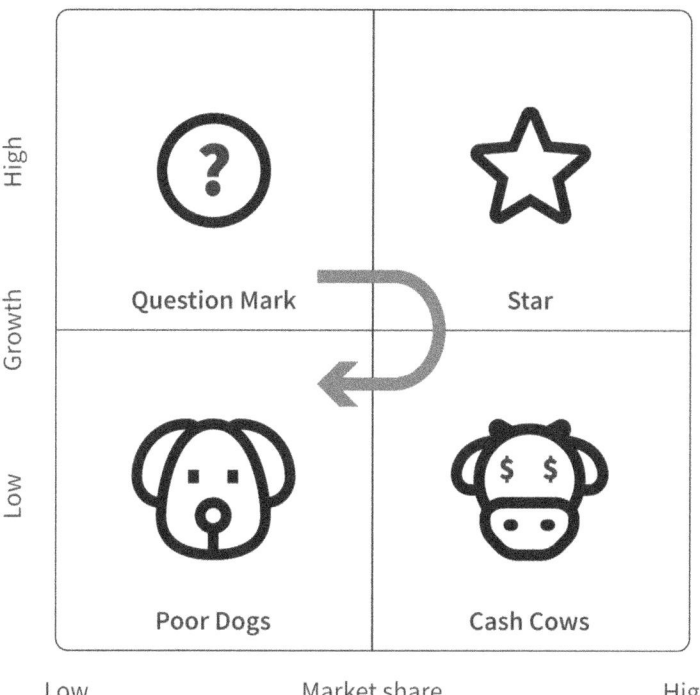

Other consulting firms have expanded on this concept to address further aspects. For example, the McKinsey Matrix (or GE-McKinsey Matrix) extends the BCG approach by assessing business units on industry attractiveness and business strength, using a 9-cell grid to suggest strategies like invest, selectively grow, or divest. And the ADL Matrix (from Arthur D. Little) combines the competitive position with the industry life-cycle stage (from embryonic to decline), highlighting how strategies should adapt over time. Both offer more nuanced portfolio analyses than the BCG Matrix by adding depth and a dynamic perspective.[81]

---

[81] McKinsey & Company (1970); Arthur D. Little Inc. (1970).

The second type of inputs is derived from the core RGM analyses to help identify areas – typically category and channel or retailer combinations – with higher or lower net revenue and profit potential. For example, using the insights from Chapter 2 on the relationship between price elasticities, gross margins, and the net revenue and profit-optimal prices, opportunities can be identified. In areas with low price elasticities and low margins, prices can be increased more easily than in areas with high price elasticities and already high margins. Likewise current price positions against competitors can be used to identify areas of opportunity. Figure 3.10 shows the net revenue targets for the example dairy company that were derived using a combination of strategic portfolio and core RGM analyses.

With traditional RGM tools like static price elasticity tables, this is typically a two- or three-step process where targets are first defined at a county or division level, then broken down by category and channel or retailer, and finally price changes are determined for individual products. With modern fully digital solutions this process can become much more

Figure 3.10 Net revenue targets per category and channel (2026)

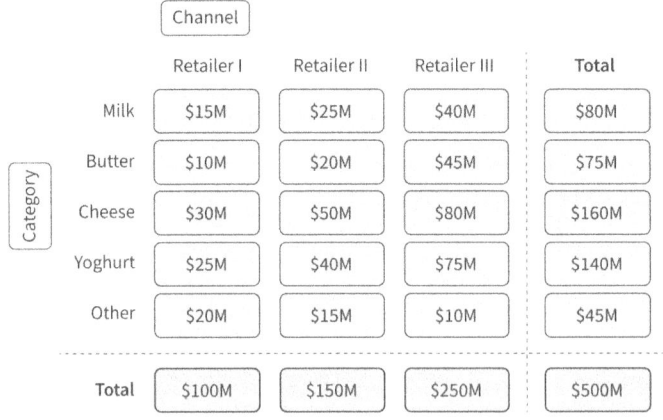

integrated, as prices, PPA, and promotions can be optimized at the most granular level already to determine opportunities on country, division, category, and channel level.

Step 1.1. 3 – RGM Levers

After differentiated objectives have been set, teams need to decide what RGM levers to use to achieve the objectives. To align instruments (e.g., RGM levers) with use cases, teams must consider the following three criteria:

- **Ease of use:** Levers that take a long time to implement are inadequate for short-term change. This differs between industries and products. Consider product feature changes. For example, increasing the data volume in a mobile plan from 40 GB to 50 GB is typically easy and fast to implement, while changing a bottle size from 1.0 liter to 1.2 liter can imply substantial changes along the whole supply chain for a soft drinks company, that can only be implemented with significant preparation. Therefore, the expected effects of levers and their ease of use need to be aligned. The results can differ greatly by industry.
- **Common practice:** Because manufacturers, retailers, and everyone else involved in the process should generally try to use established levers in their typical frequency and pattern, unless there are good reasons to deviate. For example, if it is common in a market to change prices twice a year, parties should only deviate from this pattern if there are specific reasons. For example, in 2022 inflation peaked in many countries and in some categories rapidly increasing COGS necessitated more rapid price increases.
- **Shopper expectations:** At the end of the day, shoppers need to accept offer changes and buy the product at a new price, size, with a different promotion, etc. Therefore, all changes need to consider shoppers' preferences and expectations. For example, if COGS increase, shoppers expect a price change and typically not a pack size change. If a

manufacturer prefers to reduce the size of a product rather than increase the price, there need to be specific reasons for this and the decision needs to be supported by solid analytics.

Figure 3.11 shows, for the example dairy company, the alignment of levers (instruments) with uses sorted from long term to tactical. While the details differ from company to company, most CPG companies will work with a similar setup. Trade terms are adjusted every few years, and portfolios can undergo constant change, but with significant changes not every year. List prices are changed annually or biannually, and

Figure 3.11 Overview of pricing instruments

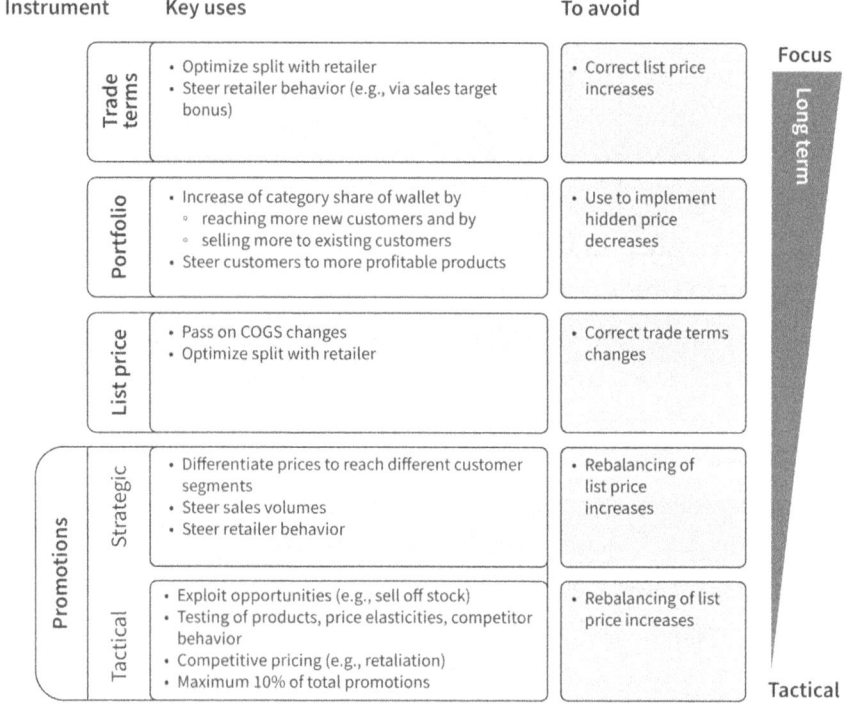

promotions are used tactically when targets need to be met or the company needs to react to short-term changes in the market.

In addition to the alignment of instruments and uses, companies often define what triggers an RGM change. Figure 3.12 provides an overview of active and reactive triggers. Active triggers include a change in the strategy – for example, a shift from growth to profitability – or product innovations that require an RGM adjustment. Reactive triggers include cost change, competitor actions, and demand changes that require an adjustment of the offer.

This concludes the strategic phase (Step 1.1) of the RGM process. It provides an overview of what is relevant and in practice this phase should result in an RGM strategy that can be formulated in three to five pages and shared with the RGM team. Note that other aspects can also be relevant in specific situations or other industries that can be added to the process if needed.

Figure 3.12   Overview of trigger events for pricing actions

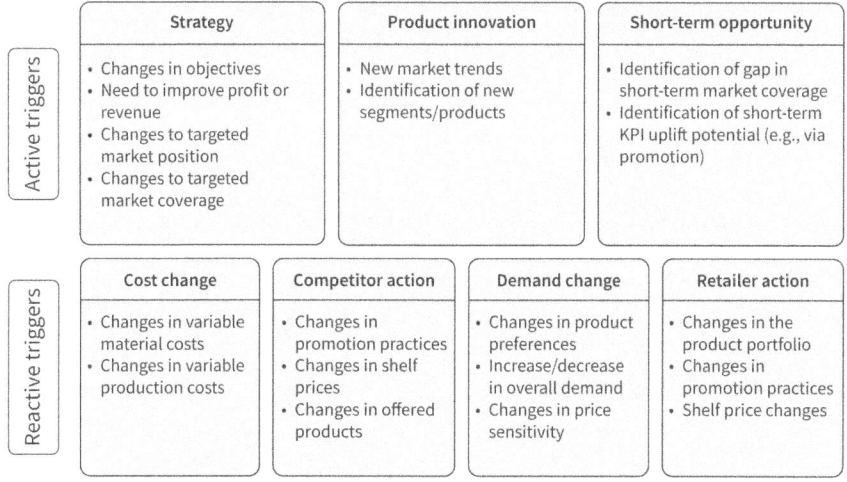

3.2.1.2 Step 1.2 – Execution

Next, the RGM strategy – including specific RGM objectives broken down by category and channel or retailer with clearly assigned levers to achieve the objectives – needs to be executed (Step 1.2). For this, three steps are important: Analytics (Step 1.2.1), Decisions (Step 1.2.2), and Implementation (Step 1.2.3).

Step 1.2.1 – Analytics

A wide range of analyses are available to RGM managers. The most important ones were discussed in Section 2.4. Teams should define which data sources they need to consider (see Figure 3.13 for an example) and what set of analyses they want to conduct for their decision-making (Figure 3.14 for an example).

It is important to define a set of analyses that is conducted on a continuous basis to get a sufficient overview of the status quo and the dynamics in a market before making decisions. If analyses stay consistent, teams

Figure 3.13   Integration of different data inputs

Figure 3.14 Key analyses per RGM lever (selection)

RGM lever	Key analyses
Pricing	• Price elasticity analysis • Competitive benchmarking • Willingness-to-pay studies • Price corridor/gap analysis • Profit pool analysis • …
Promotions	• Promotion ROI analysis • Incrementality • Depth and frequency optimization • Cannibalization/stockpiling impact • Customer-specific effectiveness • …
Trade terms	• Spend effectiveness vs. sales • Pay-for-performance analysis • Trade spend allocation • Net revenue realization • Retailer profitability assessment • …
Price pack architecture (PPA)	• Price ladder and pack size mapping • Affordability and premiumization • Segment pack preferences • Channel-specific performance • Margin by pack size/format • …
Mix	• SKU profitability • Assortment optimization • White-space analysis • Cannibalization and duplication • Portfolio complexity vs. growth potential • …

can see the evolution of results and KPIs over time to better understand changes. At the same time, it is important to not overanalyze (i.e., paralysis by analysis). Three to five analyses per RGM lever typically provide the right level of detail. For decisions with a significant impact, such as new product introductions or a full portfolio reset, it can also be useful to add external support – for example, from a consulting firm – for a focused assessment without the need to add internal resources.

Historically, analyses have been conducted by lever as shown in Figure 3.14. This, of course, ignores the potential interactions between levers – for example, between a price and a pack size change. The main reason for this has been that traditional tools like the price elasticity do not allow for an easy modeling of these interactions. Recently, more capable solutions are emerging, that allow teams to holistically look at the combined effects of lever changes. One such solution is the Virtual Shopper technology that we are building at Buynomics. In Chapter 4, we will discuss the capabilities and potential of this technology in more detail.

Step 1.2.2 – Decisions

A solid analysis is the bedrock of good decision-making. However, this is only one element of the process, as in most organizations many different departments are involved. Ideally, this is organized by RGM. Figure 3.15 summarizes the key elements of the decision-making process for the RGM levers price, PPA, trade terms, promotions, and mix as the combination of the other levers. For each it includes the objectives, departments involved, frequency of changes, and trigger events. It is useful for teams to make this explicit so that the involvement of all teams is clear, particularly when responsibilities change.

Figure 3.16 shows an example of a portfolio optimization process over a seven-month period, divided into Planning and Implementation phases. During the Planning phase (months one to three), the team focuses on data collection, performance analysis, opportunity identification, and scenario testing, leading to internal alignment on priorities and portfolio changes. The Implementation phase (months three to seven) then covers customer

Figure 3.15 Overview of the key RGM processes (example)

	Portfolio optimization	List/SRP price changes	Trade terms negotiations	Promotions	
				Strategic	Tactical
Details	Definition of offered products, product delistings, innovation opportunities per category and retailer	Definition of list prices per product and retailer	Definition of trade and shopper terms per product and retailer	Definition of promotion plan for upcoming quarter per category per retailer	Definition of promotion details of ad hoc requested/ suggested
Outcome	Optimized portfolio in structure and offered products	Optimized list prices incl. starting, target and walk away price	Optimized trade and shopper terms incl. starting, target and walk away terms	Optimized promotion calendar incl. promoted products, depths and target KPIs	Promotion evaluation incl. promoted products, depth, target and actual KPIs
Involved departments	• Category / Shopper • Marketing • RGM • KAM • Finance	• KAM • Marketing • RGM • Category/ Shopper • Finance	• KAM • RGM • Category / Shopper • Finance	• KAM • RGM • Finance	• KAM • RGM • Finance
Frequency	Ad hoc	Yearly	Yearly	Quarterly	Ad hoc
Additional trigger event	• New product development • Competitor changes • Product mix changes • Strategy change	• Cost changes • Portfolio changes • Shelf price changes • Change in strategy	• New product introduction • Significant change in promotion practice	• New product introduction • Significant change in market performance	• Promotion request / suggestion from KAM / RGM

meetings, retailer discussions, product development, distribution negotiations, and the eventual portfolio launch. Key milestones include monitoring results, internal decision points, and customer confirmations that guide the next steps. Collaboration across different functions – KAM, Finance, RGM,

Figure 3.16 Example portfolio/PPA optimization process

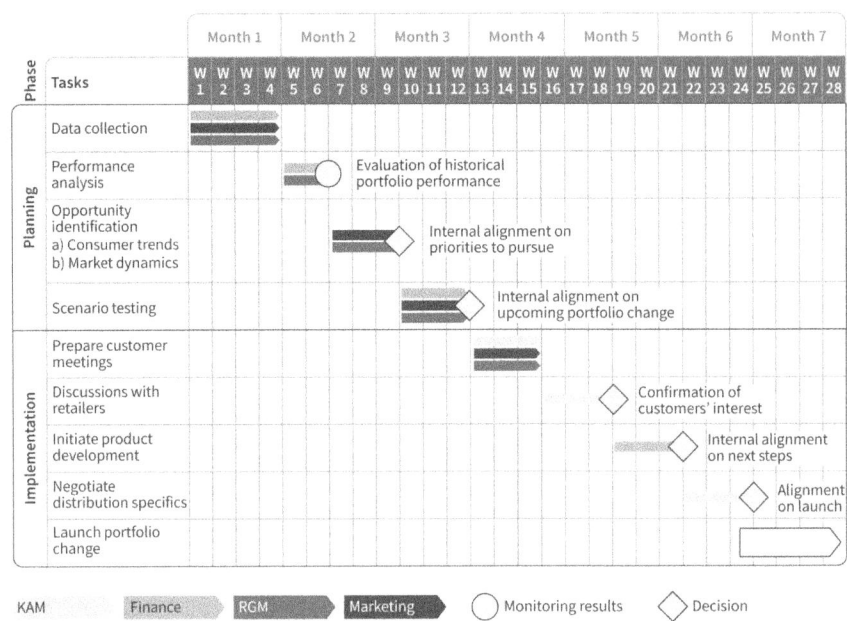

and Marketing – is essential throughout the process, as indicated by the color-coded tasks.

Figure 3.17 shows an example of the pricing optimization process carried out within a 12-week pricing cycle.[82] The process begins with data collection (weeks 2 to 6), followed by performance analysis and scenario testing to evaluate historical pricing and prepare for updates. During weeks 7 to 11, the team updates SRPs (Suggested Retail Prices) and list prices while developing a sell-in story to support negotiations. The Implementation phase (weeks 10 to 12) involves negotiations with retailers, after which new list

---

[82] Note that pricing is at the sole discretion of the retailer.

Figure 3.17 SRP and list price process

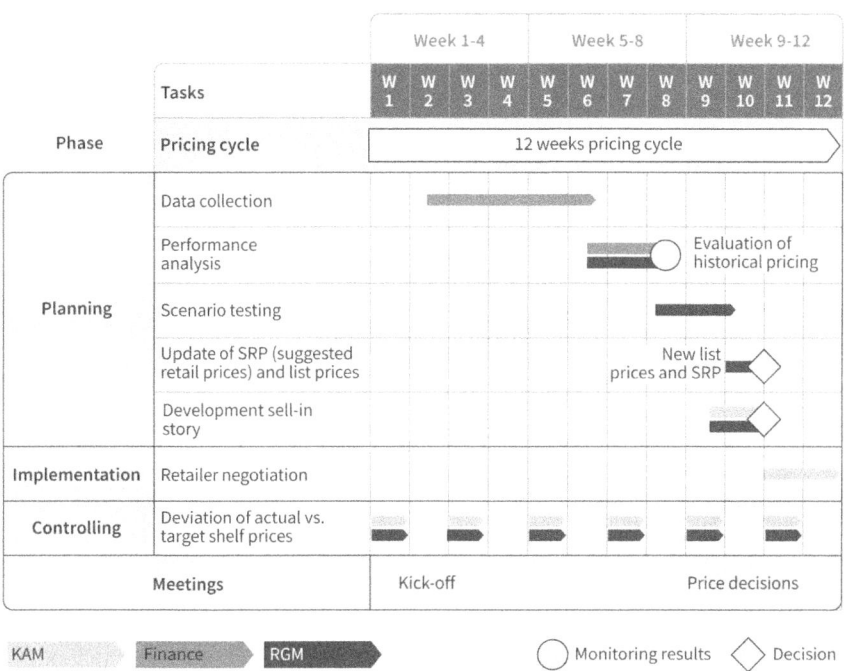

prices and SRPs are finalized. Throughout the cycle, controlling activities track deviations between actual and target shelf prices, while key decisions and monitoring checkpoints guide the next steps.

Figure 3.18 shows an example of the promotion optimization process within a 12-week promotion cycle. The process starts with data collection and preparation (weeks 1 to 5), followed by performance analysis and scenario testing (weeks 6 to 8), leading to the evaluation of historical promotions. In weeks 9 to 11, teams update promotion guidelines and formulate a promotion plan, which are finalized through decision milestones. The Implementation phase includes retailer negotiations (weeks 11 to 12), while

Figure 3.18 Promotion process

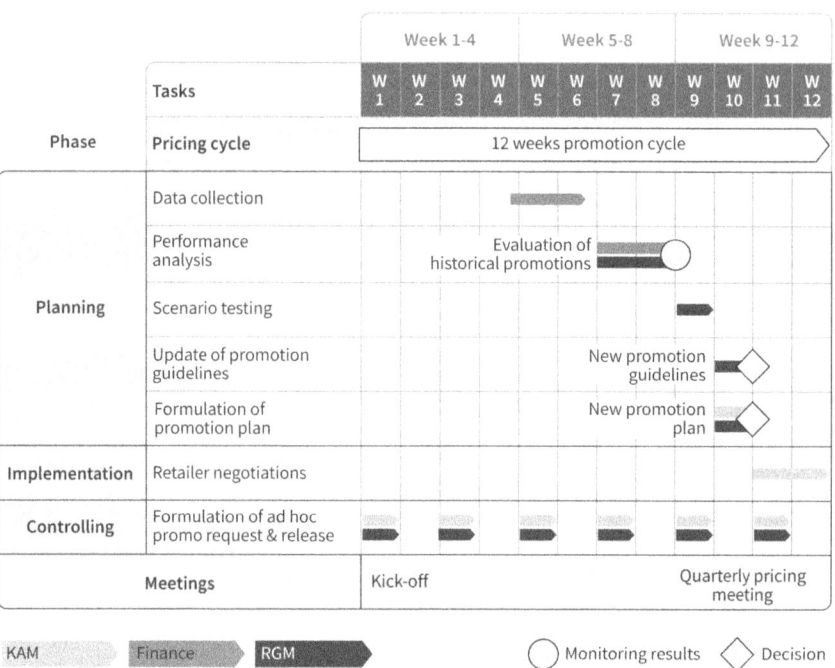

ad hoc promotions can be requested and released flexibly throughout the cycle. Regular checkpoints such as the pricing alignment meetings and quarterly pricing meeting ensure alignment, with cross-functional collaboration between KAM, Finance, and RGM.

After offer changes have been decided internally, they need to be implemented. Here, we will focus on external communication and alignment because in the example processes described here, different departments have already been involved. If this is not the case, internal communication and alignment of decisions is often required.

Step 1.2.3 – Implementation

The implementation of offer changes depends on the type of change, the category, and the industry. Here, and throughout this chapter, we will focus on CPG. The most important task of the RGM team is supporting the sell-in story – that is, the process of aligning RGM plans of the manufacturer with those of the retailer. This often involves convincing the retailer of the benefits of intended changes such as a price or portfolio change. Implementing portfolio, PPA, or promotion changes can often require substantial adjustments across the supply chain – for example, when different products need to be produced, or product sizes are changed, or if a promotion requires additional displays. While the details of these changes need to be dealt with in other teams, RGM needs to understand the cost and distribution effects of these changes – ideally early in the planning process.

A successful sell-in story is characterized by three features:

1. **It is category-led:** The retailer needs to see clear opportunities in specific categories.
2. **It is data-backed:** The retailer needs to see clear benefits of any offer changes. These must be based on the analyses conducted in the previous steps – with a focus on the retailer perspective.
3. **It is relevant for the retailer:** If the retailer believes recommended offer changes make them win with their shoppers, they are more likely to accept them.

Figure 3.19 provides a five-step framework covering the key topics and questions when designing a sell-in story. It illustrates a structured approach to building stronger business partnerships by highlighting the progression from establishing shared value, to addressing challenges, making the case for change, and recommending actionable steps. The flow concludes by

Figure 3.19　Five elements of a successful sell-in story

Step 1 — Establish the value of collaboration
- Highlight why partnership matters
- Emphasize mutual commitment
- Set the tone for joint success

Step 2 — Identify shared challenges and opportunities
- Present key market dynamics
- Discuss barriers and potential growth areas
- Show where alignment creates value

Step 3 — Build the case for action
- Explain the risks of inaction
- Illustrate benefits of change
- Provide data and insights for credibility

Step 4 — Provide tailored recommendations
- Suggest specific actions for the partner
- Connect to their business objectives
- Outline practical next steps

Step 5 — Frame outcomes as mutually beneficial
- Show how both parties win
- Highlight long-term impact
- Position it as a sustainable growth strategy

emphasizing mutually beneficial outcomes, ensuring collaboration drives sustainable growth. The case for a sell-in story is the triple-win. That is, an offer change benefits manufacturer, retailer, and shopper.

3.2.1.3　Step 1.3 – Improvement

The RGM process concludes with a recap of the previous planning cycle to gain insights on what has worked and what has not, in order to learn and improve the next planning cycle. This exercise is typically conducted after

Figure 3.20 Example set of KPIs

KPIs	Connected instruments	Connected decisions	Update frequency	Lead responsibility
Sales value	• Trade terms • Portfolio • Shelf price • List price • Promotions	• Product innovations • Changes to portfolio • Changes to shelf prices • Changes to retailer terms (trade terms and list prices) • Promotion guidelines and plans	• Monthly	• RGM
Net sales value				
Standard gross margin				• Finance
Return on investment (ROI)	• Promotions	• Promotion guidelines and plans	• Ad hoc after completed promotion	• RGM/Sales
Retailer sales value	• Trade terms • Promotions • Portfolio • Shelf price • List price	• Product innovations • Changes to shelf prices • Changes to retailer terms (trade terms and list prices) • Promotion plans	• Monthly	• RGM/Sales
Retailer margin				

Priority A   Priority B

the actual effects of previous measures can be observed and before the next planning cycle. Here, the steps are important: **Monitoring** the right KPIs (Step 1.3.1), deriving the right **Learnings** (Step 1.3.2), and if needed a **Strategy Update** (Step 1.3.3).

Step 1.3.1 – Monitoring

A well-known management proverb states that only "what gets measured, gets done!"[83] Therefore, RGM teams need to define the KPIs they want to monitor. Here, it is useful to differentiate between a tactical – more day-to-day – and a strategic – more long-term – perspective.

The **tactical monitoring** focuses on measuring the immediate effects (typically manifesting within one planning period). Figure 3.20 shows the

---
[83] LeBoeuf (1985).

selected KPIs of the example dairy company. It identifies primary and secondary KPIs together with further details such as instruments and decisions they focus on as well as the frequency of their measurement and who is responsible for the outcomes. The specific selection of KPIs differs between industries, teams, and requirements. Here, a very concise selection has been chosen that provides a good overview. The purpose of these KPIs is the assessment of the immediate effects of offer change – for example, the gross and net margins after a price change or the ROI of a promotion.

Because every team will require a different set of KPIs based on their needs, Figure 3.21 provides a long list of potential KPIs to monitor. These include general growth metrics such as net revenue growth compared to competition and a selection of important KPIs for each RGM lever. For example, for price decisions the development of price elasticities, margins, and their relationships should be monitored. Teams can use a selection of these KPI or develop their own based on their specific needs. When choosing a selection of KPIs, it is useful to apply the MECE principle.[84] That means that the selected KPIs should cover everything that is relevant, but there should not be different KPIs that measure the same effect. For example, "Revenue per SKU" and "SKU Contribution to Revenue (in %)" both measure SKU productivity, one in absolute and the other in relative terms.

Strategic monitoring focuses on the long-term development of the quality of RGM and how it aligns with the overall corporate strategy. This often requires a more advanced view on RGM, and in our experience most teams have not yet developed this, but it is an important part of RGM visibility. A useful tool for strategic monitoring is the Balanced Scorecard (BSC).[85] It is a strategic performance management framework that helps organizations translate their vision and strategy into a comprehensive set of

---

[84] MECE: mutually exclusive and collectively exhaustive.
[85] Kaplan and Norton (1996).

Figure 3.21 KPI overview for assessing RGM success

Lever	KPI	Definition
General growth	NSR growth vs. category	Net sales revenue (NSR) growth compared to overall category growth.
	Gross margin expansion	Improvement in gross margin percentage vs. prior period.
	Incremental value creation vs. baseline	Incremental revenue/profit generated over baseline performance.
	Share gain in profitable segments	Market share gains in profitable consumer/retailer segments.
Pricing	Net revenue per unit	Average net revenue earned per unit sold.
	Price index vs. competitors	Relative pricing vs. key competitors (index 100 = parity).
	Price elasticity	Measure of volume sensitivity to price changes.
	% of price pack architecture executed	Extent to which the planned pack-price architecture is implemented in market.
	Margin % (gross and net)	Gross or net margin percentage delivered per unit or overall sales.
PPA	Revenue and margin by pack type	Revenue and margin contribution by each pack type.
	Channel fit of packs	Fit of pack size/type to its intended channel use case.
	Innovation success rate	Share of new pack launches meeting revenue/volume targets.
	% of sales from strategic packs	% of sales from strategic growth packs vs. long-tail SKUs.
	Cost-to-serve by pack	Logistics and servicing cost per pack type.
Promotions	Promotional ROI	Incremental profit generated per unit of promotional spend.
	Promotional uplift	Incremental sales volume driven during promotions vs. baseline.
	% of sales sold on promotion	Proportion of total sales volume sold on promotion.
	Trade spend efficiency	Sales uplift achieved per $ of trade spend invested.
	Post-promotional dip	Drop in baseline sales after a promotion ends.
Mix	Net revenue per case by channel/customer/pack	Revenue per case adjusted for channel, customer, or pack.
	Contribution margin by mix element	Profit contribution from different mix elements (SKU/channel/customer).
	Premiumization %	Share of sales from premium products/packs.
	Portfolio profitability	Profitability analysis across full product portfolio.
	Incremental vs. cannibalized volume	Volume that is truly incremental vs. volume lost from cannibalization.
Trade terms	Trade spend as % of net sales	Total trade investment as % of net sales.
	Customer P&L / net margin per customer	Profit margin contribution by customer after trade terms.
	Pay-for-performance compliance	Extent to which customer executed agreed activities.
	Return on trade investment	Profit generated relative to trade spend with customers.
	% Spend aligned to strategic customers	Proportion of spend focused on priority customers.

measurable objectives across key perspectives. Unlike traditional performance systems that focus mainly on financial outcomes, the BSC provides a more balanced view by integrating both lagging indicators (like revenue and profit) and leading indicators (like innovation, customer satisfaction, and employee development). This holistic approach ensures that organizations not only track short-term results but also build the capabilities needed for long-term success.

In the case of RGM, the most important perspectives to look at are:

- **Financial perspective:** KPIs to measure the financial performance including (net) revenue and profit growth, and the development of margins. These are most closely related to the tactical KPIs discussed before.
- **Shopper perspective:** Provides an overview on shopper health by measuring shoppers' price sensitivity, brand strength, product satisfaction, etc.
- **Competitor perspective:** Provides an overview on the position against competition, including price and value differences – and market shares.
- **Retailer perspective:** Details the relationship with retailers. This includes measuring the mutual importance of the relationship, the balance-of-power in negotiations, and the growth at different retailers.
- **Environment perspective:** This includes the relevant external drivers such as inflation, GDP growth, COGS changes. This perspective differs from the others in that the company has no real influence on the KPIs here, but the trends measured can affect all dimensions of company performance.

The specific selection of perspectives can differ between companies, and teams need to decide what they consider relevant. For example, if

RGM is strongly involved in product development by helping identify customer needs (e.g., different pack sizes or product flavors) that are currently underserved, then it can also make sense to introduce the product perspective into the RGM BSC. KPIs might include the success rate or value of product innovations.

Figure 3.22 shows an example of a BSC for strategic RGM monitoring. It includes the five perspectives described above. Within each perspective, it lists the three to five KPIs the company wants to focus on. For each KPI, the value and the change over time should be shown together with an indication of how well it performs against some benchmark. Here, this is indicated with the traffic lights. This allows teams to transparently see where they have issues – those they can solve on their own and those they need to escalate. Further, the individual KPIs within each perspective should be aggregated into a perspective score and assessment, and a total score across all perspectives to produce an overall assessment.

To gain a more detailed picture, the BSC should allow users to zoom in to different product categories, channels, shopper segments, etc., and to zoom out to compare KPIs over time and – for global organizations – across countries.

Step 1.3.2 – Learnings

The learnings phase is a critical step in the RGM process, as it allows organizations to reflect on the outcomes of executed strategies and actions. By analyzing results and comparing them with expected objectives, companies can derive valuable insights into what worked effectively and what did not. This process includes evaluating pricing strategies, promotional effectiveness, product performance, and customer responses. The goal is to transform raw outcomes into actionable knowledge, ensuring that every initiative contributes to a deeper understanding of market dynamics, shopper behavior, and competitive responses. These insights form the

Figure 3.22 Strategic KPI monitoring (Balanced Scorecard)

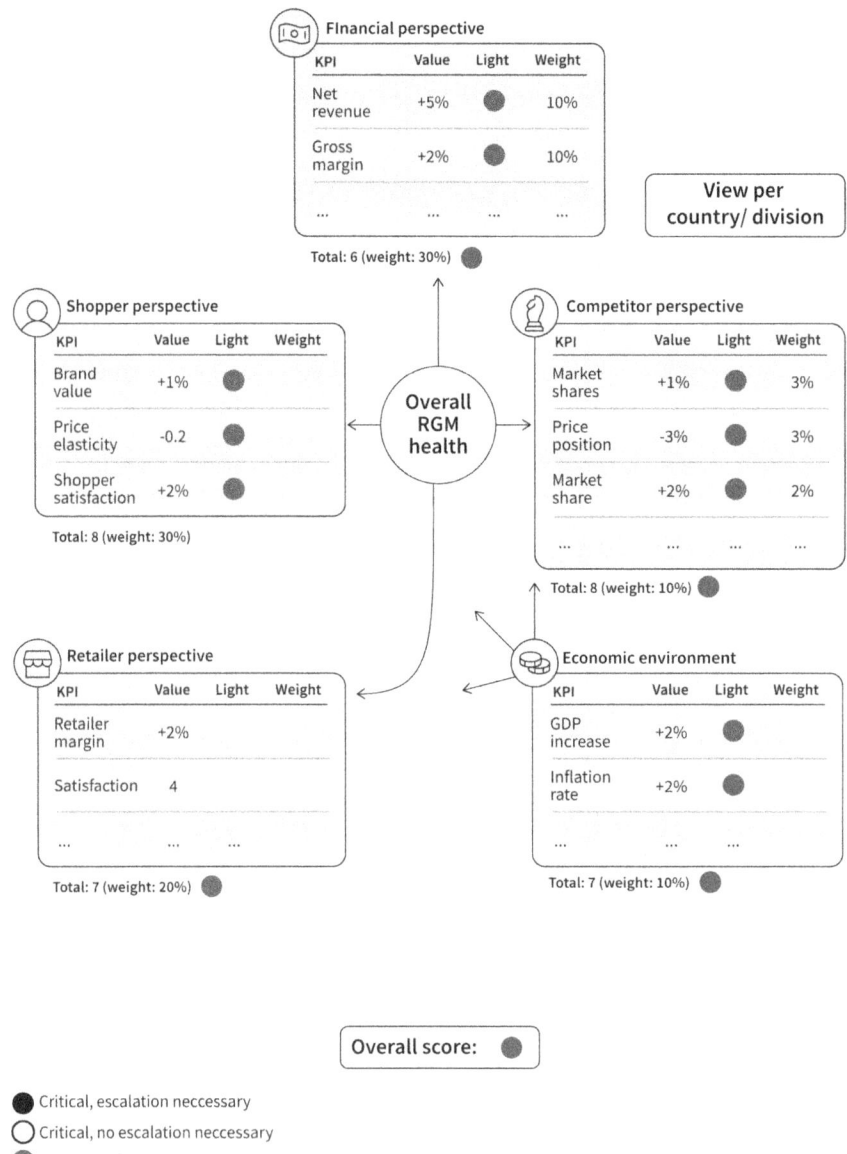

foundation for continuous improvement and better decision-making in future cycles.

There are different learning techniques to capture, analyze, and apply insights from actions taken. They ensure that organizations continuously refine strategies and execution. Some commonly used techniques include:

- **Postmortem/after-action reviews:** A structured evaluation conducted after a campaign, promotion, or pricing initiative to assess what went well, what did not, and why.
- **KPI tracking and gap analysis:** Comparing actual results against defined KPIs (e.g., sales uplift, margin growth, market share) to identify deviations and understand root causes.
- **Benchmarking:** Comparing performance against industry standards, competitors, or best-in-class internal examples to identify improvement areas.
- **Knowledge sharing sessions:** Facilitating cross-functional workshops where teams exchange lessons learned and best practices to avoid repeating mistakes.

The results of these analyses need to be aggregated and discussed in the RGM team. Here it is important to build a culture where it is normal to challenge and improve the status quo. RGM is a journey, not a destination!

Step 1.3.3 – Strategy Update

The strategy update stage ensures that RGM remains a dynamic and adaptive process rather than a static plan. Based on the insights gathered during the learnings phase, organizations refine and evolve their strategies to align with shifting market conditions, consumer expectations, and business priorities. This involves setting new objectives, revisiting the use of RGM levers, and adjusting trade terms, product focus, or promotional approaches to stay competitive and relevant. By incorporating lessons learned and external changes, the strategy update closes the loop in the RGM cycle.

After updating the RGM strategy, the next – and often more relevant – step is incorporating the RGM perspective into the overall corporate strategy. In essence, this is about making the company more market-led. That means, with stronger RGM teams, the RGM objective should move from "increase prices/(net) revenue/profit by X%" to RGM identifying the true market potential and prices, products, promotions, etc. to achieve it. With growing capabilities, the role of RGM needs to become more strategic in the overall organization. This is the RGM journey.

3.2.2 Step 2 – People and Organization

In most organizations, RGM has evolved out of other commercial teams such as sales or marketing based on the realization that activities across the RGM levers need to be coordinated better. Because of this, RGM naturally works closely with other commercial teams.

There are different ways to set up the RGM organization. A typical example is shown in Figure 3.23. Here, the organization is built around

Figure 3.23 The RGM organizational structure

three core elements: The **division-embedded RGM teams** work closely with commercial, marketing, and finance functions to apply RGM strategies directly to pricing, promotion, and portfolio decisions, adapting central frameworks to local market realities. The **analytics teams** provide the analytics foundation, working with models, tools, and dashboards that measure, for example, pricing effectiveness, promotional ROI, and mix optimization. At the center, the RGM **Center of Excellence (CoE)** defines the overall strategy, frameworks, and governance, ensuring consistency, capability building, and alignment with corporate objectives. The CoE also connects insights across divisions, standardizing tools and sharing best practices. Together, these three components create an integrated RGM structure that combines central expertise with local execution, enabling FMCG companies to drive sustainable, data-led, and profitable growth.

The size of an RGM team varies widely by company revenue and portfolio complexity. While no fixed standard exists, an internal benchmark often used by practitioners suggests approximately one full-time equivalent (FTE) per $100 million to $500 million in annual revenue. In practical terms, a $1 billion business might operate with 2–10 dedicated RGM professionals, scaling upward in organizations with multiple markets or a high degree of promotional intensity. McKinsey case examples show that global rollouts can involve more than 100 trained RGM practitioners across 20 or more markets, underscoring how headcount expands with both revenue and geographic dispersion.[86]

To organize how RGM works together with the other commercial functions, it is often useful to align clear roles. Figure 3.24 presents an example of

---

[86] McKinsey & Company (2019a).

Figure 3.24 Responsibilities for key activities

Activities	RGM	Category/Shopper	Marketing	KAM	Finance
Trade terms	Consult	Consult	Consult	Responsible	Support
Portfolio	Support	Responsible	Responsible	Support	Support
Shelf price	Responsible	Support	Support	Support	Support
List price	Responsible	Support	Support	Support	Support
Promotions	Support	Consult	Consult	Responsible	Support

a RACI type matrix,[87] where this particular table only uses "Consult," "Responsible," and "Support." Each column represents a task or process, while each row represents a commercial function. By mapping these roles across activities, the RACI matrix eliminates confusion about who does what, ensures accountability, and promotes efficient collaboration. For instance, key account management (KAM) is responsible for managing trade terms with support from finance, with other functions only having a consulting role. In the RGM playbook, all key roles for the key activities need to be clearly defined.

3.2.3 Step 3 – Technology

The key technologies to be used by RGM need to be defined in the playbook. This includes the selection of tools and the range of data inputs to be used.

---

[87] RACI is a project management tool used to clarify roles and responsibilities within a team or organization. RACI stands for responsible, accountable, consulted, and informed. For details, see Smith (2021).

Figure 3.25 Tools to use

Purpose	Tools	Related instruments		Data input	Lead responsibility
Performance analysis	• Price index tool	• Shelf prices • Promotions • Portfolio		• Sell-out data • Product data • COGS • Retailer conditions	• RGM
	• Annual price promo chart	• Shelf prices • Promotions • Portfolio			• RGM
	• Margin calculator	• Shelf prices • List prices • Trade Terms	• Promotions • Portfolio		• Finance
Scenario testing	• Deal calculator	• Shelf prices • List prices • Trade Terms	• Promotions • Portfolio	• Promotions mailer data • Retailer conditions • COGS	• RGM/KAM
Promotion setting	• Promotion guidelines tool	• Promotions		• Price elasticities	• RGM/KAM
Optimization of portfolio, pricing, promotions and retailer terms	• Advanced forecasting tool (e.g., Buynomics)	• Shelf prices • List prices • Trade Terms • Promotions • Portfolio		• Sell-out, promotions and product data • COGS • Retailer conditions	• RGM

[Advanced]   [Basis]

3.2.3.1   Tools

We have already discussed RGM tools previously in this book. Therefore, we can be brief here. Figure 3.25 shows an example for how to structure and align tools with use cases to make sure all areas are covered and it is clear who is responsible.

3.2.3.2   Data

Also, the use of data needs to be clear. Similar to the tool use, it must be clear what data are needed for what purpose. Figure 3.26 shows this for the example dairy company. Here, it must be clarified what data are used for what use cases and tools, in what frequency the data will be collected and digested, and who is responsible.

Figure 3.26   Required data inputs

Data input	Details	Following tools	Update frequency	Lead responsibility
Sell-out data	• Sell-out data per SKU per period and channel	• Price index tool • Annual price promo chart • Margin tool • Deal calculator • Promotions guidelines tool • Advanced forecasting tool	• Monthly	• RGM/Category
Product data	• Product characteristics per SKU (own and competition)		• Monthly/ at change	• RGM/Category
COGS	• COGS per SKU		• Quarterly/ at change	• Finance
Retailer conditions	• Trade term and list prices per SKU		• Quarterly/ at change	• RGM/KAM
Promotion data	• Past promotion characteristics per SKU per channel	• Deal calculator • Advanced forecasting tool	• Monthly	• RGM/Category
Price elasticities	• Price and promotion elasticities per SKU and channel	• Promotion guidelines tool	• Monthly	• Shopper/KAM
Store data	• Store placement and communication per SKUs	• Advanced forecasting tool	• Monthly	• Shopper/KAM
Consumer purchase data/studies	• E.g., panel, loyalty card data, conjoint analyses		• At occurence of specific question	• Marketing/RGM

Advanced   Basis

3.3 INTERNATIONAL RGM CONSIDERATIONS

In the previous steps, we essentially ignored the international dimension. Within the FMCG industry, this can be justified with the fact that although most companies operate globally, their RGM activities are mostly steered locally by country teams. Smaller organizations have teams that manage multiple countries, but most often they do this with a focus on the country-specific needs and less with the international coordination of offers and prices in mind. This is because compared to many other industries like consumer electronics or automotive, local differences in preferences are more important and gray markets between countries have been less relevant because of relatively higher logistics costs as a result of lower price to weight ratios (e.g., as compared to mobile phones or other electronics).

However, international considerations are becoming more pronounced lately. Here, we want to briefly touch on three relevant aspects: first, global governance options, second international price coordination, and third – as a deep dive – the effects of gray markets and how to consider them in international price coordination.

Companies have different options to set up their global RGM governance. To identify these, it is useful to look at two dimensions: decision autonomy (local flexibility vs. global consistency) and knowledge sharing (no sharing vs. free sharing among HQ and countries). The resulting 2×2 matrix in Figure 3.27 shows four typical global governance types:

- **Center of Excellence (CoE) and local execution:** A central CoE collects and develops best practices, develops advanced analytics, and identifies and makes available tools, which local teams then use to drive day-to-day execution. This ensures markets benefit from cutting-edge expertise while staying aligned with company standards. The model balances efficiency and standardization with the acknowledgment that local teams have relevant and detailed insights into their market needs and are best able to execute on them. In this case, profit and loss (P&L) responsibility is typically in the countries.
- **Global guardrails and strategy:** The global RGM organization defines the "non-negotiables" – such as overall revenue growth priorities, pricing architecture, and margin protection rules. These guardrails provide consistency and risk control across markets. They enable local teams to innovate within clear strategic boundaries. P&L responsibility is typically in the countries, but teams often

Figure 3.27   Global governance

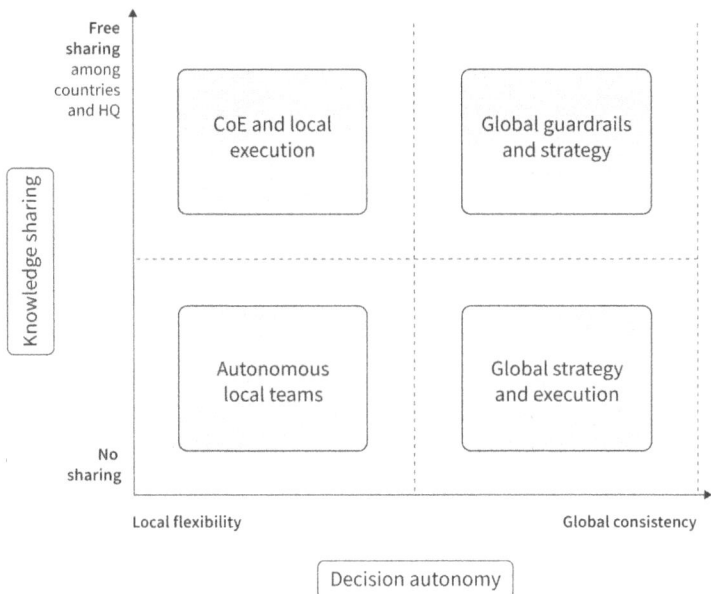

blame guardrails when they miss targets, which highlights potential conflicts in situations of shared global and local responsibilities.
- **Autonomous local teams:** Markets with deep knowledge of their shoppers, retailers, and competitive landscape can act with high autonomy. These teams design promotions, set pricing tactics, and optimize assortment with minimal global oversight. While this accelerates responsiveness, it requires strong trust and accountability mechanisms and is more common in cases with only limited insights that can be generalized across countries.
- **Global strategy and execution:** In this model, both strategy and execution are driven centrally, with little variation across regions. The global team sets direction, manages tools, and oversees implementation, ensuring tight control and consistency. Local teams

provide support, for example, with gathering data and implementing the actions set by the global team. It is most effective in highly standardized categories where brand equity requires uniformity. Also, this is often the setup for smaller companies that do not operate a full RGM team in each country or region.

To choose between the different setups, companies need to understand what aligns best with the two axes. First, we look at **decision autonomy**. Here, the setup should be more **local** if shopper and retailer dynamics differ strongly between countries, speed and responsiveness are critical, and P&L responsibility sits in the countries. Decision-making should be more **global** if brand equity, pricing architecture, or margin rules require consistency, if scale efficiencies or specialized expertise matter more than local nuance, or if the company is small or operates in highly standardized categories.

On the other axis, there should be **no or limited knowledge sharing** if markets are highly unique and best practices cannot easily be applied across countries, if sharing risks misapplication (e.g., compliance, legal, or competitive sensitivity), or if the cost of collecting/disseminating knowledge outweighs the benefit. Further, there should be **free knowledge sharing** if insights gained in one country are also useful in others, if markets are diverse, so local teams can selectively apply what is relevant, and if the company culture supports the mutually beneficial exchange of ideas.

The need for international price coordination can arise for several very different reasons:

- **Consistent brand positioning:** Price levels send strong signals about brand image and perceived quality. If prices vary too much between countries, shoppers may start to question the brand's identity. Coordinating prices helps ensure that the brand is positioned consistently across markets.

- **Avoidance of gray markets:** Large price gaps between regions can encourage unauthorized resellers to buy in one country and sell in another – or shoppers to buy in another country directly. This undermines local distributors and can damage shoppers' trust if warranties or after-sales support are affected. International coordination reduces the risk of these arbitrage opportunities.
- **International retailer buying groups:** Major retailers with operations in multiple countries may push for harmonized pricing. Without coordinated policies, companies risk losing bargaining power or being forced into unfavorable deals. Aligning prices helps firms negotiate from a stronger, unified position.
- **A company's desire for consistency:** Many firms simply want a coherent global strategy, and pricing is an important part of that. Consistency makes communication clearer for both internal teams and external partners. It also signals professionalism and reliability to customers worldwide. This is often by itself not perceived as the best reason – for example, from the perspective of profit or net revenue optimization – but it is common in many organizations.

To coordinate international prices, companies often define price corridors based on some global or regional reference price (see Figure 3.28). The corridor can be wider across broader regions and become narrower for close neighbors. Within the corridors, prices can be set based on local need. This approach typically poses a good trade off between global coordination and consideration of local flexibility. Figure 3.29 shows a stylized example of how to understand the effects of gray market activity as a function of the price difference between the import and export markets. With an increasing price difference, the gray market share in the import country increases, but profits (in this example) also increase because of the higher prices. This results in a profit-optimal price difference against the export market.

Figure 3.28   Global, regional, local price coordination

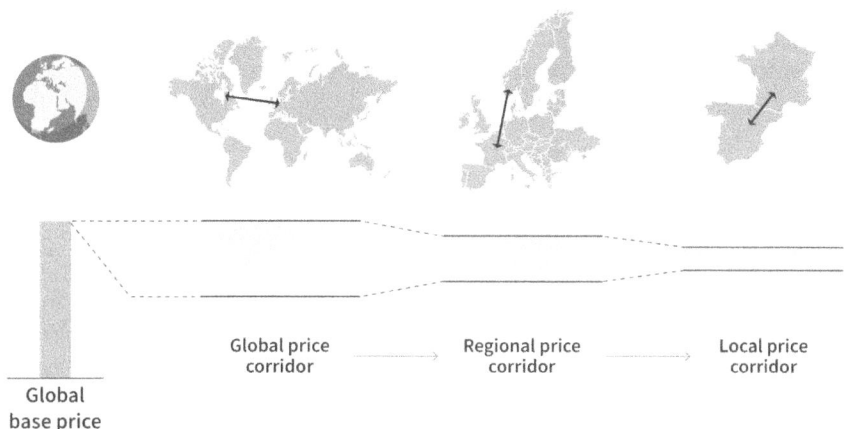

Figure 3.29   Impact of gray market share

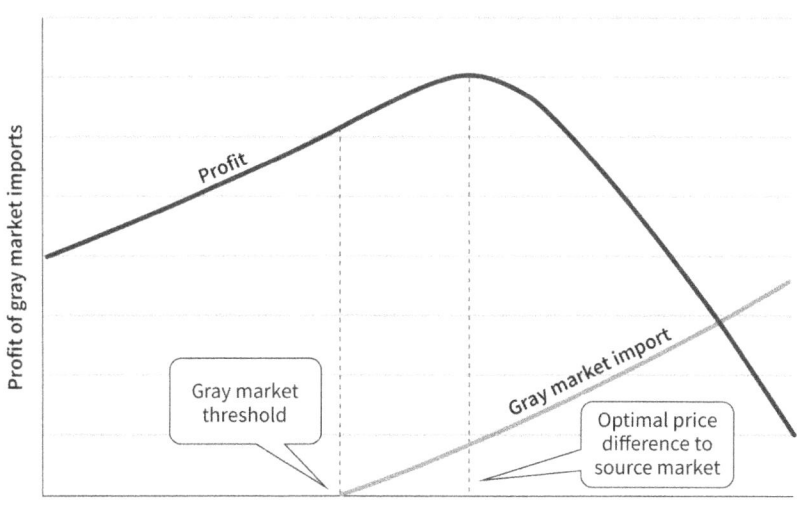

We want to close this section with a specific simple case study on the effects of gray markets for differentiated prices between countries – and how to assess and deal with the effects. For this, consider two countries, the Import market and the Export market, and a company that sells a single product. In the Import market, demand (d_I) is linear ($d = a + bp_I$) with $d_I = 150 - p_I$. At unit costs (c) of €50, the optimal price is €100 with sales of 50 units (see Chapter 2). In the Export market, demand (d_E) is $d_E = 1100 - 10p_E$. Then, with the same unit cost of €50, the optimal price is €80 with sales of 300 units. These two price optimizations were made with the assumption that there is no gray market between the two countries. This is summarized in Figure 3.30 as the *independent optimization* case. In this case, the total profit for both markets is €11,500, with most coming from the export market. If we now consider the possibility of a gray market between the two countries and how to deal with it, we have two principal options. We can harmonize prices or we can allow some degree of gray market activity. If we harmonize prices to avoid a gray market, we can do this at the price level of the low-price country (Export market), at the level of the high-price country, or some price in between. In those cases, total profits range between €7,500 and €11,100. That means, we lose at least €400 in comparison to the independent optimization case.

If we differentiate prices between the two countries and thereby allow a gray market to emerge, sales in the Export market will increase what will be exported to the Import market and reduce direct sales there. In the case shown, 10 units are sold via gray imports. This results in total profits of €11,300. That is €200 more than in the best case of price harmony between the two countries. In fact, allowing gray imports can increase to 20 units – that is, 40% of total sales in the Import market – for price differentiation to be profit optimal. This highlights that allowing gray markets can often be beneficial from a pure profit perspective compared to harmonized prices. Further, in some cases gray markets can be

Figure 3.30 Gray market assessment (case study)

Independent optimization

	a	b	Price	Cost	Sales	Revenue	Profit
Import market	150	−1	€100	€50	50	€5,000	€2,500
Export market	1100	−10	€80	€50	300	€24,000	€9,000
				Sum	350	€29,000	€11,500

Both priced low

	a	b	Price	Cost	Sales	Revenue	Profit
Import market	150	−1	€80	€50	70	€5,600	€2,100
Export market	1100	−10	€80	€50	300	€24,000	€9,000
				Sum	370	€29,600	€11,100

Both priced high

	a	b	Price	Cost	Sales	Revenue	Profit
Import market	150	−1	€100	€50	50	€5,000	€2,500
Export market	1100	−10	€100	€50	100	€10,000	€5,000
				Sum	1500	€15,600	€7,500

Independent with gray market

	a	b	Price	Cost	Sales	Revenue	Profit
Import market	150	−1	€100	€50	40	€4,000	€2,000
Gray export			€80	€50	10	€800	€300
Export market	1100	−10	€80	€50	300	€24,000	€9,000
				Sum	350	€28,800	€11,300

used as a way to allow price differentiation in a market where customers with a lower willingness-to-pay have the gray market option. This can also open up the option to introduce a higher primary price point in a market. This needs to be balanced with strategic considerations, as a large gray market share weakens the local organization and brand reputation, as the local organization loses revenue and might be less able and willing to provide proper services – especially for the gray imports.

3.4 HOW TO BUILD YOUR RGM PLAYBOOK

Over the past two decades, I have worked with dozens of teams developing and implementing pricing or RGM frameworks in organizations across many different industries and geographies. Based on this experience, here are a few guidelines on how to build your own playbook for your organization:

- **Start small and pilot:** Do not try to build the full RGM playbook in one go. Pick one market, category, or product line to pilot. Use it as a learning ground to test the framework, refine your approach, and build early wins before scaling up.
- **Involve the right people early:** Bring in cross-functional stakeholders (e.g., sales, finance, marketing, supply chain) from the start. Defining roles and responsibilities early (Step 2.1) creates ownership, avoids bottlenecks, and ensures practical execution in the market. Use the support from people who have built a pricing or RGM playbook before. These people may be colleagues from within the company or external consultants.
- **Build iteratively, not linearly:** Think of the framework as a cycle (Strategy → Execution → Improvement), not a one-time sequence. Draft a first version of your playbook, test it, collect feedback, and refine. Each loop should make the playbook more practical and aligned to business needs.
- **Keep it actionable and data-informed:** Focus on turning insights (Step 1.2.1) into clear decisions (Step 1.2.2) and practical execution steps. Use data and tools (Step 3) to guide choices, but don't overcomplicate – prioritize decisions that teams can act on.

CHAPTER FOUR
DIGITALIZATION OF PRICING AND RGM

So far, everything in this book has been technology agnostic. That means, the analytics, tools, research methods, and the outlined pricing playbook can be applied with anything from paper and pencil, Excel, or an integrated AI-based pricing or RGM tool. In this chapter we now want to direct our attention more toward the latter and discuss the role and potential of digitalization pricing and RGM. Specifically, we want to look at the promises, limitations, options, and real-world applications of AI, GenAI, and Agentic AI technologies in pricing and RGM.

To that end, we will structure the chapter into five parts. First, we will provide a general overview of digitalization. Second, we will focus on digitalization within the field of pricing and RGM. Third, we will discuss the specific challenges of current pricing methods as discussed in Chapter 2 when trying to open them up for GenAI. Fourth, we will introduce a technology that solves the addressed issues. This is the Virtual Shoppers technology we are developing at Buynomics. Here, we provide an outlook of how we think this technology will shape the role of the RGM manager of tomorrow. Finally, we will discuss use cases and applications within FMCG and other industries.

4.1 DIGITALIZATION

Before we discuss digitalization of RGM, we start with a brief clarification of the key terms and with a very short history of digitalization in general. Digitalization is often confused with related terms such as digitization and digital transformation, but the distinctions are important.

4.1.1 Terminology

Here is a definition of each term:

- **Digitization** describes the technical process of converting information from analog into digital form. For example, this includes scanning a paper record into a PDF or encoding an analog photograph as a JPEG. Digitization is about how data is represented, not about changing or evaluating it. It is the foundation on which digital technologies are built,[88] as it allows substantially faster access to much larger sets of data that are required in the AI era.
- **Digitalization**, in contrast, describes the use of digital technologies to redesign processes, enable new ways of working, and create additional value. It is the stage where organizations and societies use

---
[88] See Tilson et al. (2010).

digitized data to redesign their operations. For example, a hospital that digitizes X-rays produces digital files. A hospital that digitalizes its diagnostic process integrates those X-rays into an AI-based workflow to accelerate treatment decisions.[89]

- **Digital transformation** refers to the fundamental changes to a company's business model, culture, and value proposition based on digitalization. Therefore, digital transformation is not only about adopting new technologies, it is also about reinventing how organizations compete, innovate, and deliver value to stakeholders.[90]

Taken together, digitization enables digitalization, and digitalization drives digital transformation (see Figure 4.1). This chapter focuses on digitalization – how organizations use digital technologies to transform processes and generate new forms of value – while recognizing its foundations in digitization and its culmination in digital transformation. While we see that the current program of RGM also includes some aspects of digital transformation as described above, we also believe that the current challenges in RGM are best represented by what is defined here by the term digitalization. Maybe the next edition of this book might see a shift in focus toward digital transformation – focusing more on business model and cultural implications in pricing and RGM.

Figure 4.1   The digitalization journey

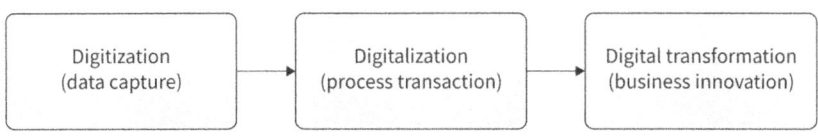

---

[89] Brennen and Kreiss (2016).
[90] Westerman et al. (2014).

4.1.2 Origins and developments

The origins of digitalization lie in the cumulative progress of digitization.[91] Once information could be converted into digital form, organizations began to recognize the opportunities for redesigning how work was done. In the late twentieth century, early adopters deployed enterprise systems, email, and online databases to speed up communication and cut costs. By the 1990s, companies like Dell and Amazon were demonstrating that entire business models could be built digitally, using the internet as a primary channel rather than a supporting tool. The twenty-first century saw digitalization move beyond efficiency gains, as cloud computing, mobile platforms, and artificial intelligence have enabled entirely new ecosystems. Scholars often describe this as the transition from an "industrial economy" to a "digital economy."[92]

Digitalization requires more than converting data. It requires reengineering processes. For example, a retailer does not merely put its catalog online. Instead, it builds an integrated e-commerce ecosystem with payment gateways, personalized recommendations, and digital supply chains. Several technologies act as enablers. Cloud platforms provide the infrastructure for scalable operations, while analytics turn raw data into insights that drive decision-making. Standards and platforms ensure that these systems interoperate, allowing businesses to build digital ecosystems rather than isolated solutions.

Digitalization is reshaping industries. In business, digital workflows and platforms have made it possible to automate supply chains, scale customer service through chatbots, and personalize marketing on an increasing scale. Financial services have been transformed by digital banking, while retail has shifted to omnichannel experiences that blend physical and

---

[91] Portions of this text were drafted with assistance from ChatGPT5 by OpenAI. This AI tool supported initial research for this sub-chapter. All AI-generated content was carefully reviewed, edited, and approved. The final analysis, conclusions, and interpretations represent my views and expertise. I take full responsibility for the content and accuracy of this work.
[92] Brynjolfsson and Kahin (2002).

digital shopping. In healthcare, digitalization extends beyond electronic health records. Hospitals use predictive analytics to allocate resources, while wearable devices allow continuous monitoring of patient health.[93]

Education has embraced digitalization through hybrid learning environments, adaptive technologies, and global platforms that democratize access to knowledge. Cultural institutions now create digital-first experiences, where a museum is not only a physical space but also a virtual platform for engagement. Meanwhile, industry has adopted digital twins, robotics, and predictive maintenance to achieve levels of efficiency and customization unimaginable in traditional settings.

The benefits of digitalization extend far beyond efficiency. Organizations gain agility, scalability, and new ways for value creation. Digital platforms enable global reach at marginal cost, while analytics empower managers to make evidence-based decisions. For customers, digitalization often translates into convenience, personalization, and transparency. However, digitalization is not without challenges. The cost of transitioning to digital platforms can be high, especially for small and medium enterprises. Cybersecurity has become a critical issue as digital systems expose organizations to new vulnerabilities. There is also the challenge of organizational change. Digitalization is not simply about technology. It requires cultural shifts, new skills, and leadership willing to rethink established ways of working.[94]

Looking forward, digitalization will continue to evolve, as AI technologies are moving to the center stage. Immersive technologies such as augmented and virtual reality will redefine interaction – and digital twins offer companies the ability to simulate entire factories, supply chains, or shopper behavior. Figure 4.2 summarizes the key developments of digitalization.

---

[93] Boston Consulting Group (2023).
[94] World Bank (2016).

Figure 4.2   The history of digitalization

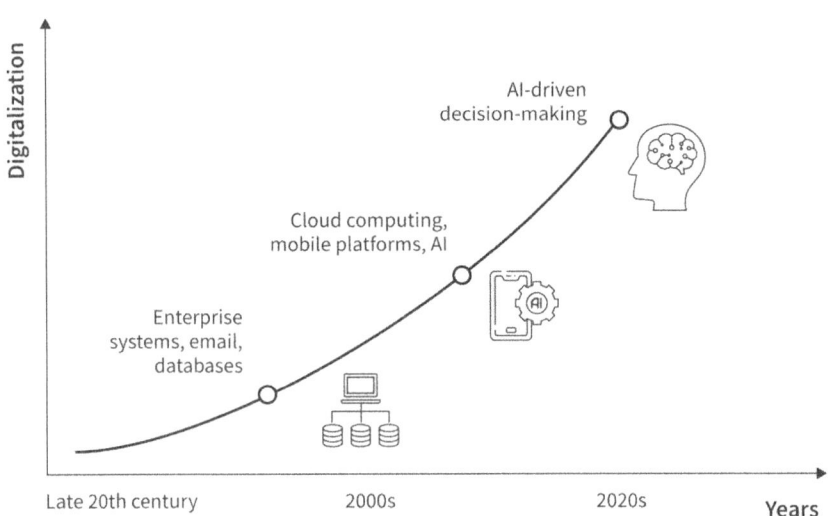

4.2   EVOLUTION OF RGM IN THE DIGITAL AGE

Now, we will focus our attention on digitalization within the RGM space. As discussed previously, revenue growth managers are at the forefront of every consumer packaged goods (CPG) business. They need to understand what shoppers and retailers want, consider cost changes, assess innovations, and anticipate competitor moves to optimize their own product offer – all in accordance with the overall company objectives. In the digital age, this is becoming both more difficult and easier. To set the scene, we start with a brief recap on the core RGM challenges.

4.2.1 Recap Core RGM Challenges

What makes RGM both difficult and interesting is the increasing complexity of the playing field on which decisions must be made. Shoppers are becoming more informed and demanding, competition is becoming fiercer, and retailers are increasing the pressure on margins. To address these challenges, many CPG companies have started to transform their revenue management in the past years by establishing dedicated RGM departments that take over responsibilities like pricing and promotion management previously dispersed across different teams. Further, companies are starting to use more powerful tools to integrate and analyze a broad range of data sources.

In this section, we will outline the RGM journey in CPG companies from the past years to the present day and present our vision of the next steps on that journey. Specifically, we will address the role of the revenue growth manager of tomorrow in the age of AI: How will tasks, roles, responsibilities, and requirements evolve in the coming years?

RGM is a strategic function within CPG companies focused on optimizing pricing, promotions, trade spend, and product and channel mix to drive sustainable and profitable revenue growth. It enables businesses to make data-driven decisions that balance volume, profitability, (net) revenue, and market competitiveness. By leveraging analytics and consumer insights, RGM helps companies maximize their revenue potential while ensuring long-term brand health.[95]

Specifically, RGM addresses and coordinates the following challenges (see Figure 4.3):

---
[95] For more details, see Chapters 2 and 3.

Figure 4.3 RGM levers

- Price optimization – Determining the right price to balance sales volume and profitability while adapting to inflation, competitive shifts, and changing consumer behavior.
- Price-pack architecture (PPA) – Ensuring the right product formats and price points meet consumer needs across different income levels and purchasing occasions.
- Promotion optimization – Structuring promotions effectively to drive demand without eroding margins or conditioning consumers to buy only at a discount.
- Trade spend management – Optimizing investments in retailer discounts, incentives, and funding to ensure they generate true incremental growth.
- Product and channel mix management – Balancing premium, mainstream, and value-tier products across different sales channels to maximize revenue and profitability.

As many market conditions become more complex, RGM is increasingly critical in driving sustainable business growth. Specifically, the following trends are key:

- Data-driven decision-making – AI, machine learning, and advanced analytics allow for more precise pricing, PPA, promotional, and trade spend strategies.
- Consumer behavior shifts – Increased visibility, economic uncertainty, and inflation make consumers more picky and price-conscious, increasing the need for optimized RGM strategies.
- Retailer and e-commerce expectations – Retailers and online marketplaces increasingly demand more efficient trade spend and promotional strategies that deliver mutual profitability.
- Margin pressures – Rising costs require businesses to manage pricing and promotions carefully to protect profitability while maintaining competitiveness.

To address these challenges, RGM has started undergoing significant change. Specifically, we see this change in two waves. In the first wave, many organizations have integrated their RGM teams (see Figure 4.4). The second wave will be all about integrating solutions. Next, we will discuss these two waves and the implications for revenue managers in more detail.

4.2.2 First Wave: From Siloed to Integrated Teams

RGM departments started emerging in many large CPG companies in the early to mid-2010s. Before that, RGM functions were often spread across different departments (see Figure 4.5). For example, price decisions were made in finance, product decisions by marketing, and promotions managed by sales. This siloed approach often resulted in poorly coordinated levers that worked against each other. For example, price increases implemented

Figure 4.4 Evolution of RGM in CPGs

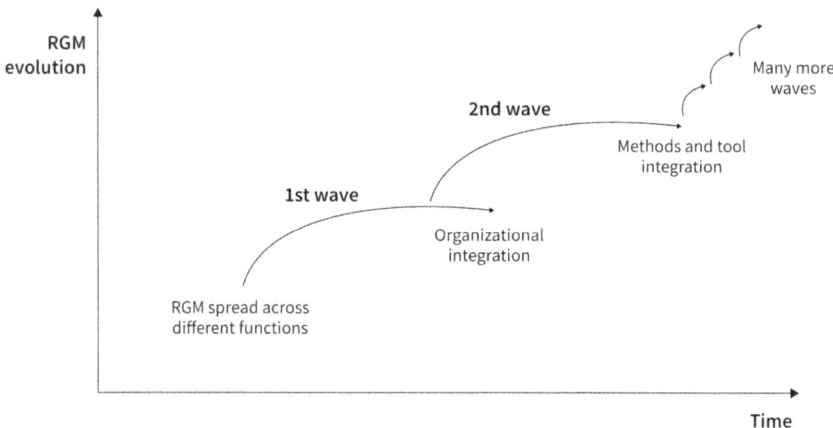

Figure 4.5 From siloed departments to integrated RGM teams

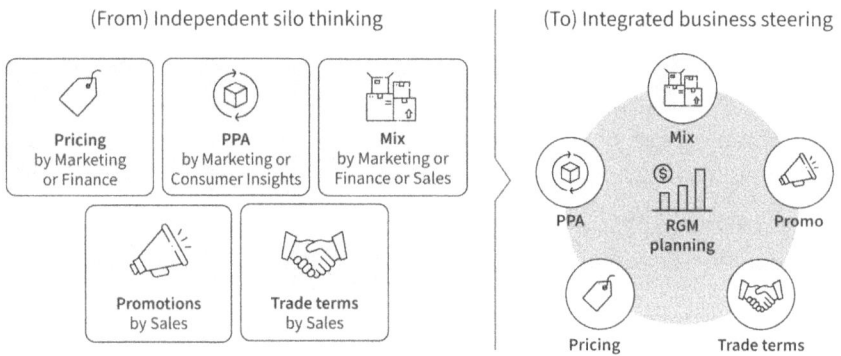

by finance were often reversed by sales with an increase in the depth and frequency of promotions if they did not consider price increases feasible. Also, many analyses were performed by different teams with finance, marketing, and sales measuring price elasticities independently using different methods (e.g., regression analyses or conjoint studies) and coming to different conclusions.

The evolution of integrated RGM departments was driven by the need to address these challenges. It was supported by consulting firms, who shared best practices among organizations. This way, RGM was built into a key function of leading CPG companies. These organizations integrated the RGM levers into RGM frameworks by pointing out the benefits of their coordinated use.

Some of the main achievements resulting from the introduction of RGM teams include:

- Coordination of key data and analytics.
- Definition of KPIs (key performance indicators) to steer RGM in one place.
- Alignment of processes across all involved teams.
- Governance set up with clearer responsibilities for outcomes.
- Sharing of best practices between teams across divisions and countries.

4.2.3 Second Wave: Toward Integrated Solutions

Although a lot has already been achieved in the first wave, the key step toward a true orchestration of the RGM levers is still missing. In our view, this requires an RGM native technology solution, which is built around the core challenges of coordinating the different levers and understanding the combined effects of all offer changes on full portfolio sales, revenue, and profits.

To illustrate the limitations of current tools and methods, consider the previous price-pack architecture example shown here in Figure 4.6. Here, two typical RGM methods are used to determine the prices of the products in a portfolio. The first method is a price ladder, which is often used to price the products in a portfolio along a key dimension, for example, product weight.

Figure 4.6 Example of PPA vs. pricing analysis

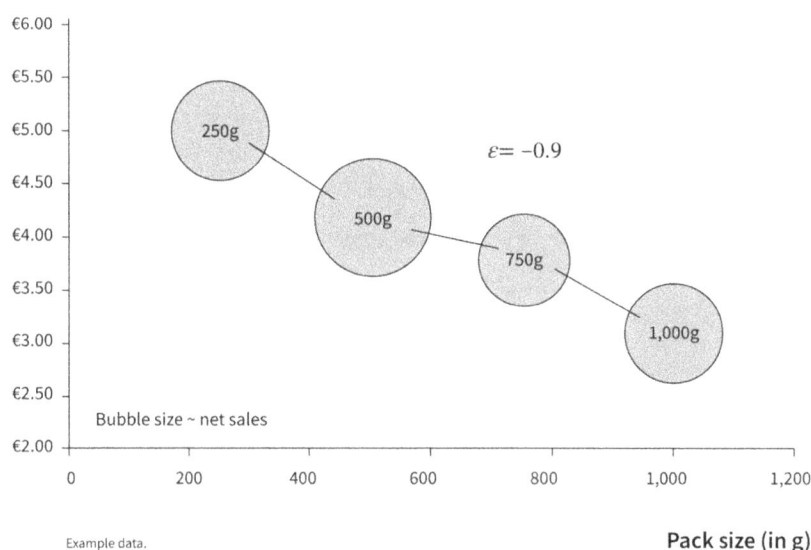

To push sales up the ladder to the larger packs and because shoppers expect lower prices per unit if they buy more, it is common to price products on a constantly declining price-per-unit curve as shown in the graph. In the example, this analysis suggests that the price of the 750g pack needs to be reduced so that all products are priced on a common curve.

The second method is the price elasticity – still the workhorse in pricing and RGM. It is used to assess how demand reacts to a price change. In the example, the price elasticity of −0.9 indicates that a price increase of 1.0% leads to a sales volume reduction of 0.9%. Hence, a price increase leads to both a revenue and a profit increase. Therefore, the price elasticity analysis supports a price increase, which results in conflicting recommendations from the two methods.

This example highlights the core problem of the tools and methods currently used by RGM teams. They are not aligned and integrated well. They mostly focus on individual levers and do not properly address interactions – both between levers and product sales. This is because methods such as price elasticities or customer segmentations come from a paper-and-pencil era that favors simplicity over precision. For anyone who needs more than these back-of-the-envelope heuristics that do not benefit from the increasingly available large and diverse data sets, these traditional methods are not the best choice.

Therefore, we believe that the second phase of the RGM evolution is about moving to an RGM native solution that will be all about integrating across these three dimensions (see Figure 4.7):

- **Data sources:** Different data sources are available to revenue managers with different strengths and weaknesses that are currently not used to their full potential (Figure 4.8). For example, sell-out data is best able to inform teams about the price and product vs. sales relationships for their full product portfolio, while surveys such as conjoint studies provide insights into attributes such as new brands or product features that have not been in the market before. A solution for wave 2 needs to be able to naturally integrate insights from all available sources.

Figure 4.7   Increasing integration

We are moving toward the integration of…

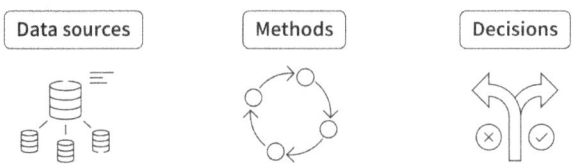

Figure 4.8 Data sources

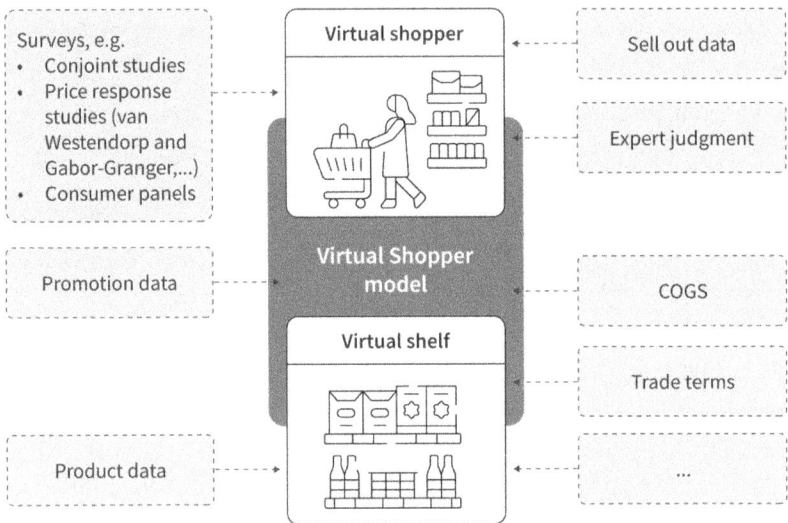

- **Sales dynamics:** Understanding the shopper movements between products after changing prices is crucial for designing and implementing an RGM strategy. However, traditional methods such as (cross) price elasticities are notoriously incapable of providing good insights into these dynamics. For example, they are not good in predicting what share of sales moves to another product from their own portfolio and what is lost to competition. A solution for wave 2 needs to be able to provide insights into all the cross-effects between products after price, PPA, or promotion changes. This is because the effects on other products often account for half of the total impact on sales, (net) revenue, and profit – and without a proper solution, RGM teams cannot see them.
- **Decisions:** With the organizational setup to have all RGM decisions in one place to allow coordinating price, PPA, and promotion decisions, teams now also need a solution that enables the holistic

optimization of all RGM levers (Figure 4.3). This includes the ability to precisely predict how sales, (net) revenues, and profits react to offer changes using a combination of levers (e.g., price, PPA, and promotions) and the ability to choose the course of action best in line with the overall company strategy.

The benefits of such an integrated solution include:

- Holistic optimization of product portfolios using all RGM levers in concert across the full portfolio, while considering all the cross-effects.
- Substantial increase in predictive accuracy of expected market behavior.
- Increased speed to insight with the ability to compare large numbers of scenarios, while reducing the time spent on forecasting significantly.
- Substantial increase in profitability and/or (net) revenue through the ability to select better offer changes.

4.2.4 Toward the Revenue Manager of Tomorrow

So, what does this mean for the revenue manager of tomorrow? The role is clearly evolving, and we need to look at it in two different ways: First, the role of the revenue manager as a change agent (revenue manager of tomorrow), and then how the role evolves as a consequence of this change (revenue manager of the day after).

4.2.4.1 Tomorrow – The Revenue Manager as a Change Agent

A core responsibility of a successful revenue manager will be to enable the transformations described in waves 1 and 2 above. Many organizations have already achieved large parts of wave 1, so the focus will now shift toward implementing an integrated RGM solution.

One of the central questions revenue managers need to answer is that of "make or buy?" Our view is clear on the right path. Teams should focus on implementing their RGM strategy and not on trying to build the next-level RGM platform themselves.[96] Such a platform must be able to predict the effects of offer changes across all RGM levers – and also support teams with optimizing price and other offer changes. The revenue manager needs to focus on enabling teams to best interact with the platform by providing training, best practices, and ensuring that the best available data are used to train the AI models that power predictive analytics.

4.2.4.2 The Day After – Hypotheses on the Changing Role

With an integrated RGM platform in place, the evolution in the role of the revenue manager will resemble the evolution from a pilot flying a plane in the 1920s versus flying a commercial plane in the 2020s. It will be more about managing a professional crew and interacting with complex and mature technology, rather than hustling through with a combination of gut feeling and firefighting. Specifically, we expect the following key effects on the work of the revenue manager:

- **Increase in the importance of data:** With better technology and the ability to use more advanced analytics, the importance of data will increase. This is not only true for the data sources that are currently in use but also other sources that help inform systems about specific aspects of shopper behavior that are difficult to identify, for example, in sell-out data alone. Here, AI technologies will become more important in helping teams gather, structure, and integrate different data sources.

---

[96] For a more detailed discussion, see the Buynomics blog on buy vs. build (2025b).

- **Less need for in-house (manual) analytics:** Also, with the establishment of best-in-class solutions, the need for laborious in-house analytics will be reduced.
- **More focus on management:** In turn, the importance of managing RGM not only within RGM teams globally, but also the interactions with other departments that rely on the best shopper and demand insights like marketing, sales, supply chain, and finance will become more important.
- **Increase in the quality of decision-making:** With better technology and organizational enablement, RGM decision-making will improve substantially, giving first movers an initial competitive advantage and later movers who continue to rely on siloed and manual analyses a clear disadvantage against their more precise and agile competitors.

This is a very exciting time for revenue managers, as the role is shifting and becoming more important within organizations. We are very much looking forward to what's next!

4.3 GENERATIVE AI FOR RGM

In this section, we will hone in on the role of Generative AI (GenAI) in RGM. Specifically, we will first provide a general introduction to the core concepts around AI as they are relevant for RGM (Section 4.3.1). Then, we will identify the core challenge for AI in RGM (Section 4.3.2) and present the different types of AI relevant for RGM (Section 4.3.3). Finally, we will specifically discuss the future role of AI agents in RGM (Section 4.3.4).

4.3.1 Introduction to AI, GenAI, and Other Variants[97]

AI, GenAI, and Agentic AI are hot topics, not just in RGM but everywhere. When I speak about these concepts at conferences, I always start with a check of where we are in the AI Hype Cycle.[98] For this, I present the most current version of Figure 4.9, which shows the Google trends. In our case, they show how many searches there have been for the terms "GenAI" and "Agentic AI" globally over the past five years. When I did this for the first time in early 2024, I only showed the graph for GenAI.

There were two key observations and one question. The first observation was that GenAI started gaining in importance with the rise of

Figure 4.9 Google searches for GenAI and Agentic AI over the past five years

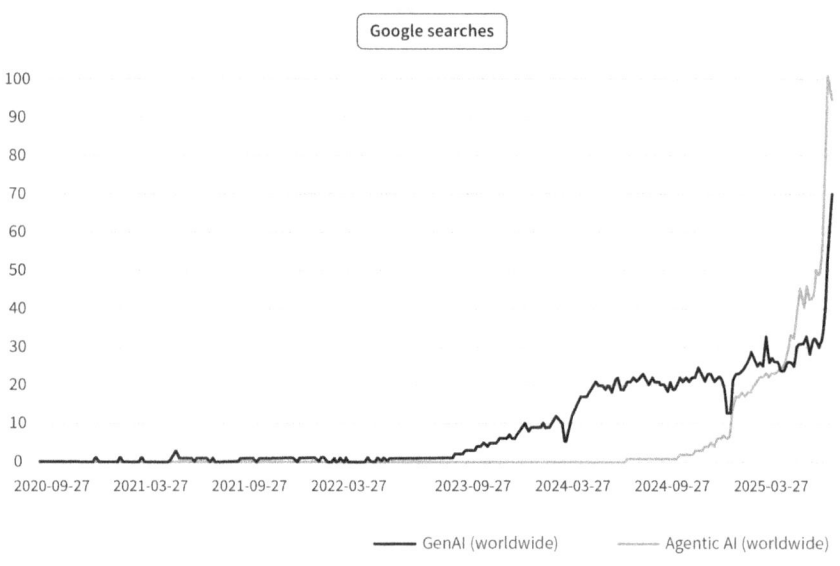

---

[97] Portions of this text were drafted with assistance from ChatGPT5 by OpenAI. This AI tool supported initial research for this sub-chapter. All AI-generated content was carefully reviewed, edited, and approved. The final analysis, conclusions, and interpretations represent my views and expertise. I take full responsibility for the content and accuracy of this work.
[98] Source: Gartner (n.d.b).

ChatGPT, which was released to the public in November 2022 and quickly gained traction in 2023 with the gradual removal of search restrictions and the introduction of free tier and subscription plans. The second observation was that the drop in the search frequency around Christmas 2023 (and then also in 2024) suggested that GenAI was mostly of professional interest. The open question then was whether GenAI would turn out to be a fad, and interest would decline after it peaked sometime in 2024. It now looks like this open question can be answered for the moment, as interest in GenAI has continued to increase throughout 2025 with an acceleration at the time of this writing in August/September.

Further, we have added a second curve in early 2025 to account for the emergence of Agentic AI, that now has surpassed searches for GenAI. This leaves us with new questions: How long will this trend continue, and what form of AI will be most relevant in general and for RGM in particular?

While it looks like AI is still in an early phase of the hype cycle, there are already some critical voices that point to the challenges of implementing AI projects in companies. Prominently, a recent MIT study found that 95% of GenAI pilot projects at large companies failed to deliver measurable financial returns. The report argued that the core problem is not the AI technology itself, but a "learning gap" – organizations lack the skills, processes, and governance to integrate AI into workflows effectively. It also noted a mismatch in investment: over half of AI budgets are directed at sales and marketing initiatives, even though the largest initial returns came more from back-office automation (e.g., reducing outsourcing or streamlining operations). Moreover, the study found that externally procured AI tools and partnerships tended to succeed more often than internally built solutions, and it warned of the risks from "shadow AI" – employees using unsanctioned tools – as well as the need to empower line managers rather than central AI labs.[99]

---

[99] Source: Fortune (2025).

In the same line of reasoning, many consultants and agencies have identified key success factors for the implementation of GenAI and Agentic AI in RGM. Here are the key findings[100]:

- **Foundations and strategy matter:** Data, governance, and an "AI-first" mindset separate leaders from laggards.
- **Human and AI partnership:** Oversight, judgment, and trust remain human responsibilities even as agents gain autonomy.
- **Redesign first, tech second:** Real impact comes from rethinking workflows and business models, not just adding agents.
- **Right tool for the job:** Agents excel in complex, multi-step decisions but are not needed everywhere.

With this overview, we define the key types of AI.

4.3.1.1 GenAI

Over the past decades, AI has evolved from a theoretical concept into one of the most transformative forces in global business and technology. The idea dates back to the 1950s, when pioneers like Alan Turing began asking whether machines could truly "think."[101] In the 1960s and 1970s, researchers built early expert systems that followed human-written rules, but progress stalled due to limited computing power and data. By the 1980s and 1990s, advances in statistical learning and neural networks began to reignite optimism.[102] The real acceleration came in the 2010s, when massive data sets, cloud computing, and deep learning drove breakthroughs in fields like speech processing and image recognition. Systems like AlphaGo demonstrated that AI could outperform humans even in complex strategic games.[103] The early 2020s marked another leap forward with large language

---

[100] Sources: McKinsey & Company (n.d.); Genpact (n.d.); EY (n.d.); BCG (2025).
[101] Turing (1950); McCorduck (2004).
[102] Russell and Norvig (2021).
[103] Silver et al. (2016).

models such as OpenAI's GPT-3, GPT-4, and GPT-5, which demonstrated the ability to reason across text, visuals, and other data to generate fluent, human-like responses.[104] In essence, AI is the science and engineering of creating machines that can perform tasks requiring human-like intelligence – learning, reasoning, perception, and decision-making.[105]

Generative AI (GenAI) is a subset of AI that focuses on creating new content – such as text, images, music, code, or video – rather than just analyzing or predicting existing data. GenAI systems, like OpenAI's GPT-5 or image models such as DALL·E and Midjourney, are powered by large models such as neural networks trained on vast datasets. These models generate new outputs based on patterns they have learned, allowing businesses to use them for a broad range of (creative) tasks.

For the following, we will use an expert's definition of the term. ChatGPT defines GenAI as: "GenAI (Generative AI) refers to a class of AI systems designed to generate new content, data, or information that is similar to, but not directly copied from, existing examples. These systems use algorithms and models to create original outputs by learning patterns and structures from the input data they were trained on."[106]

The most prominent current applications are large language models (LLMs) that are trained on large amounts of texts. These models use GPTs (generative pre-trained transformers) – as in ChatGPT. They can generate human-like texts based on the input they receive, making them capable of tasks such as text completion, translation, summarization, and creative writing. Very simplified, these models build their output texts step-by-step by predicting the next word in a sentence based on the previous text (see Figure 4.10).[107] This example highlights that answers are always probabilistic. The sentence "The price is . . ." can continue with "high," "low," or many

---

[104] OpenAI (2023, 2025).
[105] Nilsson (2010).
[106] Created with ChatGPT 3.5, February 2024.
[107] NVIDIA Developer Blog (n.d.).

Figure 4.10 Example workflow of an LLM predicting the next word

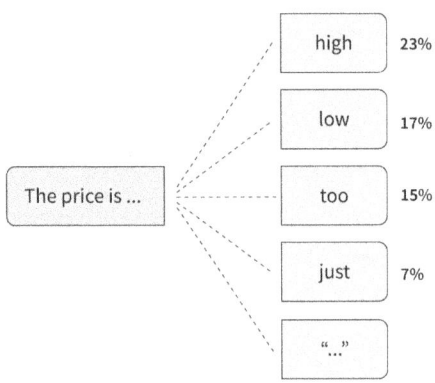

other words. So, if you ask the same question multiple times, you will likely get a (slightly) different answer each time.

Other applications of such GenAI models include the creation of pictures and music by predicting the next pixel in an image or the next note in a song (Figure 4.11). The basic idea of these models is always the same: Use available data to predict outcomes in new situations.

What is new about this technology, and what are the benefits? The ability of GenAI systems to learn structures from large amounts of data and then apply these to generate new outputs has only been made possible

Figure 4.11 Overview of different AI applications

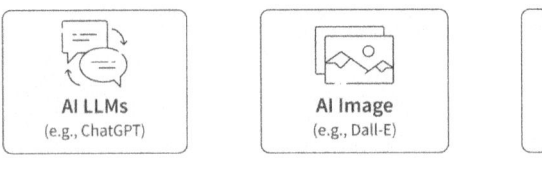

in recent years with the emergence of fast and cheap computing power that allowed the analysis of large – and often unstructured – data.

This enables the completion of creative tasks such as text or image creation, or it can be used to improve tasks that have been solved with more traditional methods before. One such example is DeepMind's weather forecasting AI.[108] Instead of modeling the physics of weather dynamics across a grid of cubes that cover the globe and interact with each other, it uses a graph-based representation of the atmosphere that is trained on decades of historical weather data. This leads to a more precise and faster prediction of mid-range forecasts (up to 10 days), and once trained, the AI model is so efficient that it can run on a laptop, where traditional solutions required the largest servers available.

To summarize, AI models excel in situations with large, complex, and unstructured data, where they can provide fast, new, cheap, creative, and more precise answers than traditional methods or humans. The question for us is then: How can these models be best applied to RGM – particularly to better solve the main task of understanding how demand reacts to offer changes? This will be answered in the following sections. Before that, we outline the core idea of Agentic AI.

4.3.1.2 Agentic AI

In recent years, AI has evolved from a tool that executes predefined instructions into systems capable of independent decision-making – that is, Agentic AI. Unlike traditional automation, which relies on explicit programming, Agentic AI operates through adaptive models that perceive environments, set goals, and take actions to achieve them with minimal human oversight. This transition marks a profound shift in how businesses conceptualize work, strategy, and value creation.

---

[108] Science.org (n.d.).

Agentic AI systems (also called AI Agents) can plan, reason, and coordinate across digital and physical domains, effectively becoming digital employees capable of managing complex workflows or even entire business functions. For example, an Agentic AI might autonomously negotiate supplier contracts, manage marketing campaigns, or optimize logistics in real time. As such, businesses adopting agentic systems are moving toward what some analysts describe as autonomous enterprises – organizations where AI acts not merely as an assistant but as an active participant in operations and innovation.[109] For RGM, we are not there yet and AI Agents – where in place – are currently doing much smaller tasks such as collecting data or supporting with the selection of promotions.

4.3.1.3 Agent-Based Modeling

Agent-based modeling (ABM) has emerged as a powerful technology for understanding complex systems – whether markets, organizations, or entire economies – by simulating the interactions of individual agents that follow simple behavioral rules. Unlike traditional top-down models that assume equilibrium or uniform behavior, ABM operates from the bottom up: it allows dynamic, heterogeneous agents to interact within virtual environments, producing emergent outcomes that mirror real-world behaviors and complexity.[110]

In business contexts, ABM enables managers to explore how local decisions and micro-level preferences and behaviors give rise to macro-level patterns such as market demand or competitive dynamics. For example, a team can model how shoppers respond to price changes or how disruptions propagate through global logistics networks. Rather than relying solely on statistical inference, ABM offers an experimental environment, where decision-makers can test scenarios before committing to action.

---

[109] Brynjolfsson and McAfee (2017); Bubeck et al. (2023).
[110] Bonabeau (2002).

The integration of AI has significantly expanded the capabilities of ABM. Advances in machine learning now allow models to better learn from a broad range of empirical data, thus allowing more realistic simulations.[111] For example, AI-enhanced agents can incorporate reinforcement learning to optimize behaviors. This convergence of ABM and AI effectively transforms simulation from a descriptive tool into a predictive and exploratory one that is capable of informing specific actions, strategy, and innovation.

The key ideas of GenAI, Agentic AI, and ABM are summarized in Figure 4.12.

Figure 4.12 Summary of AI types

Generative AI (GenAI)	Agentic AI[a]	Agent-based modeling (ABM)

• Produces new content (text, images, code, …) from a prompt • One-off interaction, no goal orientation **Example:** Drafting an email, generating an image **Key distinction:** Created outputs but does not act	• Autonomous agents that observe, act, adapt in cycles • Goal-driven, can chain multiple steps and use tools independently **Example:** AI assistant booking travel end-to-end **Key distinction:** Acts autonomously to achieve goal	• Simulation of many agents, each following simple rules • Used to study interactions and emergent system-wide patterns **Example:** Simulating shoppers' reaction to pricing changes, traffic flows in a city **Key distinction:** Models collective behavior, not individual intelligence

[a] Consists of several layers: LLM (reasoning) + Memory (context) + Planner (goals/steps) + Tools/Actions (execution) + Orchestrator (control/safety).

---

[111] Epstein (2014).

4.3.2 The RGM Core Challenge for AI

There are many potential applications for AI tools in RGM and pricing. We will address these more broadly in the next section. However, the most important challenge for AI to address is predicting how demand reacts to offer changes across the RGM levers – and then being able to explain why it does so. We argue here that this is not only the core challenge, but also the one that needs to be solved from within the RGM field. This is because predicting demand reactions to complex offer changes is a very specific challenge to which solutions from other domains such as physics or biology cannot easily be applied. Further, it becomes quickly clear to everyone who has tried it that a naïve and direct use of LLMs such as ChatGPT to answer the core challenge of demand prediction does not lead to good results. From reading large amounts of text, an LLM cannot know if increasing the price of a chocolate bar by 5% or 7% will be better for revenue or profit optimization. It might be able to use and steer predictive tools, but it is not built to predict demand reactions to offer changes.

Therefore, we in RGM need to build our own model. The natural starting point for building an RGM AI model are the tools and methods discussed in Chapter 2 to analyze the RGM levers. Because it is the workhorse of pricing, we will use the price elasticity as an example to highlight the challenges in building an RGM AI model – all the other tools face similar challenges. Figure 4.13 shows the standard way that price elasticities are computed. In the graph, each dot represents the total sales and average sales price of these sales in a channel for a week. To determine the price-sales relationship, a linear regression is applied. In its simplest form, it uses two parameters, the intercept and the slope, to describe the relationship between price and sales. This is because the linear regression was developed at a time about 150–200 years ago, when computation was expensive and data was scarce, as all analyses had to be done by hand. The complete methodological

Figure 4.13   Price elasticity measurement via regression analysis

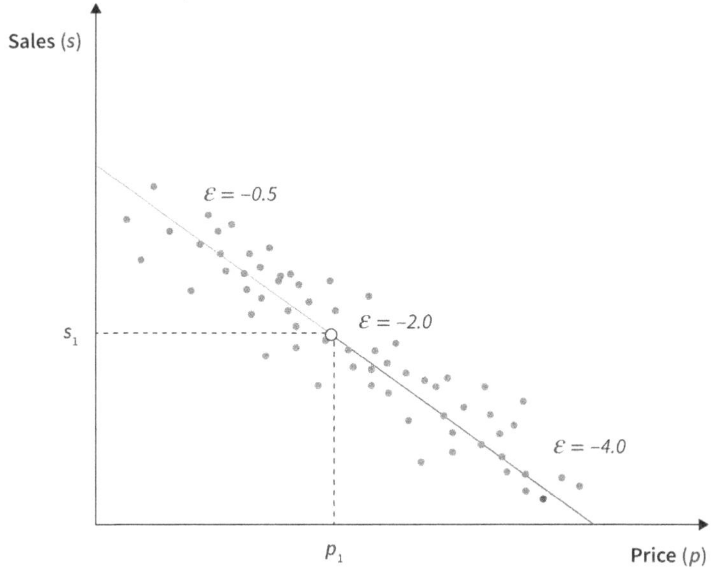

[Chart showing Sales (s) on y-axis vs Price (p) on x-axis, with scatter points and a downward-sloping regression line. Labels on the line indicate $\varepsilon = -0.5$ at the upper region, $\varepsilon = -2.0$ near the middle point (p_1, s_1), and $\varepsilon = -4.0$ at the lower region.]

Note: Basis for example: Linear demand with $a = 100$, $b = 25$.

framework of traditional statistics is built around the idea of reducing effort. For example, the normal distribution – that under some simple assumptions can explain a broad range of phenomena with just two parameters (mean and standard deviation) – can be estimated decently from small (representative) samples. Methods like least-square, used to determine the parameters in a regression analysis, use elegant procedures to reduce the computational effort to determine parameters. Further, Karl Popper's research approach of hypothesis testing[112] comes from this reductionist view that aims at reducing effort, because empirical research was manual and slow. The motto can be captured in the phrase "Think before you act!"

---

[112] Popper (1959).

However, there is a downside to this approach that becomes apparent in the AI age. Methods and tools from this era do not necessarily scale well into a data and computationally rich environment.

The regression analysis in Figure 4.13, which is used to determine the price elasticity of the product at different price points, is based on about 100 data points (weekly total sales vs. average price). If the number of data points were expanded to 1,000 or 1,000,000, then the quality of the parameter estimates for the intercept and the slope would not improve meaningfully.[113] By contrast, AI models such as LLMs, require vast amounts of data to parameterize very large models before they can deliver any meaningful results. Figure 4.14 shows the progression in the number of model parameters against the model quality from ChatGPT-2 to ChatGPT-5. Compare the 1.5 billion parameters of GPT-2 with the 2 parameters of a simple linear regression, and the further model expansion from GPT-2 to GPT-5. To get from basic text generation to near human comprehension and planning, a more than 3,000-fold increase in the number of model parameters was required. Therefore, ML models require large amounts of parameters and benefit massively from further expansion in the number of parameters. This is a very different basic approach from classical statistics that is probably best summarized by von Neumann's dislike of large-parameter regression models expressed in his statement: "With four parameters I can fit an elephant, and with five I can make him wiggle his trunk."[114]

Therefore, a core AI model for RGM that can benefit from the increasing amount of data and advancements in machine learning, must be able to benefit from an increasing number of parameters to capture additional insights from more data. This is clearly not the case for any of the methods and tools presented in Chapter 2.

---

[113] For example, if at $n = 100$ the estimate of a price elasticity is -2 ± 0.2, then for $n = 1,000$ it is -2 ± 0.06, and for $n = 1,000,000$ it is -2 ± 0.002.
[114] Dyson (1949), quoted in Dyson (2004).

Figure 4.14   Model parameters vs. model performance

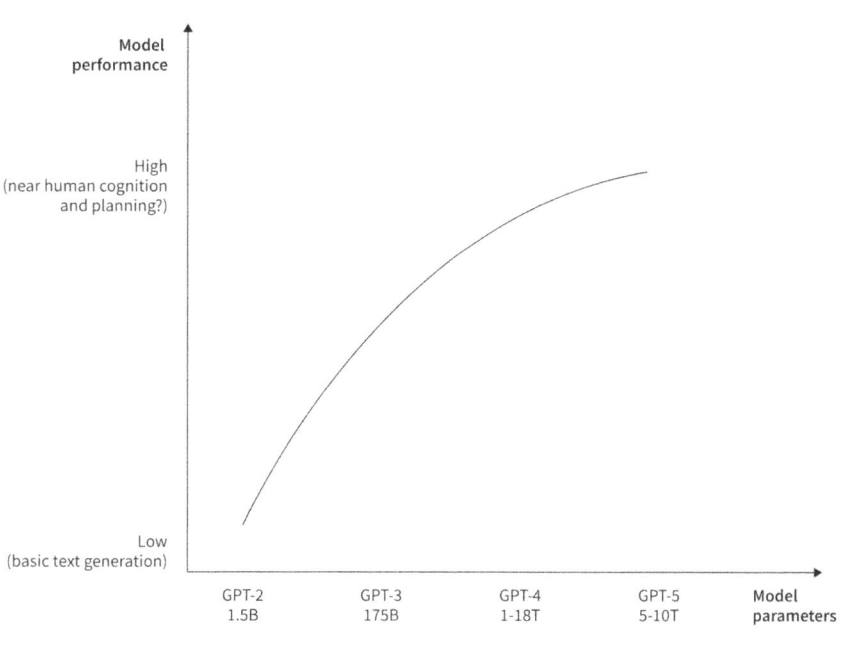

B: Billions, T: Trillions

With this and some further previous ideas on how to work with data in RGM, we define the requirements that an RGM AI model that predicts demand reactions after offer changes needs to satisfy:

- The quality (precision and scope of cases covered) of the model benefits from access to more data by meaningfully expanding the scope of model parameters.
- The model can integrate and learn from key RGM data sources (e.g., aggregated sales data, surveys, shopper panels).
- The model can simulate the joint effects of all RGM levers (e.g., price, PPA, and promotion changes together).
- The model can simulate all relevant cross-effects – for example, between products, over time, and between channels.

There are likely different ways to build such a core RGM AI model. The one we are developing at Buynomics seems to me to be the most obvious one – we call the technology Virtual Shoppers. For this, look at Figure 4.15, which is based on the previous Figure 4.13, but now we have included the shoppers standing in equal distance at the bottom, sorted by their willingness to pay (WTP) for the product. Those with the highest WTP are to the very right and those with the lowest WTP to the left – then everyone right of the product's price buys it and everyone left does not. This is what a demand function implies. The idea of the Virtual Shoppers technology that we will outline next is that we generalize this understanding of the basic shoppers implied by a demand function. They are basic, because they only have one property: their WTP for this one product. We generalize this

Figure 4.15 Demand and Virtual Shoppers

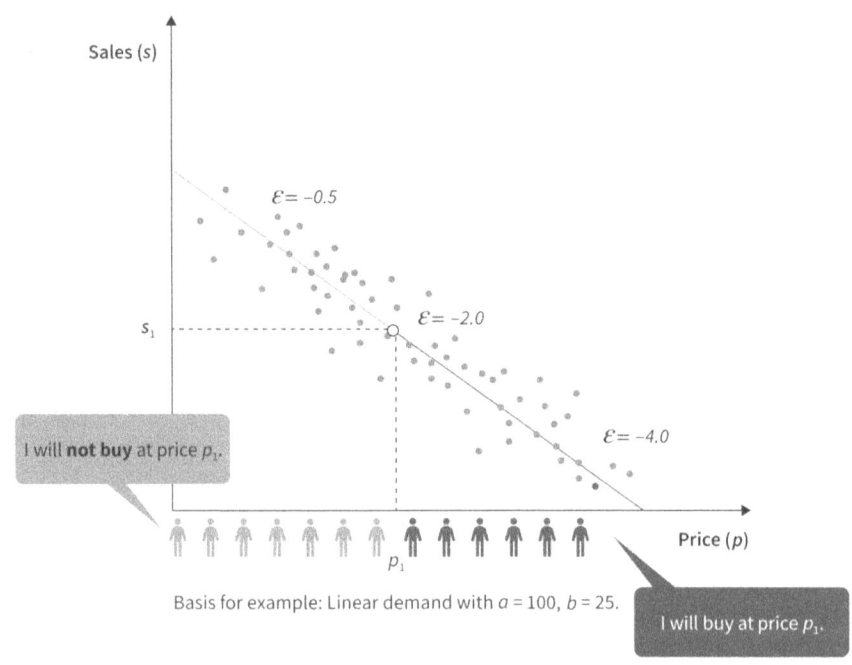

by giving them further preferences for different product attributes and behavioral features – such as how susceptible they are to price thresholds or how easily they can be nudged toward specific purchases.

The idea of the Virtual Shoppers technology is to replicate the actual buying situation as closely as possible. First, this includes the shoppers with behaviors and preferences, who buy products. Second, it includes a close replication of the competitive situation – specifically, what products are available to which shoppers in a period. For example, in supermarkets, not all products are available each week, promoted products differ from week to week, etc. To best model the shopping situation, these differences must be replicated in a simulation. So, we will discuss these two aspects in a bit more detail: the virtual shopper and the virtual shopping situation.

4.3.2.1 Virtual Shoppers

Figure 4.16 summarizes the principal approach of the Virtual Shoppers technology. First, Virtual Shoppers have behaviors – just like real shoppers. For example, some respond to price thresholds such that they are much more likely to buy a product at €9.99 than at €10.00, while for others there is no difference between a price change from €9.98 to €9.99 and a price change from €9.99 to €10.00. With sufficient data, Virtual Shoppers can learn all the behaviors that are described in Chapter 2 (behavioral pricing) and their strengths, such as how they respond to specific promotions or their preference for the middle option in a good-better-best portfolio. Second, Virtual Shoppers can have preferences for different product features such as the brand, the size, the material and other properties that are important for shoppers.

Figure 4.17 shows how sales dynamics are derived from Virtual Shoppers' preferences. We will outline later how the preferences and behaviors are determined. In the example here, each Virtual Shopper #1, #2, #3, etc. has a set of behaviors and preferences for product attributes. Based on their behaviors and preferences, Virtual Shoppers choose between the offered products A, B,

Figure 4.16 The Virtual Shoppers technology

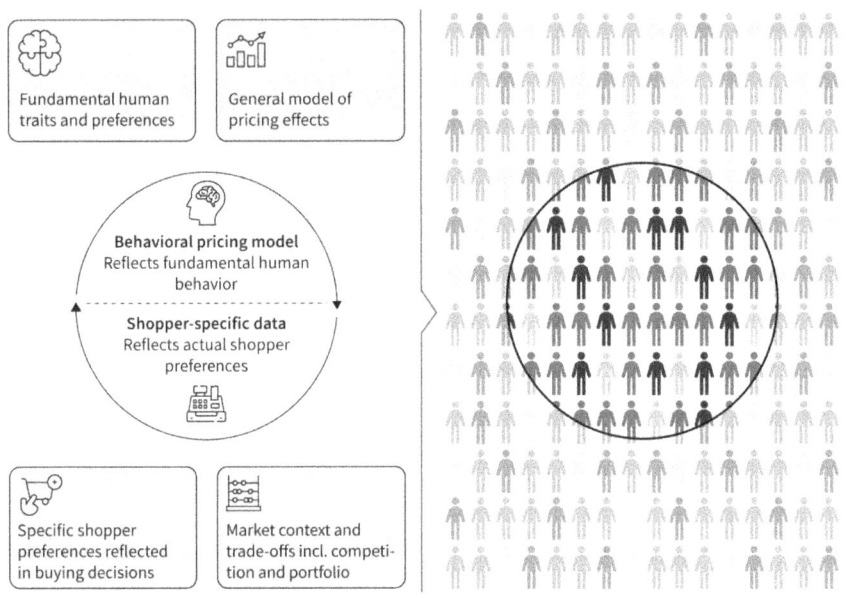

and C, considering their specific product features and prices. Each Virtual Shopper chooses the product that gives them the greatest value – by comparing products' utilities against their prices, given the Virtual Shopper's preferences and specific behaviors. The right side of the figure shows for the example of price changes, how Virtual Shoppers can be used to determine the implications of offer changes. If the price of product A is constantly being increased, more and more Virtual Shoppers will choose to buy something else or nothing at all. The result for product A is the demand curve shown. The shape and slope of the demand curve depend on how preferences for product A are distributed among Virtual Shoppers relative to those of the other products offered. Once a demand function is determined, everything else of interest to the pricing or RGM manager, such as price elasticities, revenue, and profit functions can be deduced.

Figure 4.17 From Virtual Shoppers to demand prediction

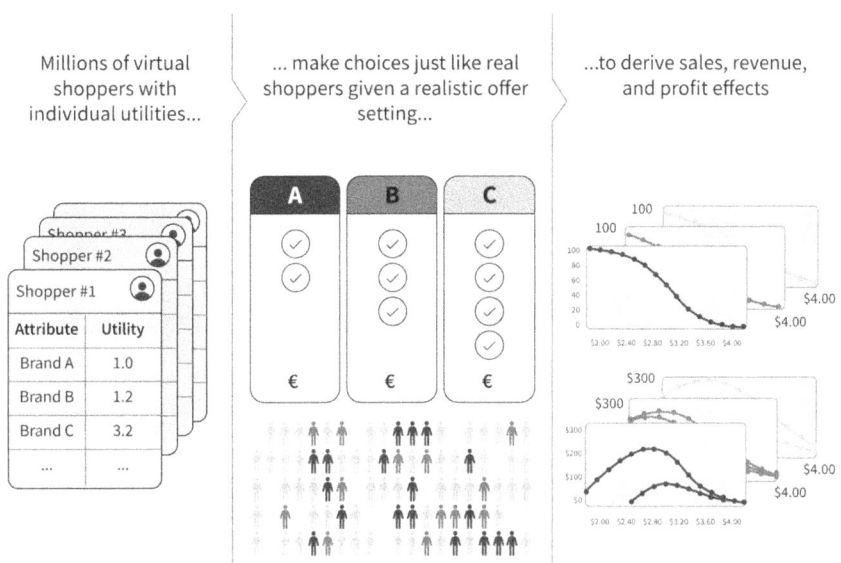

It is important to note that the Virtual Shoppers cannot only be used to produce independent demand functions for each product. Rather, they can also model interdependencies between the price changes of different products. For example, if in Figure 4.17 the price of product B is increased, then the demand curve for product A shifts upward, so that at each price, more Virtual Shoppers will buy product A. Also, the effects of changes in product features can be modeled. If, for example, the size of product A is increased and the product becomes more valuable, then this shifts the demand curve of product B downwards and at each price point fewer Virtual Shoppers will buy product B. Of course, the effects of combinations of RGM lever changes (e.g., price, product, promotion) differentiated across products can also be modeled.

For real applications, up to millions of Virtual Shoppers are created to determine the sales, revenue, and profit implications of offer changes.

This is required to replicate the actual shopping dynamics in large product categories such as soft drinks in large countries.

4.3.2.2 Virtual Shopping Situation

Further, the Virtual Shoppers technology allows users to model specific shopping situations at a granular level. Figure 4.18 shows the example of a product category (nuts) and the same sample of Virtual Shoppers shopping in two consecutive weeks with different products on promotion. As a result, sales units are very different in both weeks. However, sales in both weeks are well predicted by the same sample of Virtual Shoppers, who with the same preferences and behaviors in both weeks

Figure 4.18 Virtual Shoppers predict demand for different offers

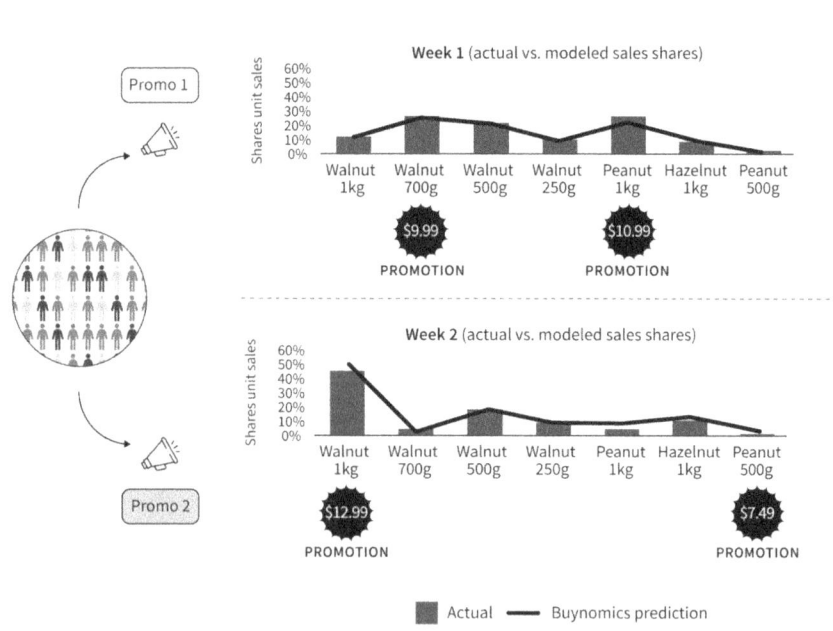

buy different products because promotions and prices differ. Further details of a shopping situation can change. For example, not all products are available in all periods, or products are replaced with specific seasonal variants, or products are displayed differently over time. This is particularly important in online sales, where display changes can be implemented very easily. Also, the number of Virtual Shoppers considering the products in a category can vary with long-term trends or seasonal changes. Finally, preferences can change over time. For example, brand value can grow or decline over time, or product features can increase or decrease in importance.

4.3.2.3 Further Considerations

The key to a good prediction of sales dynamics is the right parametrization of the Virtual Shoppers. For this, all the typical data sources used in pricing and RGM can be used. For example, sales data reveal how many units were sold at what prices (as in Figure 4.18). Therefore, historical sales data can be used to parameterize a Virtual Shopper model. Other data sources such as surveys can provide further insights on the value of features that have not been tested in the market. For example, if a manufacturer wants to introduce a new brand, then it is not possible to assess the value of that brand from historical sales data. However, the new brand can be evaluated via a conjoint study, and the insights are then added to a Virtual Shoppers model primarily parameterized from historical sales data. In general, different data sources have different advantages and disadvantages. With the legacy methods described in Chapter 2, these could not be fully exploited to form a coherent picture of shoppers' preferences and buying decisions.

The Virtual Shoppers technology can integrate different data sources naturally into one coherent model. Different data sources such as sales data, transaction data, survey, or shopper panels can be understood as different tools to measure buyer preferences and behaviors. Each has different advantages and disadvantages that can be combined to paint an increasingly complete picture of a market. In this book, we will not focus on the details of parametrization. Here, we only provide an outline, show use cases, and discuss our perspective on what the technology can deliver next. For example, the Virtual Shoppers can be enriched with demographic or other shopper insights, so that models do not only predict how many units are sold of a specific offer, but also who buys it. From this, marketing can derive better who their customers are, what is needed to attract specific target demographics, and how to attract new customers more consistently.

4.3.3 AI in RGM

In the previous section, we outlined the core pricing and RGM technology we are developing at Buynomics to predict the sales implications of offer changes. Although we argue that this is the most important task in RGM, it is clearly not the only area that can benefit from the use of AI technology. In this section, we discuss the range of relevant applications and provide some guidance on which technology is relevant for each. Further, we will argue that there are four layers that are built on top of each other and need to be solved by teams in sequence. But before we do this, we first need to bust a common myth that exists not only within the RGM field but more broadly.

From our conversations, we often get the impression that some in the RGM field expect to be able to simply ask a ChatGPT or Microsoft Copilot: "How do I best increase my net revenue by 4%?" and receive the price, promotion, and PPA changes required for this outcome. Is this possible? Yes and no. "No," if you expect ChatGPT or Microsoft's Copilot to answer these questions directly once they have access to the right data. These LLMs are not built to predict how sales react to offer changes or to optimize prices. "Yes," if you stack together the right specialized GenAI models. For example, an LLM can use sales prediction and price optimization engines for that task in the same sense as it can use – for example – chess

Figure 4.19 The GenAI halo effect in RGM

He is a good writer. Therefore, he must also be good at math!

It can summarize my emails. Therefore, it also knows how I should increase my prices!

engines to play at the level of the world champion, while the LLM cannot itself play chess very well.[115]

What is often at play here is a version of the Halo effect as shown in Figure 4.19.[116] The Halo effect is a cognitive bias where our general impression of a person, company, brand, or product is too much affected by our perception in specific (narrow) areas. Specifically, if we think someone (or something) is good in one area, we tend to assume they are also good in others, even without evidence. We find that there is a strong GenAI Halo effect at work in the pricing and RGM space at the moment, where some think that because tools like ChatGPT or Microsoft's Copilot produce very convincing results in some tasks such as preparing email replies, they can also solve their other challenges such as optimizing their prices for next year. This is not the case.

---

[115] ChatGPT5 on its chess-playing skills (October 2025): "Without an engine, my play is roughly in the 1800–2000 Elo range (strong club player level). I understand openings, middlegame plans, and endgames, but I can still blunder occasionally – like a human. With an engine's help, I can play at any strength you want, from beginner to super-GM (2800+)." Note that here "engines" refers to specialized chess engines such as Stockfish or AlphaZero.

[116] Nisbett and Wilson (1977).

Figure 4.20 Four core layers for using (Gen)AI in RGM

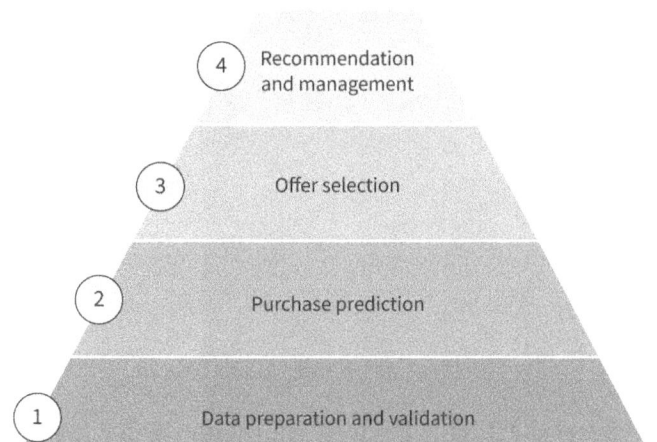

Next, we will first discuss each of the four layers for using (Gen)AI in RGM shown in Figure 4.20 separately and then show how they build on top of each other. Specifically, we will discuss how AI technologies can be applied to make RGM teams more effective and efficient.

4.3.3.1 Data Integration

RGM, like many practical fields, relies on a broad range of relevant data sources that are used for decision-making (Figure 4.21). Making these different data sources useful requires several steps including data cleaning (e.g., identification of errors or outliers) or harmonization of sales data coming from different sources that need to be mastered before the data can be analyzed. Also, different forms of data – for example sell-out and survey data – need to be aligned. With traditional methods, this often happens as a last step: The sales data analysis yields a price recommendation of €5.00, and the conjoint study yields €10.00 – then, teams often go for the middle, that is €7.50.

Figure 4.21   Integration of key data sources into a single model

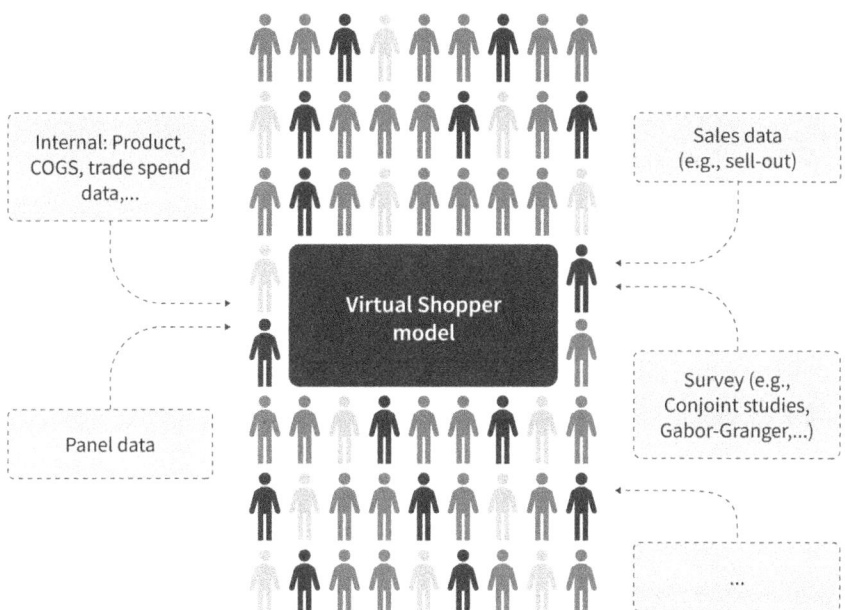

Here are many opportunities for GenAI to support with (1) preparing, (2) visualizing, and (3) integrating different relevant data sources. (1) and (2) are not specific to RGM, and as a field, we should use and integrate the best solutions available. Here, (1) is proving to be notoriously difficult to automate and it still frequently requires meaningful manual work. (2) is a commodity and is available via tools such as Microsoft's Copilot. (3) is the challenge that needs a specific RGM solution. Currently, the most successful solution is the Virtual Shoppers AI, which can learn shopper preferences and behaviors from different data sources, as described previously.

One note of caution is important here. Some in the RGM field seem to expect that LLMs can be used for market research and soon replace, for example, surveys such as conjoint studies. Recent tests of this idea suggest that we should be more cautious about this idea. In a recent study,

Brand et al. (2024) show that large language models like ChatGPT can generate synthetic consumer survey responses that are like human responses, especially for familiar product attributes. However, their analysis suggests that specific attribute valuations can differ significantly, particularly for new categories.[117] Therefore, they are not yet fit for high-stakes decision-making in companies. One observation in this and other studies like it is that they work with small sample sizes. In small samples, it is easy to generate the impression of human-like survey responses, as differences typically only become apparent when comparing large samples. Therefore, the difficult part is matching the full distribution of real human responses within and across attributes (including cross-effects). Therefore, we do not expect LLMs to replace human surveys soon. However, potentially they can be used to augment human surveys.

4.3.3.2 Sales Forecasting

We have already discussed the traditional RGM tools and their current limitations, and we outlined the Virtual Shoppers AI technology we are developing at Buynomics in the previous section. When moving to GenAI in RGM, it is important to recognize that traditional tools like price elasticities are also unfit as a basis for a GenAI future. This is because they are rooted in microeconomic thinking that was built around the need to simplify the modeling of market dynamics so much that they could be studied with paper and pencil. This is reflected in the use of linear or isoelastic demand functions, mostly single product markets, the use or regression analyses to determine the price-sales relationship, and the use of price elasticities, which summarize a market reaction to a price change in a single number. These simplifications fit well into the time about 200 years ago, but not into today's environment with access to large data sets and cheap computing power, which will not, however, make a simple linear regression analysis – and with this derived price elasticities – much better.

---

[117] Brand et al. (2024).

Therefore, a GenAI approach to sales forecasting after an offer change needs to build on a different foundation. Like text, picture, or music models, such an RGM GenAI for sales forecasting must aim to replicate human-like behavior to predict the next purchases of shoppers after an offer change. This can be achieved with the Virtual Shopper AI, that creates large groups of virtual shoppers that make purchasing decisions just like real shoppers. This allows the model to holistically forecast the effects of all RGM lever changes, in isolation and together, and not only of a price or promotion change in isolation. Further, it allows users to understand the interactions between products – for example, the difference between a price change of a single product against the whole portfolio, or against a price change in combination with a size change or delisting of a product.

The Virtual Shoppers can be trained on all available historical RGM data including sales, survey, and panel data. For sales data, the AI identifies the virtual shoppers' preferences that produce the observed sales across products, channels, and over time, given the specific prices and offers during the training period. Further, survey results on a new potential brand can be integrated into a model built from sales data for all already existing value drivers and attributes. This allows teams to assess the potential of a new brand using a robust model based on historical sales data and new insights from a survey.

In summary, this technology provides users with an integrated assessment of all data sources, RGM levers, and product sales changes (considering cross-effects). This results in:

- **Increased accuracy:** Virtual Shoppers make decisions just like real shoppers. They consider the entire category, including your other products and competing ones. This often results in forecasts of up to 95% accuracy.[118]

---

[118] Depending on data quality.

- **Increased speed-to-insight:** Virtual Shoppers can be asked about their purchasing decisions thousands of times within minutes. This allows users to find the optimal portfolio combination from very large sets of alternatives.
- **Better scalability:** Virtual Shoppers react exactly like their real-life counterparts, even in new channels and markets. This allows the solution to be deployed in any context, in any market, by any team. This is not possible with an Excel model some consultant built three years ago.
- **A new way of working:** Virtual Shoppers empower teams to engage in a fully digitized way of working. With their immense speed-to-insight, users can answer more hypotheses in a shorter amount of time. Instead of waiting for the results of an eight-week market study, revenue managers can iterate their hypotheses in minutes to get more insights faster.
- **Reduced data needs:** Unlike other methods, Virtual Shoppers can already work well with limited amounts of data. There is no need to add an endless number of studies or AB tests to finetune the model.
- **Top- and bottom-line improvements:** The result of these improvements often leads to net revenue and/or profit increases of up to 2–4%.

Accurate and fast sales forecasting are the necessary foundation for the two next key layers of an RGM GenAI solution.

4.3.3.3   Offer Optimization

The next step is enabling the system to recommend offer changes that, for example, optimize net revenue or profit, or that achieve a desired profit or net revenue improvement, if this is possible. In principle, this process is straightforward. You only need to produce a sufficiently large set of offer change scenarios and then choose the best ones according to the defined objective function. However, there are several challenges here:

- **Complexity:** In a product portfolio, there are very many potential price, promotion, and product feature changes available to RGM managers. In a portfolio with 10 products and 10 potential change options for each, there are 10^{10} = 10 billion potential variations. In a portfolio with 30 products and 30 change options for each, there are $30^{30} = 2.06 * 10^{44}$ combinations, which is a lot more than the number of potential possible positions in chess ($\approx 10^{40}$). Because most changes are discrete (e.g., product features, promotion weeks, specific price points), analytic optimization is difficult.
- **Constraints:** The complexity challenge coming from the large number of cases is further increased by various constraints that need to be considered. These include regulatory limitations. For example, not every price increase, promotion, pack size may be allowed. Further, retailers may limit the frequency or type of promotions that are available. Finally, many price-architecture constraints often need to be considered. For example, more valuable products also need to be more expensive, while the price per gram is expected to decrease for larger packs. Such constraints make it difficult to search efficiently through the options space.
- **Definition of the objective function:** It is often difficult to precisely define the objective function that is to be optimized. First, most organizations do not simply aim to maximize profit or net revenue, but some combination of both. Also, other softer criteria often need to be considered. For example, between two RGM plans that yield the same profit and net revenue improvement, most teams prefer the one that requires the smaller number of promotion changes, as these are often hard to negotiate.

Because of these challenges, there is a role to play for GenAI in identifying and recommending the right offer changes that optimize the organization's KPIs. We find that the best way for a GenAI solution to support RGM teams is not by simply proposing a single optimal answer but rather by providing a range of preselected, very good options, and then letting teams choose from those. As an example, Figure 4.22 shows how this is implemented in the Buynomics solution. Here, the graph shows a large number of potential differentiated price changes and the profit and revenue implications of each. These plans can also be filtered by further criteria – for example, by showing only plans that satisfy some price structure or competitive positioning. From these, users can choose the ones that best fit their overall strategy and present those to their top management for final decision-making.

This approach addresses the three challenges discussed above, and it allows the system to learn what offer changes produce the best outcomes and are preferred by teams and senior management. (Discrete) optimization is

Figure 4.22   Offer optimization using AI

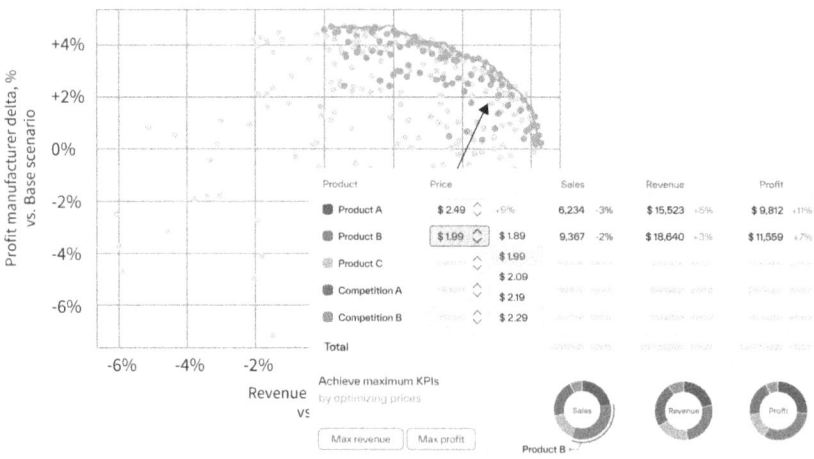

Screenshot Buynomics price optimization tool (Decision Guide).

an established discipline within ML and AI. Here, the main task for the RGM field is to structure the RGM optimization challenge such that it can best be used by existing tools. There is nothing new that needs to be invented here.

4.3.3.4 Recommendation and Management of Offer Changes

The last key step for GenAI in RGM is also the currently most prominent and visible one in the general discussion. It is the prompt-based interaction with a solution such as ChatGPT or Microsoft's Copilot. Here it is most important to recognize that such an interface can only be as good as the solution that it interacts with, as the LLM cannot perform key RGM tasks on its own. For example, Microsoft's Copilot can use Excel to create a Graph from a data table or do some data aggregation using pivot tables. However, it cannot do much that a versed user could not also do with Excel. For RGM, this means Copilot will not any time soon go beyond Excel's capabilities – that is, predicting sales changes after a price increase using price elasticity values from a table, usually provided by some agency. We already discussed the limitations of this approach.

Therefore, the LLM mainly serves as an interface between the user and the GenAI that can predict how sales react to offer changes and identify optimal offer changes from that (the two previously discussed layers). Figure 4.23 shows an example of a typical question posted by leadership to an RGM team. For the AI to provide a useful answer, it must identify which offer changes yield a 5% net revenue increase and, of those, which will be considered "best" by leadership. Therefore, a prompt-based interface must satisfy the following requirements:

- It needs to precisely understand technical terminology of the domain. In the case of RGM, this means that it needs to be trained on the – often company specific – definitions of key terms such as net revenue, gross profit, or fall through rate.

Figure 4.23 Example of prompt-based RGM optimization

> We are starting our annual RGM planning. Can you provide me with an overview of options we have for the UK market for next year?

Yes, you can achieve a maximum net revenue increase of 6.7% with a combination of pricing, PPA, and promotion adjustments, and an increase of 4.6% with only price changes.

> That is a good starting point. Can you tell me the best way to increase net revenues for the UK market by 5%?

Yes, I have identified one option, where we need to add one additional pack size and work with only price changes otherwise, and one option without PPA changes, but a change in the promotions we run and only price changes otherwise. Both options yield an expected 5.0% net revenue increase with maintaining the current percentage gross margins.

> Thanks. Please show me the details for both together with our assumptions on competitor offer changes.

Here you go!

...

- It must be able to assess which options are considered "better" by an organization. Let's say that an optimization algorithm identified two offer changes that each produce a 5% net revenue improvement against the status quo, and use very different levers to achieve the improvement. How does the AI present the two options to the user and how does it choose between them if needed? For this, it needs to be able to consider a range of further criteria. For example, to achieve the same net revenue increase, an RGM team might prefer the one that requires fewer promotion week changes or not too much or too little price differentiation. These criteria are often not explicitly available but must rather be learned from the interaction of the AI with the team. Areas where LLMs can provide particular benefits include: (1) deriving specific and consistent RGM strategy

implications from annual reports, CEO statements, and internal strategy documents; and (2) providing consistency in pricing practices specifically in teams with high fluctuations.
- It must avoid hallucinations, a typical problem in many LLMs. That means that they make up answers that are false or misleading. Particularly in a professional environment, where the solution is used for high-value decisions as is the case of RGM, they need to be highly reliable. This cannot be achieved by the LLM layer alone but must be supported by the data integration, prediction, and optimization layers together. Only this ensures that the LLM does not have access to false results.

In sum, GenAI in RGM must combine different AI layers. LLMs such as ChatGPT or Copilot cannot answer key RGM challenges end-to-end by themselves. Rather, such systems need to have access to specifically designed and trained models for the key tasks of data integration, sales forecasting, and offer optimization. For the LLM itself it is more important to specifically focus on understanding the key terminology of the RGM domain than being able to rephrase a question about net revenue optimization in the form of a Shakespearean sonnet – which would be ChatGPT's specialty.

4.3.3.5 Integrating the RGM GenAI Layers

Figure 4.24 shows the overview of how the four GenAI layers for RGM are stacked on top of each other. The basis are data preparation and validation – for example, via offering users the option to perform *ex post* analyses and to visualize time-series of data. The next layer centers on the Virtual Shopper AI, which integrates all data sources into a central model to predict what shoppers will buy. Then, the offer optimization AI identifies the best offer changes based on the defined preferences. Only in the final step comes the text-based interface, which can range from trivial requests ("Show me what happens, when we increase all prices by 5%") to requests

Figure 4.24 Strategic importance of AI layers

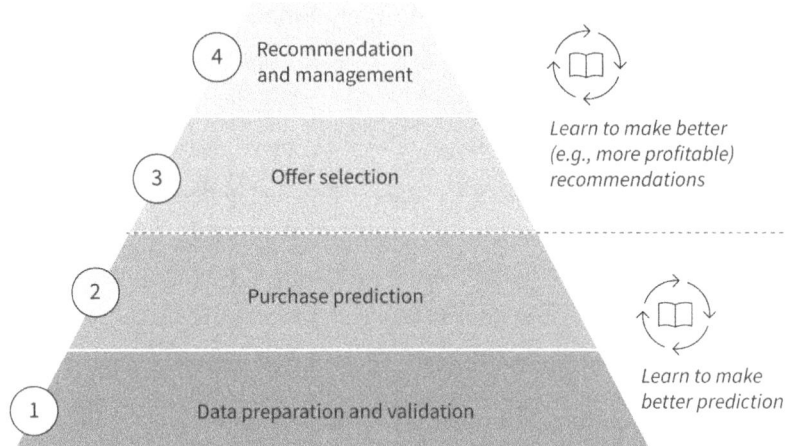

more challenging for the system ("What is the best way to increase net revenue by 5%?").

The bottom two layers need to be trained for precision, both in preparing historical data and using it best for predictions. The top two layers need to be trained to make the most useful recommendations for the organization. Such recommendations not only need to identify options that improve profit and net revenue, but they also need to fit into the overall strategy and consider what can be implemented by sales teams and produced in the factory.

4.3.4   Are AI Agents the Future of RGM?

Over the past months, we have talked to many decision-makers across a broad spectrum of companies, who have been tasked with developing a GenAI strategy for RGM. More recently, Agentic AI – that is the use of AI agents for RGM tasks – has become an increasingly important part of those discussions. This begs the question: Are AI agents the future of RGM, that will automate larger shares of the work currently done by humans or not done at all?

Our perspective, based on the discussions on the previous pages, is summarized in Figure 4.25, which integrates the different forms of AI discussed so far. Here, an AI agent orchestrates the different tasks required for RGM, linking human decision-makers, diverse data sources, and specialized analytical tools to drive integrated, data-driven strategy and execution.

At the top, human stakeholders – such as RGM, marketing, finance, and sales teams – define the objectives and provide strategic context. These inputs, stored in the agent's memory and context layers, ensure that all analytical outputs remain aligned with business goals, such as revenue optimization, market share growth, or trade efficiency. The AI agent continuously ingests and harmonizes data from multiple sources: internal systems (e.g., ERP, POS, CRM), sales data (e.g., sales and promotion data), and external market intelligence (e.g., competitor prices, consumer trends, macroeconomic indicators). This unified data foundation enables the

Figure 4.25 Integration of GenAI, Agentic AI, and agent-based models

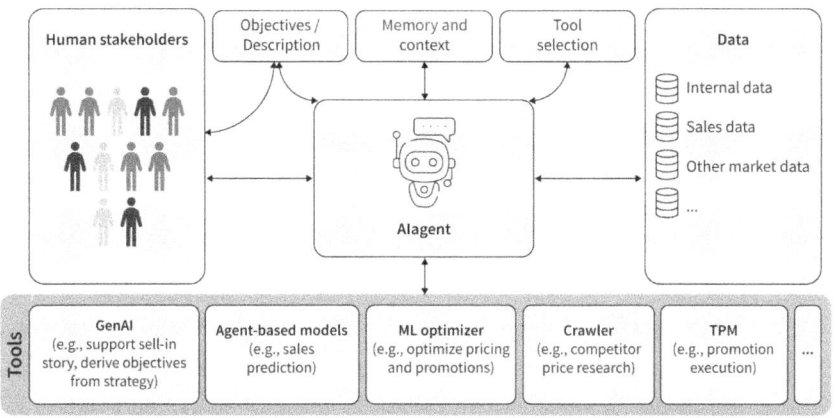

agent to generate actionable insights. Using this information, the AI agent uses a suite of specialized tools, each serving a specific RGM function:

- **GenAI:** Supports storytelling and strategy formulation by generating sell-in stories, executive summaries, and business rationales. It can translate complex analytics into human-readable narratives and derive objectives or KPIs from high-level strategies.
- **Agent-based simulations (e.g., Buynomics' Virtual Shoppers):** Simulates individual shoppers and market behaviors to predict aggregate outcomes, such as sales, (net) revenue, and profit implication under different offer changes. These models capture real-world dynamics like brand switching, cannibalization, and competitive reactions.
- **ML optimizer:** Uses machine learning algorithms to identify the best price, portfolio, and promotion combinations based on the predictions from the agent-based simulations.
- **Crawlers:** Automatically scan, for example, competitor websites, online retailers, and digital platforms to collect pricing, availability, and promotional data. It uses this data in combination with the other data sources such as internal data. This ensures the AI agent stays updated on market shifts and competitive moves in real time.
- **TPM (trade promotion management):** Manages promotion planning, execution, and post-event analysis. It allows the AI agent to implement the identified optimal promotion plans and track actual spend and performance against forecasts, creating a closed feedback loop for continuous improvement.

Together, these tools can form an integrated RGM system, with the AI agent orchestrating many of the activities and preparing actionable recommendations. It acts as a digital copilot that augments human expertise and enables a smarter, more agile approach to RGM. To our knowledge, in 2025 such systems are still mostly in an experimental phase in companies.

However, it should be clear that these systems – most likely combining AI agents, GenAI, and agent-based simulation models – will play an increasingly larger role in pricing and RGM. We expect that specialized solutions for the different tasks will be combined by some integrator or by companies themselves. What parts of these integrated systems are most relevant and strategic will soon become clear.

Will such systems be fully automated without human input? Most likely not anytime soon. Let us look at the process in another field that is easier to digitalize and already went through the complete cycle. In 1997, Deep Blue, the supercomputer built by IBM, beat Garry Kasparov in a six-game competition 3.5–2.5. This was the first time a machine won against a reigning chess world champion. This was a specialized machine built and trained to play against Kasparov. Later, commercially available machines won against subsequent world champions. However, for another 10–15 years, so-called centaurs – teams of computers and humans – outperformed both humans and the best computers alone. Only with the emergence of AI chess engines (such as AlphaZero developed by DeepMind) in the 2010s did machines get better than centaurs – when at the highest level, humans were only adding noise and making the performance of the strongest engines worse. Chess is much narrower in scope than RGM and therefore easier to master for AI. Therefore, we expect humans managing AI tools via AI agents and so on, will be the setup of the most successful companies in the next 10–20 years.

4.4 USE CASES IN RGM FOR CPG COMPANIES

This technology – particularly its prediction and prescription (e.g., optimization) layers – enables numerous use cases beyond pure price changes for practical applications. Here is a selection of use cases.

4.4.1 Trade offs Between RGM Levers

A global snacks producer in the food and beverages industry, with annual revenues exceeding €3 billion, leveraged the Buynomics solution to optimize its pricing and product architecture in the US market. The company faced margin pressure due to a steady rise in cost of goods sold (COGS). Its goal was to better understand price and size elasticities and the pricing implications for both its own and its main competitor's product portfolio changes.

Buynomics was implemented within three months by the company's RGM team. The setup involved integrating key data sources such as sell-out, survey, and product data. The tool enabled the team to model shopper reactions to various pricing and product configuration scenarios, including price-pack architecture (PPA) adjustments.

The use of the Buynomics solution led to a profit uplift of more than 5% and approximately 60% time savings on pricing analyses. The tool empowered teams to test numerous pricing and product-change scenarios efficiently and supported advanced modeling of product dependencies – such as understanding cross-effects and flowback into the company's own brands.

One key insight uncovered was that it was more profitable to reduce pack size rather than increase prices (see Figure 4.26). Traditional pricing tools, relying on static elasticity models, suggested a price increase from $2.49 to $2.79 per 1.0 kg pack, which would have led to suboptimal results. In contrast, the Buynomics solution identified that reducing the pack size to 0.9 kg while keeping the price at $2.49 achieved a higher profit increase from $5.0 million to $5.3 million. This finding demonstrated that de-gramming (reducing pack size) aligned better with shopper price perceptions and preferences, offering a more favorable approach for profit optimization.

Figure 4.26   Price increase vs. de-gramming

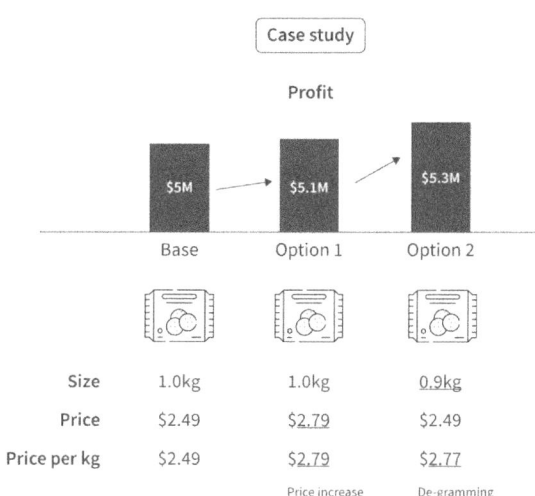

By adopting Buynomics, the snacks producer enhanced its pricing intelligence and strategic decision-making, achieving a sustainable improvement in profitability and operational efficiency. The case highlights how data-driven, simulation-based pricing tools can reveal opportunities traditional methods often cannot identify.

4.4.2   Promotion Fine-Tuning

A leading European beverage company with global operations and annual revenues exceeding €20 billion sought to optimize its promotional strategy. The case was based on the company's German operations, which relied heavily on promotions through top-tier retailers.

The company faced challenges due to its large dependence on promotional sales and the limitations of traditional price elasticity tools. Existing methods lacked precision and flexibility to assess complex promotional variations – such as different combinations of discount levels, product selections, and promotional types. Specifically, they could not capture the cross-effects such as cannibalization between promoted and unpromoted products. This made it difficult to accurately predict shopper reactions and optimize profit outcomes.

Buynomics implemented its simulation-based RGM solution within 12 weeks. The platform integrated key data sources, including sell-out, promotion, and product data, allowing the RGM team to model shopper responses to changes in pricing and promotional mechanics. By leveraging this advanced modeling approach, the company could systematically analyze how different variables – product selection, promotion type, and discount level – interacted to influence sales, revenue, and profit (see Figure 4.27). Buynomics enabled the company to move beyond static metrics like price elasticity or uplift factors. Instead, it evaluated the combined effects of multiple factors, such as:

- Selection of promoted products (e.g., single vs. multiple SKUs)
- Promotion type (e.g., leaflet vs. shelf)
- Discount level (e.g., 20%, 30%, etc.)

Through simulation, the company identified optimal combinations that delivered superior performance compared to status quo promotions, yielding a profit uplift of 3%–5%.

4.4.3 Strategic Pricing Shift from High-Low to EDLP

This case study examines the impact of a strategic shift from a High-Low pricing model to an Every Day Low Price (EDLP) strategy for a leading snacks producer in a large European market. The goal was to understand how the change would affect sales volumes, consumer behavior, and portfolio dynamics within the snacks category.

Figure 4.27　Promotion optimization

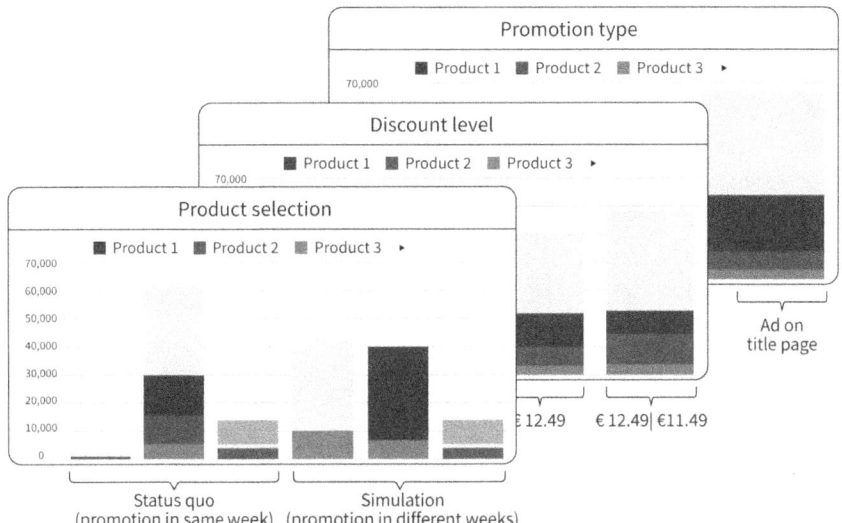

Under the High-Low pricing model, the company alternated between regular prices and periodic promotions. This approach created sales spikes during promotion weeks, as seen in the sharp peaks in Figure 4.28, followed by declines during non-promotional periods. While effective for short-term boosts, this strategy often led to volatility in sales volumes, consumer stockpiling, and inconsistent demand forecasting.

The shift to EDLP aimed to stabilize sales by offering a consistent low price throughout the year, reducing the peaks caused by promotions, while there were still smaller peaks driven by competitors' promotions. The key question for the team was: How would the shift affect (net) revenues and profits? This is difficult to assess with traditional price elasticity and promotional uplift-based solutions. This is, among other effects, because these solutions have difficulties capturing the

Figure 4.28 High-Low pricing vs. EDLP

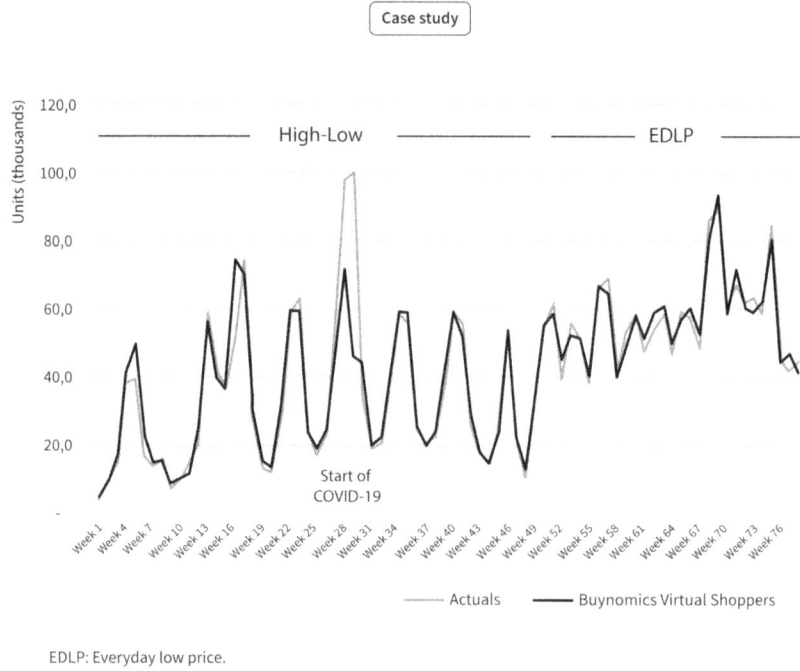

EDLP: Everyday low price.

stocking effects of shoppers after promoted sales that affect unpromoted sales and the cross-effects between promoted and (typically more profitable) unpromoted products in the portfolio. This particularly makes the assessment of the impact on profits very difficult.

According to the analysis modeled with Buynomics' Virtual Shoppers technology and validated by actual results, the transition produced two major outcomes:

- Sales volume increased by approximately 50% for the focus snack product. Consumers responded positively to the consistent low pricing, perceiving it as fair and reliable, which encouraged repeat purchases and improved baseline demand.

- About 40% of the sales gain came from cannibalization within the company's own snack portfolio. In other words, part of the growth in the focus product's sales was offset by declines in smaller or related products, as some consumers shifted their purchases within the same brand family rather than increasing total consumption.

However, this resulted in an overall (net) revenue and profit improvement. The case demonstrates that difficult to assess cases such as moving from a High-Low to an EDLP strategy can strongly benefit from the more precise agent-based modeling – resulting in better decision-making.

4.5 USE CASES IN OTHER INDUSTRIES

So far, this book has focused mostly on the CPG industry. There are many good reasons for this. First, everyone has bought and knows their products. When we present an example with a bar of chocolate, we do not need to explain the importance of its product features. When we used a B2B example with some specific machinery, this is very different. Further, from a pricing and RGM perspective, CPG operates in one of the most data-rich environments. Therefore, we can draw from a broad set of examples including sales prices, surveys, panels, etc. In many other industries, not all of these are available. However, there are also important differences between industries that are relevant for pricing and RGM. Therefore, we want to discuss these for some important examples.[119]

---

[119] Portions of this text were drafted with assistance from ChatGPT5 by OpenAI. This AI tool supported initial research for this sub-chapter. All AI-generated content was carefully reviewed, edited, and approved. The final analysis, conclusions, and interpretations represent my views and expertise. I take full responsibility for the content and accuracy of this work.

4.5.1 Telecommunications (Telco)

RGM in telco is defined by high capital investments and low marginal cost. Operators manage vast fixed-cost infrastructures, while competing in markets where price transparency is high and customer switching costs are low. This creates a structural challenge. The marginal cost of serving another gigabyte of data is low; however, pricing power is limited by intense competition, regulation, and consumer price sensitivity. The core strategic lever for telcos has historically been differentiation through bundling and segmentation. Operators design layered offerings – mixing voice, data, content, and device subsidies – to capture different willingness to pay levels while minimizing churn. However, excessive complexity and legacy plans have led to large catalogs, revenue leakage, and poor price realization. The price waterfall from list price to realized revenue is eroded by promotional discounts, retention offers, and dealer commissions. Best-in-class operators implement disciplined price governance and rely on advanced pricing analytics integrating insights from a wide range of data sources. They aim to improve ARPU (average rate per user) while maintaining perceived price fairness.

Recently, the focus has shifted to monetizing 5G and fiber investments. Telcos globally are experimenting with speed-tiered plans, low-latency enterprise SLAs (service level agreements), and hybrid monetization models for network slicing. Advancements in analytics are enabling micro-segmentation, predictive churn management, and more tailored upselling. The potential next frontier in telco pricing lies in experience-based differentiation – moving from "GB sold" to "value delivered" – as networks become smarter, more automated, and more embedded in digital ecosystems. The Virtual Shoppers technology helps decision-makers address all of these challenges by providing clear visibility on how customers choose between different offers, including variations of existing features, segment-specific offers, and the assessment of innovations.

4.5.2 Automotive

Automotive pricing has long been characterized by high list prices, deep discounts, and structural complexity. RGM must reconcile manufacturing economics, dealer incentives, and consumer price perception. Original equipment manufacturers (OEMs) operate within a multi-tiered distribution chain that makes control over end-user pricing more difficult. The traditional model – that is, the manufacturer recommended retail price (MSRP) is set by OEMs, transaction prices are determined by dealer negotiation – often results in chronic value leakage and poor pricing discipline. Fleet sales, trade-in allowances, and subsidized financing create further dispersion between MSRP and realized price. The typical tool to understand margin leakage is the "price waterfall." It helps identify where incentives, logistics, and dealer markdowns consume margin. Further, OEMs use price elasticity-based pricing to calibrate incentives by trim, region, and vehicle lifecycle.

Globally, the automotive landscape is currently undergoing one of its largest pricing paradigm shifts in decades. The transition to electric vehicles (EVs), direct-to-consumer digital retailing, and software-defined cars is changing what customers pay for – and how. Tesla's dynamic pricing and BYD's rapid market entry have forced incumbents to rethink their offer structure. Agency sales models, pioneered by Mercedes-Benz and Toyota in selected markets, are centralizing pricing authority back to OEMs while preserving dealer relationships for delivery and service. Further, some OEMs experiment with subscription-based features and over-the-air upgrades to add recurring revenue streams. These require careful value communication to avoid customer backlash. With their complex offer structures including vehicle sales using different payment forms, the multitude of options, bundles, trimlines, and aftermarket sales, OEMs can benefit largely from the advanced analytics described in this chapter to better understand the effects of offer changes on sales than the traditional price elasticity solutions still widely in use.

4.5.3 Retail

RGM in retail centers on orchestrating millions of SKUs, frequent price changes, and promotions across digital and physical channels. Challenges arise from high price transparency and the prevalence of discounting. Retailers must balance EDLP strategies against High-Low promotion cycles while managing their price image on known value items (KVIs). The analytical backbone of retail RGM is still price elasticity modeling, including the effects on basket sizes and cross-category substitution. However, effective implementation remains difficult due to incomplete transparency on retail competitors and shoppers' behavior outside the own system. Strategically, leading retailers use price-role frameworks that define which categories drive traffic, which build margin, and which sustain brand positioning.

In recent years, global retail pricing has become both more dynamic and more algorithmic. Inflationary aftereffects, cost volatility, and digital competition are pushing retailers toward AI-enabled dynamic pricing engines and integrated retail media monetization. The most advanced practitioners view RGM not as price optimization in isolation but orchestrating all RGM levers including pricing, assortment, shelf placement, promotions, and supplier collaboration. As loyalty data become more valuable, retailers aim to offer more differentiated prices and rewards for shoppers while protecting their own margins. The Virtual Shoppers technology outlined in this chapter is the ideal framework to better understand and steer these activities to improve performance.

4.5.4 B2B (Business-to-Business)

In B2B industries, RGM is often less about setting the right price than about ensuring that the price is implemented. Complex contract structures, negotiated deals, and unstructured rebates create many opportunities for poor pricing. Sales teams are constantly under pressure to hit volume targets. Therefore, they frequently grant discretionary discounts or extended terms that erode profitability. A strategic RGM approach begins with transparency. The starting point for this is the "price waterfall" from list to pocket price to identify where value is lost. Segmentation based on willingness to pay, cost to serve, and strategic importance can replace simple cost-plus methods. Further, pricing governance frameworks combined with deal-level analytics and CPQ (configure price quote) systems give sales leadership control over approval workflows and negotiation parameters. Value-based pricing is often seen as a strategic lever to link price to measurable outcomes or usage, rather than cost.[120]

In the last years, B2B industries – from industrial components to SaaS and professional services – are converging around data-driven and subscription-based pricing models. Algorithmic quoting tools are surfacing deal anomalies and guiding sales reps toward target corridors. The challenge for practitioners is both technical and cultural: technical, because data transparency, especially on competition, is very low, making it

---

[120] See also our discussion of value-based pricing in Chapter 2.

difficult to determine the right offer; and cultural, because aligning sales incentives to achieve the intended behavior under high intransparency and uncertainty is very difficult. RGM in B2B cases can benefit from the AI-based advancements discussed in this chapter in many ways: first, by integrating insights from the large variety of data sources typical for B2B, and second by providing a framework to properly assess competitive situations with sparse data that allows for systematically more profitable offers.

4.5.5 Hospitality

The hospitality industry embodies yield management complexity with its perishable inventory, high fixed costs, and highly variable demand. Every room-night not sold is lost revenue. RGM here revolves around dynamic pricing, segmentation, and channel management. Hotels must continuously balance rate, occupancy, and distribution cost. Strategically, RGM in hospitality is aimed at optimizing revenue and profit per available room, using predictive analytics and demand forecasting to manage booking curves and overbooking risk. Price integrity remains a key challenge as online travel agencies and search engines create increasing transparency.

Recently, recovery in global travel has reignited competitive pressure, particularly in urban and resort markets. AI-powered revenue management systems are now adjusting rates in real time based on competitor data, demand signals, and local events. Increasing emphasis is put on combining room revenue with ancillary streams such as F&B, experiences, and co-branded credit card partnerships. The future of pricing in hospitality lies in personalization at scale. This includes offering micro-segmented experiences and rates while maintaining a coherent brand promise and avoiding customer distrust. In a next evolutionary stage, when individual Virtual Shoppers are addressable – for example, based on their purchase history – individual optimized offers considering occupancy can be determined at scale to support hotels in steering their offer.

CHAPTER FIVE

WAY AHEAD: THE MARKET-LED ORGANIZATION

We founded Buynomics in 2018 to build the Virtual Shoppers technology and make it accessible to our customers. One of the key moments that motivated me to start developing this technology was a conversation I had with someone in the automotive industry a long time ago. Their pricing challenge was the following: They were a few months before start of sales for a new model series and had a sudden pricing challenge. Before, they had gone through the following process. First, they built a new factory that produced about 200,000 cars per year. This fixed the total sales volume for the series per year. Then, about two to three years before start of production, all the major product details such as engine types were decided. With this, the product portfolio was fixed. Then, about six months before they started selling cars, they noticed that the relationship between their products, sales volumes, and planned prices did not work out. This was when they started thinking about the RGM topics, price and promotion – mostly as a firefighting exercise.

My question then was: How can we improve this process by introducing the RGM perspective earlier. For example, the decisions on what equipment to include in the base model and what to sell as extras, what engine types to start with and how to price them were mostly made from an engineering and procurement perspective – not from an RGM and market perspective. From an RGM perspective, we would, for example, ask how adding features to the base model versus making them optional affects sales distributions across the lineup – and with that revenue and profit. If the market perspective is included from the start, better and more profitable product offers can be decided, which also better consider developments in the competitive landscape during the time from product development to start of sales.

Some years have passed since this conversation, and many fascinating things have happened. The emergence of GenAI technologies has accelerated the progress in RGM. First, it is drawing top management attention to the benefits of and need for technological advancement in RGM using AI and ML solutions. Second, we see real benefits from the application of AI and ML solutions as described in the previous chapter. Specifically, these technologies allow us to better include the market perspective in product development and offer design. This is essential for all industries. To me, this is the true story of RGM: Building the RGM native AI-powered technology that allows teams to better understand what their customers want and design the offers that best align their company's and customers' needs.

Every once in a while, we have the opportunity to witness a fundamental technological shift in a field. This is one of those moments. The technologies outlined in the previous chapter allow companies for the first time to truly understand their customers – not via simplifications such as 3–4 buyer personas, but in their full distribution – and use that knowledge to optimize their offers. With this, companies can become truly market led. A market-led organization is a company whose strategy, products, and operations are driven primarily by the needs and wants of its customers, rather than by internal goals, costs, supply chain, or production needs – as exemplified in the automotive example above.

At Buynomics, we are happy to be a driving force of this paradigm shift – and we hope that others will follow and advance the quality of RGM across industries and regions. RGM is an essential profit and revenue driver in companies. However, as shown in this book, traditional methods and solutions are overly simplistic and lead to expensive mistakes and suboptimal product offers – and they do not scale well into the age of AI. The Virtual Shoppers technology can solve the fundamental problem of how to understand customers and address new use cases essential to the company's commercial success. This results in more accurate, faster, more scalable, leaner, and more data-efficient RGM analytics.

This is just the beginning. I'm looking forward to what's next!

BIBLIOGRAPHY

AlphaSights. (2025). https://www.alphasights.com

Ansoff, H.I. (1965). *Corporate Strategy: An Analytic Approach to Business Policy for Growth and Expansion*. New York: McGraw-Hill.

Ariely, D. (2008). *Predictably Irrational: The Hidden Forces That Shape Our Decisions*. New York: HarperCollins.

Ariely, D. (2009). *Predictably Irrational: The Hidden Forces That Shape Our Decisions*. Revised and expanded edition. New York: Harper Perennial.

Ariely, D. and Kreisler, J. (2017). *Dollars and Sense: How We Misthink Money and How to Spend Smarter*. New York: Harper.

Arthur D. Little Inc. (1970). *The Strategic Condition Matrix*. Arthur D. Little Inc.

Automotive World. (2023). Subscription Services and the Future of Automotive Revenue. *Automotive World*, March.

Baker, W.L., Marn, M.V., and Zawada, C.C. (2010). *The Price Advantage: How to Estimate, Create, and Deliver Superior Value*. 2nd ed. Hoboken, NJ: John Wiley & Sons.

Barron's. (2025). Food Giants' Mergers, Spinoffs & Activism (including Kraft Heinz). [online] Available at: https://www.barrons.com/articles/food-giants-mergers-spinoffs-activist-constellation-nestle-kellogg-kraft-heinz-46dbb75b (accessed November 4, 2025).

BBC News. (2007). Apple in iPhone Price Cut Apology. Available at: http://news.bbc.co.uk/1/hi/business/6982717.stm.

Belobaba, P., Odoni, A.R., and Barnhart, C. (2015). *The Global Airline Industry*. 2nd ed. Chichester: Wiley.

Beverage Marketing. (2025). Bottled Water. Available at: https://www.beveragemarketing.com/shop/bottled-water.aspx.

Bonabeau, E. (2002). Agent-Based Modeling: Methods and Techniques for Simulating Human Systems. *Proceedings of the National Academy of Sciences*, 99(3), pp. 7280–7287.

Boston Consulting Group (BCG). (2023). How Digital & AI Will Reshape Health Care in 2025. Available at: https://www.bcg.com/publications/2025/digital-ai-solutions-reshape-health-care-2025 (accessed September 19, 2025).

Boston Consulting Group (BCG). (2025). Agentic AI Redefines Consumer Journeys. Available at: https://www.bcg.com/publications/2025/agentic-ai-redefines-consumer-journeys.

Bradford, A. (2021). Lyft vs. Uber: Which Is Better? *Investopedia*. Available at: https://www.investopedia.com/lyft-vs-uber-which-is-better-5186795 (accessed November 7, 2025).

Brand, J., Israeli, A., and Ngwe, D. (2024). Using LLMs for Market Research. *Harvard Business School Working Paper No. 23-062* (revised July 2024). Available at: https://www.hbs.edu/ris/Publication%20Files/23-062_ed720ebc-ec4d-4bc3-a6ba-bad8cfbd9d51.pdf.

Brennen, S. and Kreiss, D. (2016). Digitalization. In K. Jensen, R. Craig, J. Pooley, and E. Rothenbuhler (Eds.), *The International Encyclopedia of Communication Theory and Philosophy*. Hoboken, NJ: Wiley.

Broeder, P. and Wentink, E. (2022). Limited-time Scarcity and Competitive Arousal in E-commerce. *Journal of Electronic Commerce Research*, 32(5), pp. 549–567.

Brynjolfsson, E. and Kahin, B. (2002). *Understanding the Digital Economy: Data, Tools, and Research*. Cambridge, MA: MIT Press.

Brynjolfsson, E. and McAfee, A. (2017). The business of AI: What it can — and cannot — do. *Harvard Business Review*, 95(4), 3–11.

Bubeck, S., Chandrasekaran, V., Eldan, R., Gehrke, J., Horvitz, E., et al. (2023). Sparks of Artificial General Intelligence: Early Experiments with GPT-4. *arXiv preprint* arXiv:2303.12712. https://doi.org/10.48550/arXiv.2303.12712.

Buynomics. (2023). The Truth About Elasticities. Webinar.

Buynomics. (2025a). Webinar Surveys 2025. [online] Available at: https://www.buynomics.com/ (accessed November 4, 2025).

Buynomics. (2025b). Buy vs. Build: What Is Right for Your RGM Team. [blog] Available at: https://www.buynomics.com/articles/buy-vs-build-what-is-right-for-your-rgm-team.

Camerer, C.F. (2011). *Behavioral Game Theory: Experiments in Strategic Interaction*. Princeton, NJ: Princeton University Press.

Chen, H., Hardesty, D.M., Rao, A.R., and Bolton, L.E. (2021). Introduction to Special Issue on Behavioral Pricing. *Journal of the Association for Consumer Research*, 6(1), pp. 4–9.

Chow, S.-C., Shao, J., and Wang, H. (2017). *Sample Size Calculations in Clinical Research*. Boca Raton: CRC Press.

Chrzan, K. and Orme, B.K. (2019). *Applied MaxDiff: A Practitioner's Guide to Best–Worst Scaling*. Provo, UT: Sawtooth Software.

Clarke, M. and Smith, B. (2004). Impact of Operations Research on the Evolution of the Airline Industry. *Journal of Aircraft*, 41(1), pp. 62–72.

Cohen, J. (1988). *Statistical Power Analysis for the Behavioral Sciences*. 2nd ed. Hillsdale, NJ: Lawrence Erlbaum Associates.

Danu, N. (2021). *Dynamic Pricing Strategies: Uber and Lyft Compared*. SmartData Collective.

Deloitte. (2025). Revenue Growth Management Magnifying for the Consumer Products Industry. Available at: https://www.deloitte.com/us/en/Industries/consumer/articles/revenue-growth-management-magnifying-for-consumer-products-industry.html (accessed December 24, 2025).

Dholakia, U. (2017). *How to Price Effectively: A Guide for Managers and Entrepreneurs*. Houston, TX: Rice University Business.

Dyson, F.J. (1949). *Advanced Quantum Mechanics*. Lecture notes, Princeton University.

Dyson, F. (2004). A Meeting with Enrico Fermi. *Nature*, 427(6972), p. 297.

Eisen, M. (April 22, 2011). Amazon's $23,698,655.93 Book about Flies. *Michael Eisen Blog*. https://www.michaeleisen.org/blog/?p=358.

Epstein, J.M. (2014). *Agent_Zero: Toward Neurocognitive Foundations for Generative Social Science*. Princeton, NJ: Princeton University Press.

European Commission. (2023). Annual Inflation More Than Tripled in the EU in 2022. Eurostat. Available at: https://ec.europa.eu/eurostat/web/products-eurostat-news/w/DDN-20230309-2.

EY. (n.d.). Agentic AI: The Future of Autonomous Consumer Products. [online] Available at: https://www.ey.com/en_us/insights/consumer-products/agentic-ai-the-future-of-autonomous-consumer-products (accessed December 24, 2025).

Foley, J. (2025). What Eggflation Teaches Us About Must-Have Goods. *Financial Times*, February 15.

Forrester. (2025) *The Forrester Wave™: Recurring Billing Solutions, Q1 2025*. Forrester Research.

Fortune. (2025). MIT Report: 95 Percent of Generative AI Pilots at Companies Failing, CFO. [online] Available at: https://fortune.com/2025/08/18/mit-report-95-percent-generative-ai-pilots-at-companies-failing-cfo/ (accessed November 4, 2025).

FRED Blog. (2024). FRED Blog. Available at: https://fredblog.stlouisfed.org/2024/05/page/2/.

Gabor, A. and Granger, C.W.J. (1979). Price Sensitivity of the Consumer. *Management Decision*, 17(8), pp. 569–575.

Gartner. (2024). Market Guide for Retail Unified Price, Promotion & Markdown Optimization (UPPMO).

Gartner. (2025a). Market Guide for B2B Profit Optimization Software, April 9.

Gartner. (2025b). Market Guide for CSP Revenue Management and Monetization Solutions, March 5.

Gartner. (n.d.a). Configure, Price and Quote (CPQ) Application Suites. Available at: https://www.gartner.com/reviews/market/configure-price-quote-applications (accessed October 2025).

Gartner. (n.d.b) Gartner Hype Cycle Methodology. [online] Available at: https://www.gartner.com/en/research/methodologies/gartner-hype-cycle (accessed November 4, 2025).

Genpact. (n.d.). How Consumer Goods Companies Can Use Agentic AI. [online] Available at: https://www.genpact.com/insight/how-consumer-goods-companies-can-use-agentic-ai (accessed December 24, 2025).

GLG Insights. (2025). https://glginsights.com.

Green, P.E. and Srinivasan, V. (1975). Conjoint Measurement for Quantifying Judgmental Data. *Journal of Marketing Research*, 12(1), pp. 103–107.

Green, P.E. and Srinivasan, V. (1990). Conjoint Analysis in Marketing: New Developments with Implications for Research and Practice. *Journal of Marketing*, 54(4), pp. 3–19. https://doi.org/10.1177/002224299005400402.

Hawkins, A.J. (2015). How Does Uber's Surge Pricing Work? The Verge.

Henderson, B.D. (1970). The Product Portfolio. *Boston Consulting Group (BCG Perspectives)*, January 1, 1970.

Hinterhuber, A. (2016). The Six Pricing Myths That Kill Profits. *Business Horizons*, 59(1), pp. 71–83. https://doi.org/10.1016/j.bushor.2015.09.002.

Husemann-Kopetzky, M. (2017). *Handbook on the Psychology of Pricing*. Norderstedt: Books on Demand.

IDC (2024). Retail Promotions Management 2024–2025. IDC MarketScape Report.

International Cocoa Organization. (2025). *Statistics*. https://www.icco.org/statistics (accessed May 16, 2025).

Johnson, E.J. and Goldstein, D. (2003). Do Defaults Save Lives? *Science*, 302(5649), pp. 1338–1339.

Kahneman, D. (2011). *Thinking, Fast and Slow*. New York: Farrar, Straus and Giroux.

Kahneman, D. (2017). *Thinking, Fast and Slow*. London: Penguin Books.

Kahneman, D., Knetsch, J.L., and Thaler, R.H. (1990). Experimental Tests of the Endowment Effect and the Coase Theorem. *Journal of Political Economy*, 98(6), pp. 1325–1348. https://doi.org/https://doi.org/10.1086/261737.

Kaplan, R.S. and Norton, D.P. (1996). *The Balanced Scorecard: Translating Strategy into Action*. Boston: Harvard Business School Press.

Kennedy, P. (2008). *A Guide to Econometrics*. 6th ed. Malden, MA: Blackwell Publishing.

Klein, B. (2020). The Subscription Software Economy. *Harvard Business Review*, June.

Kohavi, R., Tang, D., and Xu, Y. (2020). *Trustworthy Online Controlled Experiments: A Practical Guide to A/B Testing*. Cambridge: Cambridge University Press.

Kotler, P. and Armstrong, G. (2020). *Principles of Marketing*. 18th ed. Boston: Pearson.

Kotler, P. and Keller, K.L. (2005). *Marketing Management*. 12th ed. Harlow: Prentice-Hall/Pearson.

Kotler, P. and Keller, K.L. (2022). *Marketing Management*. 16th ed. Harlow: Pearson Education.

Lang, A. (2014). *Quoted in The Oxford Dictionary of Quotations*, 8th ed. Oxford: Oxford University Press.

LeBoeuf, M. (1985). *The Greatest Management Principle in the World*. New York: G.P. Putnam's Sons.

Lindstrom, M. (2008). *Buyology: Truth and Lies About Why We Buy*. New York: Doubleday.

Liozu, S.M. (2020). *The Pricing Journey: Leading and Transforming Your Pricing Function*. New York: Routledge.

Louviere, J.J., Flynn, T.N., and Marley, A.A.J. (2015). *Best–Worst Scaling: Theory, Methods and Applications*. Cambridge: Cambridge University Press.

Malik, S.-A. (2010). *Optimising Supermarket Promotions of Fast Moving Consumer Goods (FMCG)*. Saarbrücken: LAP Lambert Academic Publishing.

Marn, M.V. and Rosiello, R.L. (1992). Managing Price, Gaining Profit. *Harvard Business Review,* 70(5), pp. 84–94.

Mars. 2024. Mars to Acquire Kellanova. [online] Available at: https://www.nasdaq.com/press-release/mars-acquire-kellanova-2024-08-14 (accessed November 4, 2025).

Marshall, A. (2009)[1890]. *Principles of Economics.* 8th ed. London: Palgrave Macmillan.

Marx, K. (1867). *Das Kapital.*

Mas-Colell, A., Whinston, M.D., and Green, J.R. (1995) *Microeconomic Theory.* New York: Oxford University Press.

McCorduck, P. (2004). *Machines Who Think: A Personal Inquiry into the History and Prospects of Artificial Intelligence.* Natick, MA: A.K. Peters.

McKinsey. (n.d.). One Year of Agentic AI: Six Lessons from the People Doing the Work. [online] Available at: https://www.mckinsey.com/capabilities/quantumblack/our-insights/one-year-of-agentic-ai-six-lessons-from-the-people-doing-the-work (accessed November 4, 2025).

McKinsey & Company. 1970. *The GE–McKinsey Nine-Box Matrix.* New York: McKinsey & Company.

McKinsey & Company. (2019a). *Revenue Growth Management: The Next Horizon.* McKinsey Insights, 16 October. Available at: https://www.mckinsey.com/capabilities/growth-marketing-and-sales/our-insights/revenue-growth-management-the-next-horizon.

McKinsey & Company. 2019b. *Revenue Growth Management: The Strategy That Unlocks Profitable Growth.* New York: McKinsey & Company.

Mohammed, R. (2013). *The Art of Pricing: How to Find the Hidden Profits to Grow Your Business.* New York: McGraw-Hill.

Monroe, K.B. (2003). *Pricing: Making Profitable Decisions.* 3rd ed. New York: McGraw-Hill.

Mordor Intelligence. (2025). Price Optimization Software Market Report, 2025.

Mullainathan, S. and Shafir, E. (2013) *Scarcity: Why Having Too Little Means So Much.* New York: Times Books.

Nagle, T.T., Hogan, J.E., and Zale, J. (2016). *The Strategy and Tactics of Pricing.* 5th ed. New York: Routledge.

Nagle, T.T. and Müller, G. (2018). *The Strategy and Tactics of Pricing: A Guide to Growing More Profitably.* 6th ed. New York: Routledge/Taylor & Francis Group.

Nagle, T.T., Müller, G., and Gruyaert, E. (2017). *The Strategy and Tactics of Pricing: A Guide to Growing More Profitably.* 6th ed. London: Routledge.

Nagle, T.T., Müller, G., and Gruyaert, E. (2023). *The Strategy and Tactics of Pricing: A Guide to Growing More Profitably*. 7th ed. London: Routledge.

Ng, I.C.L., Parry, G., and Wild, P. (2013). Innovation in Services and Hybrid Offerings: Rolls-Royce's Power by the Hour. *Cambridge Service Alliance Working Paper*, University of Cambridge.

Nilsson, N.J. (2010). *The Quest for Artificial Intelligence: A History of Ideas and Achievements*. Cambridge: Cambridge University Press.

Nisbett, R.E. and Wilson, T.D. (1977). The Halo Effect: Evidence for Unconscious Alteration of Judgments. *Journal of Personality and Social Psychology*, 35(4), pp. 250–256.

NVIDIA Developer Blog. (n.d.). How to Get Better Outputs from Your Large Language Model. Available at: https://developer.nvidia.com/blog/how-to-get-better-outputs-from-your-large-language-model/.

OpenAI. (2023). GPT-4 Technical Report. March. arXiv:2303.08774. https://arxiv.org/abs/2303.08774.

OpenAI. (2025). Introducing GPT-5. August 7. https://openai.com/index/introducing-gpt-5/.

Orme, B.K. (2014). *Getting Started with Conjoint Analysis: Strategies for Product Design and Pricing Research*. 4th ed. Madison, WI: Research Publishers LLC.

Osborne, M.J. (2003). *An Introduction to Game Theory*. Oxford: Oxford University Press.

Osterwalder, A. and Pigneur, Y. (2010). *Business Model Generation: A Handbook for Visionaries, Game Changers, and Challengers*. Hoboken, NJ: John Wiley & Sons.

Phillips, R.L. (2021). *Pricing and Revenue Optimization*. 2nd ed. Stanford, CA: Stanford Business Books.

Popper, K. (1959). *The Logic of Scientific Discovery*. New York: Basic Books.

Promotion Optimization Institute and Deloitte. *Reshaping Commercial Priorities: A Guide to Help Consumer Packaged Goods (CPG) Manufacturers Craft Their Path to Trade Transformation in a Time of Changing Consumer Preferences*. Bardonia. NY: Promotion Optimization Institute, 2023.

Ramanujam, M. and Tacke, G. (2016). *Monetizing Innovation: How Smart Companies Design the Product Around the Price*. Hoboken, NJ: John Wiley & Sons.

Reuters. (2025). Kraft Heinz Splits Itself in Bid to Revive Growth. [online] Available at: https://www.reuters.com/sustainability/sustainable-finance-reporting/kraft-heinz-splits-itself-bid-revive-growth-2025-09-02.

Ricardo, D. (1817). *On the Principles of Political Economy and Taxation*. John Murray.

Rumelt, R.P. (2011). *Good Strategy, Bad Strategy: The Difference and Why It Matters*. Boston: Crown Business.

Russell, S. and Norvig, P. (2021). *Artificial Intelligence: A Modern Approach*. 4th ed. Boston: Pearson.

Science.org. (n.d.). Author Tokens: ST-155. Available at: https://www.science.org/stoken/author-tokens/ST-1550/full (accessed October 8, 2025).

Shipley, D. and Jobber, P. (2012). *Marketing and Pricing Strategy*. London: Routledge.

Shotton, R. (2018). *The Choice Factory: 25 Behavioural Biases That Influence What We Buy*. London: Harriman House.

Silver, D., Huang, A., Maddison, C.J., Guez, A., Sifre, L., et al. (2016). Mastering the Game of Go with Deep Neural Networks and Tree Search. *Nature*, 529(7587), pp. 484–489. https://doi.org/10.1038/nature16961.

Simon, H. (2015). *Confessions of the Pricing Man: How Price Affects Everything*. Cham, Switzerland: Springer-Gabler.

Simon, H. and Fassnacht, M. (2019). *Price Management: Strategy, Analysis, Decision, Implementation*. Cham, Switzerland: Springer.

Simon-Kucher and Partners. (2019). *A Practical Guide to Pricing*. Bonn: Simon-Kucher & Partners.

Singh, S. and Sharma, R.D. (2019). Impact of Sales Promotion Techniques on Consumers Towards FMCG. *International Journal of Research and Analytical Reviews*, 6(1), pp. 923–930.

Smith, J. (2021). Understanding the RACI Matrix: Defining Roles and Responsibilities. *Project Management Journal*, 52(3), pp. 45–52.

Smith, T.J. (2013). *Pricing: The Third Business Skill: Principles of Price Management*. London: Kogan Page.

Statista. (2025). Unadjusted Monthly Inflation Rate in the U.S. Statista. Available at: https://www.statista.com/statistics/273418/unadjusted-monthly-inflation-rate-in-the-us/.

Strategy&/PwC. (2017). *Zero-Based Trade for CPG Leaders*. Available at: https://www.strategyand.pwc.com/gx/en/insights/2017/zero-based-trade-for-cpg-leaders/zero-based-trade-for-cpg-leaders.pdf (accessed December 24, 2025).

Tegus. (2025). https://www.tegus.com/.

Thain, G. and Bradley, J. (2016). *FMCG: The Power of Fast-Moving Consumer Goods*. London: Kogan Page.

Thaler, R.H. (1980). Toward a Positive Theory of Consumer Choice. *Journal of Economic Behavior and Organization*, 1(1), pp. 39–60. https://doi.org/10.1016/0167-2681(80)90051-7.

Thaler, R.H. and Sunstein, C.R. (2008). *Nudge: Improving Decisions About Health, Wealth, and Happiness*. New Haven, CT: Yale University Press.

Tilson, D., Lyytinen, K., and Sørensen, C. (2010). Digital Infrastructures: The Missing IS Research Agenda. *Information Systems Research*, 21(4), pp. 748–759.

Trading Economics. (n.d.). Global Economic Indicators. [online] Available from: https://tradingeconomics.com/ (accessed November 4, 2025).

Turing, A.M. (1950). Computing Machinery and Intelligence. *Mind*, 59(236), pp. 433–460.

Tversky, A. and Kahneman, D. (1974). Judgment Under Uncertainty: Heuristics and Biases. *Science*, 185(4157), pp. 1124–1131.

UK Government. (2025). Restricting Promotions of Products High in Fat, Sugar or Salt by Location and by Volume/Price: Implementation Guidance. Available at: https://www.gov.uk/government/publications/restricting-promotions-of-products-high-in-fat-sugar-or-salt-by-location-and-by-volume-price/restricting-promotions-of-products-high-in-fat-sugar-or-salt-by-location-and-by-volume-price-implementation-guidance.

Van Westendorp, P.H. (1976). NSS Price Sensitivity Meter (PSM) – A New Approach to Study Consumer Perception of Price. *Proceedings of the 29th ESOMAR Congress*, Venice, 5–9 September 1976, pp. 139–167.

Vriens, M., ed. (2014). *Applied Conjoint Analysis*. Heidelberg: Springer. https://doi.org/10.1007/978-3-642-56706-7

Wall Street Journal. (2025). Kraft Heinz Is Splitting into Two Companies. [online] Available at: https://www.wsj.com/business/retail/kraft-heinz-is-splitting-into-two-companies-2b632fa7 (accessed November 4, 2025).

Westerman, G., Bonnet, D., and McAfee, A. (2014). *Leading Digital: Turning Technology into Business Transformation*. Boston, MA: Harvard Business Review Press.

Wilde, O. (1891). *The Picture of Dorian Gray*. London: Ward, Lock and Company.

Winer, R.S. (1986). A Reference Price Model of Brand Choice for Frequently Purchased Products. *Journal of Consumer Research*, 13(2), pp. 250–256. https://doi.org/10.1086/209067.

Wooldridge, J.M. (2020). *Introductory Econometrics: A Modern Approach*. 7th ed. Boston: Cengage Learning.

World Bank. (2016). *World Development Report: Digital Dividends*. Washington, DC: World Bank.

Zatta, D. (2022). *The Pricing Model Revolution: How Pricing Will Change the Way We Sell and Buy On and Offline*. Hoboken, NJ: John Wiley & Sons.

Zatta, D. and Kraus, M. (2022). *Pricing Decoded: How Leading Pricing Practitioners Manage Price to Boost Profits*. London: Kogan Page.

Zhou, J., Lu, J., and Shallah, A. (2023). All About Sample-Size Calculations for A/B Testing: Novel Extensions & Practical Guide. *Proceedings of the 32nd ACM International Conference on Information and Knowledge Management (CIKM '23)*, Birmingham, UK, October 21–25, pp. 3574–3583. https://doi.org/10.1145/3583780.3614779.

ABOUT THE AUTHOR

Dr. Ingo Reinhardt is a recognized expert in pricing and revenue growth management (RGM). He holds Master's degrees in management and mathematics, and earned his PhD in management from the University of Cologne. He was a postdoctoral researcher at the University of Oxford and has published in leading journals, including the *Strategic Management Journal*.

Ingo began his industry career at global consultancy Simon-Kucher & Partners, where he advised international clients on pricing and commercial strategy. He later co-founded Buynomics, a SaaS company revolutionizing RGM decision-making through its Virtual Shoppers AI technology.

Ingo frequently speaks at industry conferences and holds expert webinars on pricing and RGM topics. He has authored numerous thought leadership whitepapers and academic publications on RGM and pricing strategy.

INDEX

A

ABM. *See* agent-based modeling (ABM)
AB test, 54–58, 128
active triggers, 157
ADL Matrix, 153
agent-based modeling (ABM), 210–211
agent-based simulations, 236
Agentic AI, 204, 209–210, 234–237
AI. *See* artificial intelligence (AI)
align channel strategy, 114
AlphaGo, 206
AlphaSights, 71
analytics, 158–160
   data and, 114
   teams, 175
Ansoff, H. Igor, 144
AOL, pricing strategy, 140
Apple, 4
arc elasticity, 33
Ardensi's Pricing Strategy Summits, 132, 133

Ariely, Dan, 92
ARPU. *See* average revenue per user (ARPU)
artificial intelligence (AI), 1, 5, 205, 250
   applications, 208
   holistic optimization, 10
   model for RGM, 214
   powered revenue management systems, 248
   in RGM, 222–224
      core challenges, 212–222
   types, 211
      agent-based modeling (ABM), 210–211
      Agentic AI, 204, 209–210
      Generative AI (GenAI), 203–209
automated price elasticity engines, 118
automotive landscape, 245
automotive pricing, 81, 245–246, 248
autonomous local teams, 180–181
average revenue per user (ARPU), 81

INDEX

B

B2B. *See* business-to-business (B2B)
bad pricing strategy, 136
balanced scorecard (BSC), 168, 170–172
BCG growth-market share matrix, 153
behavioral economics, 40–44
behavioral effects, 128
behavioral pricing, 43, 91–97
benchmarking, 173
BMW, 116
bonus elements, 110, 112
Brand, J., 226
BSC. *See* balanced scorecard (BSC)
business-to-business (B2B)
    cases, 38
    industries, 81
    pricing, 71, 119
    profit and price optimization
        software, 119
    RGM in, 247–248
business-to-consumer (B2C) cases, 38
Buynomics, 5, 96, 98, 100, 142, 160, 188, 216, 222, 226, 230, 236, 238–240
    Virtual Shoppers
        technology, 242–243

C

capital markets, 45–46
Carmakers, 116
CBC. *See* choice-based conjoint (CBC)
Center of Excellence (CoE), 175
    and local execution, 179

Certified Pricing Professional (CPP)
    credential, 131
channel mix approach, 113–114
ChatGPT, 205, 207
choice-based conjoint (CBC), 70
churn reduction, 81
cloud platforms, 190
COGS. *See* cost of goods sold (COGS)
commodity price volatility, 147
company
    desire for consistency, international
        price coordination, 182
    RGM roles in, 18–19
competitive pricing, 85–87
competitor, 77
    analysis, 79–80
    insights, 81–82
    matrix of competitive advantages, 77
    perspective, 170
    value map, 77–78
competitor price change
    effects of, 35
    price elasticity dependent on, 36
complexity, optimization, 229
configure-price-quote (CPQ)
    applications, 119
conjoint analysis method, 66–70
consistent brand positioning,
    international price
    coordination, 181
constraints, optimization, 229
consumer behavior shifts, 195
coordinating prices, 181

Index

corporate objectives, statements of, 147
corporate strategy, 141, 144, 145, 168, 174
cost of goods sold (COGS), 238
cost-plus pricing, 84–85
costs matter, for profit optimization, 121–122
cost-to-serve, profitability and, 114
crawlers, 236
cultural institutions, 191
customer
   differentiation, 82
   leveraging, 9
   segments/markets, 8–9
cutting prices, 10
cybersecurity, 191

D

data and analytics, 114
data-driven decision-making, 195
data integration, 224–226
data sources, 199, 200
decision, 160–164, 200–201, 250
decision autonomy, 181
decision-making, 42
   data-driven, 195
   good, 3
decoy pricing, 43
Deep Blue supercomputer, 237
default nudge, 92
demand
   elastic, 31
   isoelastic, 23, 27–29
   inelastic, 31
   linear
      function, 21, 22, 27, 29
      point price elasticity for, 31–32
   price elasticity of, 29–34
   and virtual shoppers, 216
demand functions, 24
   empirical, 24
   linear, 21, 22, 27, 29
   microeconomics, 21–29
differentiation, RGM strategy, 151–155
digitalization, 188
   benefits of, 191
   in education, 191
   in healthcare, 191
   history of, 192
   journey of, 189
   origins of, 190
   requirement, 190
digital platforms, 191
digital transformation, 189
digitization, 188–189
discount elements, 110, 111
division-embedded RGM teams, 175

E

ease of use, RGM levers, 155
economics
   behavioral, 40–44
   microeconomics, 20–40
ecosystem, global, 131
education, digitalization in, 191
elastic demand, 31

elasticity-based pricing, 118
electric vehicles (EVs), 141, 245
empirical demand functions, 24, 27
endowment effect, 95
environment perspective, 170
EPP, 131, 134
    Global Pricing and Revenue Management Forum, 133
Every Day Low Price (EDLP) strategy, 240–242
EVS. *See* explained variance in sales (EVS)
Excel tools, 118
execution, RGM, 158
    analytics, 158–160
    decisions, 160–164
    implementation, 165–166
expert judgment, pricing research, 71–79
    price elasticity assessment, 72–74
    value driver/attribute assessment, 74–79
explained variance in sales (EVS), 50
isoelastic demand, 23, 28, 29
export market, 184

F

fast moving consumer goods (FMCG), 11, 80–82, 113–115, 118, 134
fear of missing out (FOMO), 94
financial perspective, 170
financial services, 190
fixed costs, 122
FMCG. *See* fast moving consumer goods (FMCG)
FOMO. *See* fear of missing out (FOMO)
food pricing, 84
foundations and strategy matter, 206
free knowledge sharing, 181
free-market societies, modern, 1

G

Gabor, André, 62–63
Gabor–Granger method, 62–64, 96
GenAI. *See* Generative AI (GenAI)
Generative AI (GenAI), 203–209, 250
    layers for RGM, 233–234
Gerson Lehrman Group (GLG), 71
global ecosystem, 131
global guardrails and strategy, 179–180
global pricing community, 132
global, regional, local price coordination, 183
global retail pricing, 246
global RGM governance types, 179–181
global strategy and execution, RGM governance, 180–181
global team, RGM, 180–181
good pricing strategy, 136
good strategy, 136, 137, 140
Good Strategy, Bad Strategy (Rumelt), 137
Granger, Clive W.J., 62–63

gray market
  assessment, 185
  avoidance of, 182
  share, 182, 183
gross margin growth, 149

H
Halo effect, 223
healthcare, digitalization in, 191
Heinz, Kraft, 145
heuristics
  anchoring, 43
  substitution, 42–43
high fat, sugar, or salt (HFSS), 45
High-Low pricing model, 240, 241
  vs Every Day Low Price (EDLP) strategy, 242
high price elasticities, 154
homo oeconomicus vs homo sapiens, 41
hospitality industry, RGM in, 248
human and AI partnership, 206

I
immersive technologies, 191
implementation phase, portfolio optimization, 160, 165–166
import market, 184
improvement, RGM, 166–167
  learning, 171–173
  monitoring, 167–171
  strategy update, 173–174
independent optimization, 184

indifference price point (IPP), 61
inelastic demand, 31
inflation, 4, 45–47, 54–56, 80, 81, 155, 195
INFORMS Revenue Management and Pricing Section Conference, 133
integrated e-commerce ecosystem, 190
integration of different data inputs, 158
international price, 182
  consistency, 151
  coordination, 179, 181
international retailer buying groups, 182
IPP. See indifference price point (IPP)

J
Jobs, Steve, 4

K
Kahneman, Daniel, 40–42
key account management (KAM), 176
key performance indicators (KPIs), 138, 167, 169
key products, performance of, 75
knowledge sharing sessions, 173
known value items (KVIs), 246
KPIs. See key performance indicators (KPIs)
KPI tracking and gap analysis, 173
KVIs. See known value items (KVIs)

L

Lang, Andrew, 127
large language models (LLMs), 207, 208, 212, 222, 231
launching new products/services, 9
learning, RGM, 171–173
lifecycle pricing, 81
lifetime value, 81
limited-time promotions, 94–95
linear demand
  function, 21, 22, 27, 29
  point price elasticity for, 31–32
linear regression analysis, 49, 51
list prices, 156, 162, 163
LLMs. *See* large language models (LLMs)
local teams, autonomous, 180–181
low price elasticities, 154
Lyft, 3

M

machine learning (ML), 1, 5, 48, 250
  algorithms, 118
  optimizer, 236
macroeconomic effects, on pricing and RGM, 44–46
manager
  pricing, 19, 43
  revenue. *See* revenue manager
RGM, 97, 104, 158, 188, 218, 229
manufacturer recommended retail price (MSRP), 245
marginal cost, 244

margin pressures, 195
market
  avoidance of gray, 182
  capital, 45–46
  export, 184
  gray market
    assessment, 185
    share, 182, 183
  import, 184
market data assessment, 48–58
  AB tests, 54–58
  multivariate regression analysis, 52–54
  regression analysis, 48–52
market dynamics, price elasticity depends on, 36–37
marketing campaigns, 10
market-led organization, 251
market price, 3
market share optimization, 16
Marshall, Alfred, 2, 20
Marx, Karl, 38
maximum difference (MaxDiff) survey method, 63–66
McKinsey & Company, 100
McKinsey Matrix, 153
mental accounting, 41
microeconomics, 20–21
  demand functions, 21–29
  multiple products, challenges, 34–37
  note on value, 38–40
  price elasticity of demand, 29–34
Microsoft Copilot, 222, 223, 231

Index

micro-transactions, 116
minimum margin, 151
minimum prices, 151
ML. *See* machine learning (ML)
model parameters vs model performance, 215
modern free-market societies, 1
monitoring, key performance indicators, 167–171
monopoly (one supplier), 20
MSRP. *See* manufacturer recommended retail price (MSRP)
multiple products, challenges with, 34–37
multivariate regression analysis, for promotion analysis, 52–54

N

net revenue, 149, 152
    targets per category and channel, 154
new product pricing, 4
non-negotiables, 179
no or limited knowledge sharing, 181
Nudge: Improving Decisions About Health, Wealth, and Happiness (Thaler and Sunstein), 42

O

objective function, 229
OBPPC framework, 100
OEMs. *See* original equipment manufacturers (OEMs)

offer optimization, 228–231
oil lamps, pricing strategy, 141–142
oligopolistic competition (few suppliers), 20
OLS analysis. *See* ordinary least square (OLS) analysis
OPP. *See* optimal price point (OPP)
optimal price point (OPP), 61
optimization
    costs matter for profit, 121–122
    criteria, 28
    price, 2
optimize profit, 26
optimizing prices
    profit, 24–26
    revenue, 24, 26
orchestrate portfolio and execution, 114
ordinary least square (OLS) analysis, 49–50
organizers, societies and professional, 131–132
original equipment manufacturers (OEMs), 245

P

pay-per-unit, pricing models, 115–116
The Picture of Dorian Gray (Wilde), 38
planning phase, portfolio optimization, 160
playbook, 11–12, 186
POI. *See* Promotion Optimization Institute (POI)
point elasticity, 31

271

point of sale (PoS), 104
point price elasticity, for linear
        demand, 31–32
polypolistic competition (many
        suppliers), 20
Popper, Karl, 213
Porsche, 116
portfolio, 156
    optimization, 160, 162, 165–166
PoS. *See* point of sale (PoS)
postmortem/after-action reviews, 173
power of free, 92–93
PPA. *See* price-pack architecture (PPA)
PPS. *See* Professional Pricing
        Society (PPS)
Predictably Irrational (Ariely), 92
price
    anchor, 93–94
    decisions, 195
    increases, 195, 198, 199
        vs de-gramming, 239
    levels, 181
    monitoring and competitor
        intelligence tools, 119
    profit-optimal, 121
    profit optimizing, 24–26
    recommendations from pricing
        methods, 98
    revenue optimizing, 24, 26
    setting, 8
price changes, competitor
    effects of, 35
    price elasticity dependent on, 36

price elasticity, 4, 35, 48, 97–98,
        198, 213, 214
    assessment, 72
    input, 72–73
    output, 73
    profit and revenue curves, 73–74
    defined, 30
    of demand, 29–34
    dependent on competitor's price
        change, 36
    depends on market dynamics, 36–37
    margin and, 121
    pricing, 87–88
    of product, 2–3
    product's, 36
    tables, 127
    tools, 118
    visualization of, 30
price optimization, 2, 194
    with competition, 27
    through data analysis and market
        research, 9
price-pack architecture (PPA), 36–37,
        100–104, 194, 197
    vs pricing analysis, 198
Price Sensitivity Meter (PSM), 59–63
price thresholds, 56, 94, 97, 127, 217
price waterfall, 108–109, 244, 245, 247
pricing, 83–100, 136
    analysis, 198
    ancient roots of, 2
    automotive, 81
    B2B, 71, 119

behavioral, 43, 91–97
coherent action, 138
competitive, 85–87
cost-plus, 84–85
decoy, 43
defined, 8
diagnosis, 138
elasticity-based, 118
evolution of, 18–19
examples, 138–142
food, 84
framework for, 137–138, 143
guiding policy, 138
importance of, 12
instruments, 156
logic, 117
manager, 19, 43
methods, integration of, 97–100
models, pay-per-unit, 115–116
new product, 4
optimization, 162
price elasticity-based, 87–88
professionals, 5
reference, 95
relevance of, 12–14
urgency-based, 94–95
value-based, 89–91, 97
    implementing, 122
    proponents, 122–123
    rise of, 120
pricing and RGM, 8, 17, 38
    competitor analysis, 79–80
    conferences for, 132–134
    cost analysis, 80
    current technology solutions, 117–119
    customer differentiation, 82
    differences between industries, 80–81
    macroeconomic effects on, 44–46
    pay-per-unit: pricing models, 115–116
    in practice, 47–82
    pricing myths, 120–128
    pricing research, 47–48
        expert judgment, 71–79
        market data assessment, 48–58
        surveys, 58–71
    professionals, 11, 20, 32, 35
    tool categories, 119
    traditional RGM methods, 82–115
        channel mix, 113–114
        price-pack architecture (PPA), 100–104
        pricing, 83–100
        promotions, 104–108
        trade terms, 108–113
pricing myths, 120
    costs do not matter in pricing, 120–122
    differentiate prices between customers, 124–126
    identified behavioral effects can be applied directly, 127–128
    price elasticity is a single number, 126–127
    pricing is all about value to "the customer", 122

pricing research, 48
   expert judgment, 71–79
      price elasticity assessment, 72–74
      value driver/attribute assessment, 74–79
   market data assessment, 48–58
      AB tests, 54–58
      multivariate regression analysis, 52–54
      regression analysis, 48–52
   survey methods, 58–71
      conjoint analysis, 66–70
      Gabor–Granger method, 62–64
      MaxDiff method, 63–66
      Van Westendorp method/PSM, 59–63
pricing software, rule-based, 117–118
Pricing Strategy Summits, Ardensi, 132, 133
product
   price elasticity, 2–3, 36
   price set for, 8
product and channel mix management, 194
Professional Pricing Society (PPS), 131–133
profit
   contribution, 152
   growth, 149
   mathematical optimization of, 2
   maximization, 17, 18
   optimizing prices, 24–26
   optimum, 28, 35

profitability and cost-to-serve, 114
profitable growth objective, 17
profit and loss (P&L) responsibility, 179, 181
profit and revenue, trade-off between, 146
profit-optimal price, 121
profit optimization, costs matter for, 121–122
promotion, 104–108
   dynamics, 105
   effectiveness, 106
   fine-tuning, 239–240
   levers, 108
   limited-time, 94–95
   multivariate regression analysis for, 52–54
   optimization, 163, 164, 194, 241
   price elasticity, 105
Promotion Optimization Institute (POI), 132, 133
promotion return on investment (Promotion ROI), 106
prompt-based RGM optimization, 232
PSM. *See* Price Sensitivity Meter (PSM)

R

raw materials, cost of, 4
reactive triggers, 157
recommendation and management of offer changes, 231–233
redesign first, tech second, 206

reference pricing, 95
regression analysis, 213, 214
    linear, 49, 51
    market data assessment, 48–52
    multivariate regression analysis, 52–54
regulatory changes, 45
relevant value, importance of, 75
retail centers, RGM in, 246–247
retailer and e-commerce expectations, 195
retailer perspective, 170
retail price, promotion and markdown optimization, 119
return on investment (ROI), 9, 10
    promotion, 106
revenue
    mathematical optimization of, 2
    maximization, 16–18
    optimizing prices, 24, 26
revenue growth management (RGM), 8–11, 146
    artificial intelligence in, 222–224
    in automotive, 245–246
    challenges of, 82–83
    data sources, 199, 200
    development, history, 10
    evolution in digital age, 192–203
        in consumer packaged goods, 196
    framework, 142
    functions, 195
    GenAI layers for, 233–234
    Generative AI for, 203
    global RGM governance types, 179–181
    goal of, 8–10
    guidelines, 150
    increasing integration, 199
    international considerations, 178–185
    levers, 8, 10, 83, 113, 142, 155–157, 159, 194
    managers, 97, 104, 158, 188, 218, 229
    organizational structure, 174
    people and organization, 174–176
    playbook, 11–12, 186
    pricing and. *See* pricing and RGM
    process, 144, 161
        execution, 158–166
        improvement, 166–174
        strategy, 144–157
    professionals, 11–12
    responsibilities for key activities, 176
    roles in companies, 18–19
    in second half of 2025, 148
    from siloed departments to integrated RGM teams, 196
    technology, 176
        data, 177–178
        tools, 177
    use cases for CPG companies, 237
        promotion fine-tuning, 239–240
        strategic pricing shift from High-Low to EDLP, 241–243

revenue growth management (RGM) (continued)
   trade-offs between RGM levers, 238–239
  use cases in industries, 243
   automotive, 245–246
   business-to-business, 247–248
   hospitality, 248
   retail, 246–247
   telecommunications, 244–245
Revenue Management and Pricing Section of INFORMS, 131
revenue manager, 19, 83, 192, 195, 199
  as change agent, 201–202
  hypotheses on changing role, 202–203
RGM. *See* revenue growth management (RGM)
Ricard, David, 38
ride-sharing industry, 3
right tool for the job, 206
Rockefeller, John D., 141
ROI. *See* return on investment (ROI)
Rolls-Royce's "Power by the Hour" model, 116
rule-based pricing software, 117–118
Rumelt, Richard, 137

S

sales dynamics, 200
sales forecasting, 226–228
sales share optimization, 16
sales teams, 247
sales volume, 242
sell-in story, 165, 166
service providers, 116
share optimization, sales/market, 16
shopper, 193
  behavior, 113
  expectations, 155–156
  perspective, 170
societies and professional organizers, 131–132
specific net revenue, 149
SRPs. *See* suggested retail prices (SRPs)
stock-keeping units (SKUs), 114
strategic monitoring, 168–171
strategic pricing shift from High-Low to EDLP, 241–243
strategy update, 173–174
strategy workshops, 136
subscription and recurring billing/monetization, 119
suggested retail prices (SRPs), 162, 163
Sunstein, Cass, 42
supply and demand, dynamics of, 20
surplus profit (Ricardian rent), 38
survey methods, pricing research, 58–71
  conjoint analysis, 66–70
  Gabor–Granger method, 62–64
  MaxDiff method, 63–66
  Van Westendorp method/PSM, 59–63
sustainable revenue growth, 8
SWOT framework, 139

T
tactical monitoring, 167–168
Tegus, 71
telecommunications, 116
  companies (telco), 81
  RGM in, 244–245
term creep, 113
Tesla, 116
Thaler, Richard, 41, 42
Thinking, Fast and Slow
  (Kahneman), 41
time-limited offers, 94–95
tool
  price elasticity-based, 118
  price monitoring and competitor intelligence, 119
  RGM technology, 177
total variance in sales (TVS), 50
TPM. *See* trade promotion management (TPM)
TPO. *See* trade promotion optimization (TPO)
trade-offs
  between profit and revenue, 146
  between RGM levers, 238–239
trade promotion management (TPM), 118, 119, 236
trade promotion optimization (TPO), 118, 119
trade spend management, 194
trade terms, 108–113, 156
transaction prices, 245

trigger events for pricing actions, 157
Turing, Alan, 206
TVS. *See* total variance in sales (TVS)

U
Uber, 3
upper management and marketing, 136
urgency-based pricing, 94–95

V
value-based pricing, 89–91, 97
  implementing, 122
  proponents of, 122–123
  rise of, 120
value creation vs value capture, 15–18
value driver/attribute assessment, 74–79
"value to the customer", 39
Van Westendorp method, 59–63
Virtual Shoppers, 216–221, 226, 242–244, 249, 251
virtual shopping situation, 220–221
Volvo, 116

W
Wilde, Oscar, 38
willingness to pay (WTP), 39–40, 70, 216

Z
zero price effect, 92